MASTERING BOSTON HARBOR

ECCE

Hieronymus Bos.
inuentor

MASTERING BOSTON HARBOR
Courts, Dolphins, and Imperiled Waters

Charles M. Haar

HARVARD UNIVERSITY PRESS

Cambridge, Massachusetts

London, England

2005

Copyright © 2005 by the President and Fellows of Harvard College
All rights reserved
Printed in the United States of America

Library of Congress Cataloging-in-Publication Data

Haar, Charles Monroe, 1920–
Mastering Boston Harbor : courts, dolphins, and imperiled waters /
Charles M. Haar.
    p. cm.
Includes bibliograpical references and index.
ISBN 0-674-01528-2 (alk. paper)
1. Quincy (Mass.)—Trials, litigation, etc. 2. Massachusetts. Metropolitan
District Commission—Trials, litigation, etc. 3. Marine pollution—Law
and legislation—Massachusetts—Boston Harbor. 4. Massachusetts Water
Resources Authority—History. I. Title.
KF228.Q56H32 2005
344.744'7046343—dc22   2004059910

On title page: Pieter van der Heyden (after Pieter Bruegel the Elder),
Big Fish Eat Little Fish, 1557. All rights reserved, The Metropolitan
Museum of Art.

For Suzanne

As the shining light,

That shineth more and more

Contents

Illustrations

Abbreviations

BWSC   Boston Water and Sewer Commission

CSO   Combined Sewer Overflow (of stormwater and sewage)

DEQE   Department of Environmental Quality Engineering
       (within EOEA)

DWPC   Division of Water Pollution Control (within DEQE)

EOEA   Executive Office of Environmental Affairs

EPA   U.S. Environmental Protection Agency

I/I   Infiltration/Inflow (of extraneous water into the sewer
       system)

MDC   Metropolitan District Commission

MSD   Metropolitan Sewerage Division (within MDC)

MWRA   Massachusetts Water Resources Authority

NPDES National Pollution Discharge Elimination System

QLP   Quincy Litigation Papers, Harvard Law School Library

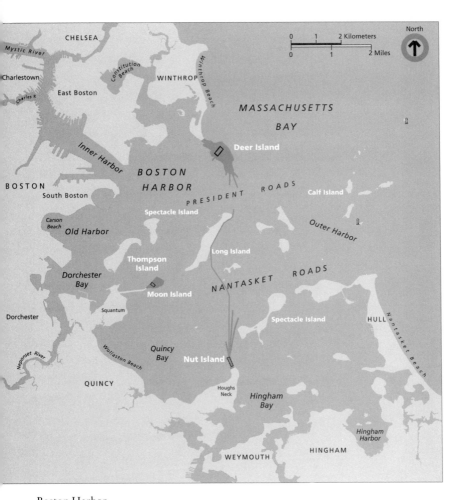

Boston Harbor

INTRODUCTION
Troubled Waters

Our government is the potent, the omnipresent teacher. . . . If the government becomes a lawbreaker, it breeds contempt for law; it invites every man to become a law unto himself, it invites anarchy.

—Louis Dembitz Brandeis

More than a national treasure, Boston Harbor is a veritable theater of American history—the setting for some of the nation's most resonant dramas. It was here that a uniquely American identity took root upon the consolidation of the Massachusetts Bay Colony with the new settlement on the Shawmut Peninsula in 1630. In 1773 the Boston Tea Party signaled the hardening of resistance to British rule. Two years later, the battle at Bunker Hill, which overlooks the strategically important harbor, became a rallying cry for the revolutionaries. Two centuries after her construction, the USS *Constitution*, the ship known to generations of schoolchildren as "Old Ironsides," still finds its home in Boston Harbor. More recently, the harbor was an obvious destination for the majestic Tall Ships procession that marked the Bicentennial celebration in 1976.

And in 1988 it was the scene of an event that shifted the tides of that year's presidential campaign. On a brilliant morning in early September, Vice President George H. W. Bush, the Republican Party candidate to succeed Ronald Reagan, launched a daring daylight raid in the home waters of his Democratic opponent, Massachusetts governor Michael S. Dukakis. With the Boston skyline looming in the background, Bush stood on the deck of the excursion craft *Bay State,* pointed to the water below, and squarely blamed Dukakis for the harbor's notorious status as "the dirtiest" in America and "the harbor of shame."[1]

The Bush charges touched a raw nerve. Indeed, the decay of the harbor had persisted unabated over the decades. Its problems received little attention at best, and even less funding. Although the "Sacred Cod" had been the totem of Boston and Massachusetts since colonial times, a symbol of the debt the city and the Bay State owed the sea, by the early 1980s many of the fish taken from the harbor were cancerous, or suffering from fin rot and other diseases and deformities caused by pollution. The seals, dolphins, and harbor porpoises had disappeared.

The state's ongoing failure to meet its legally mandated sewage disposal responsibilities jeopardized the health, safety, and welfare of every person who lived and worked in communities abutting the harbor. Furthermore, the polluted condition of Boston Harbor threatened those who used it for commerce, recreation, and other purposes, and caused substantial and long-term damage to the environment, marine animals, and vegetation. The ecological death of these waters seemed imminent.

While Bush's trip to Boston Harbor was a brilliant move—one of the defining moments in the 1988 presidential contest—it did nothing to make the harbor any cleaner. The fate of Boston Harbor was determined by another kind of drama, one that had begun several years earlier and was less flashy than those featured in presidential campaigns but perhaps of more lasting importance.

In December 1982 the city of Quincy filed suit against the Metropolitan District Commission (MDC). This was the regional agency entrusted with the huge responsibility of operating the sewerage system that served more than two million residents in forty-three cities and towns comprising the Boston metropolitan area—and whose end products flowed into the harbor and the bay beyond. When the trial began in July 1983, Paul Garrity was the presiding judge, and I was appointed by the

Massachusetts Superior Court as special master in the case. This permitted me to be a direct witness to events as they unfolded, as well as an actor in them.

The initial charge from the Superior Court was to ascertain the source and extent of the pollution that afflicted one particular beach on the edge of the harbor, and to recommend remedies. This required the organization of a special master's office to collect and marshal a trove of data. An increasingly concerned public demanded information, as did a wide range of interest groups working toward a shared understanding that their common problem extended far beyond one befouled beach in Quincy.

As part of the preparation for the work ahead, I explored the conditions of the harbor, visited the fabulous islands, both those developed and the many untouched, within its borders, and took walks on the Boston pathways bordering the sea. I also reviewed laboratory evidence concerning the qualities of its waters. And, of course, there was much reading to do: ardent salvos in statements by public commissions and dire reports by expert consultants assessing the extent of harm to the waters and to the natural order. These experiences left no doubt that the warnings of the deterioration of Boston Harbor were definitely warranted and that the time to act had come.

As revealed in my findings of fact, garnered in day-and-night sessions during July and August, Boston's harbor was the most degraded in the United States, with twelve billion gallons of raw or partially treated sewage going directly into its waters each year. This finding stunned the people of the Boston region because the evidence demonstrated beyond any doubt that the state's inability to meet its sewage disposal obligations jeopardized the public's health and safety, as well as economic development.

The judicial decisions, the tactics of the attorneys and parties, the differing bills debated in the legislature, the responses of the federal and state agencies charged with the care of the harbor, are seen in this book through the prism of the judge and the special master. This rarely invoked perspective gives a unique picture of the momentous events that followed.

The harbor's degradation was not only thoroughgoing; it was also the result of a systemic problem that required a systemic solution. At the same time, the inherent parochialism of state and federal bureaucracies created a stubborn barrier to holistic approaches to cleaning up the harbor. Massachusetts politicians historically resented spending their time on an issue likely to win them few votes, and avoided upsetting the extant applecart that offered opportunities for exercising their powers of patronage and purse.

The plight of Boston Harbor and the struggle to reclaim it forced to the surface significant ideological issues concerning the maintenance of public lands and waters. It was a contemporary example of the tragedy of the commons.[2] In principle, the harbor belonged to everyone. But with the mixture of commercial and industrial users, environmental advocates and recreational enthusiasts, as well as a tangle of federal, state, and local agencies, no single entity felt duty-bound to care for it.

Thus the task of the court was to understand not only the scope of the environmental degradation that had occurred but also the institutional breakdown that had for so many years stood in the way of change. Such institutional failure required drastic innovations, including the creation of an independent agency that superseded the existing web of jurisdictions and could plan and implement for the future of Boston Harbor.

As the controversy over the harbor's pollution reached a crisis point, the public officials best positioned to heed the mounting public call for action were a handful of state and federal judges. These judges represented the interests of the public in the broadest sense, filling roles that should have been occupied by the members of the executive or legislative branches. The abdication of responsibility by the governor and legislators who were unable or unwilling to resolve the problems afflicting the harbor left it to the judiciary to rise to the challenge. The energetic judicial response to prior legislative inertia was the most extraordinary and precedent-setting feature of Boston Harbor's journey from a national disgrace to a symbol of national pride.

The innovative judicial approaches introduced by the *Quincy* litigation were truly far-reaching. The case raised crucial questions about the role of the court in a democratic state, which are explored in Chapters 14, 15, and the Conclusion. The way that the court reached its unprecedented environmental remediation represents a model for future litigation in its procedures, the techniques employed by the court, and in its mandated remedies.

As always, money was crucial. The financial plan worked out for the new water resources authority went beyond any of the proposals advanced by the plaintiff or the defendants; it entailed (as Chapters 11 and 12 indicate) the court and financial specialists setting forth the form of a special revenue bond, controls over rates, and a complex billing, collection, and enforcement system. A remarkable "procedural order," devised to replace the stringent consent decree, enabled the parties to work together in implementing a program for regenerating the harbor (Chapters 10 and 14). Extensive use of a special master, a striking feature of the case, enabled the court to complement adjudication with mediation, the formal with the improvised (Chapters 3 and 15). Perhaps the most dramatic use of judicial power was the judge's order of a moratorium on new sewer system hookups that brought construction to a halt in the Boston metropolitan area (Chapter 13). Still later, his threat to put the MDC into judicial receivership broke a political logjam.

Another lesson to be taken from the case is the use of scientists, engineers, and other professional experts—how else can a lawyer or judge grasp technical and scientific matters or evaluate the opinions of contending specialists? (This issue is treated in Chapters 4 and 7.) The ban on court-appointed experts should be lifted and the Federal Rules limiting the appointment of a special master to "extraordinary" cases need modification (see Chapters 3 and 15).

The cumbersome adversary process was eased in *Quincy* by substituting trial by affidavit, relaxing strict rules of evidence, and allowing direct questioning of witnesses by the master and the judge. Another important and controversial step (as analyzed in Chapter 6) was waiving the ex parte rules, thereby permitting the special master to discuss matters privately with the parties, experts, or other individuals—even the presiding judge—without requiring the presence of lawyers from both sides. And the successful outcome of *Quincy* put another conventional doctrine into question—the role of the media in a courtroom case. To rely solely on the isolated judicial opinion was not adequate. Without the clarification of issues by conscientious media, including dialogues with the judge and special master, there would not have been the public understanding and support crucial to achieving the Boston Harbor renewal (Chapters 6 and 15).

The approach adopted by the judge in *Quincy* will be especially appreciated by lawyers and others who are mindful of the reach of a powerful judiciary in a constitutional democracy. A thesis of this book, argued in Chapter 14 and the Conclusion, is that once a court finds it appropriate, perhaps inescapable, to salvage an institutional breakdown, it will most likely achieve success if its remedy is bold in its decisions and firm in its implementation. Once again, form follows function. Conventional adjudication processes are not suited to the multidimensional task of complex public litigation. Returning to the original separation of powers doctrine propounded by the Founding Fathers, the court's role sometimes demands direct and forceful action to thaw frozen political barriers. Traditional constraints on the judge's action may no longer fit modern society and its discontents.

Reflecting on my years of teaching and legal practice, it has struck me that judges impose far too narrow limitations on their own roles in the great dramas of public life. Too often, out of a commendable concern to practice restraint in political controversies, they defer to other levels and branches of government to formulate vital public policies. But here one judge shed this occupational reluctance to assert visible public leadership.

Judge Paul Garrity had demonstrated his willingness to challenge conventional limits on the scope of judicial action with his landmark 1980 decision to place the corrupt, dysfunctional Boston Housing Authority into receivership. He showed the same pioneering spirit in the *Quincy* litigation. In the process, he expanded a noble judicial tradition of ensuring that promised rights would be vindicated in the face of political resistance, a tradition exemplified by the courageous judges who did so much to advance the cause of civil rights in the 1950s and 1960s. Where other judges might see a threat to the separation of powers, Garrity saw an opportunity to harmonize the law with society's changing standards and priorities. Based on early land-use laws, furthermore, his bold actions were not so much a departure from established practice but rather an effort to reactivate submerged trends that judges could no longer ignore.

The *Quincy* lawsuit set in motion events that produced a major environmental triumph. By a circuitous and perilous route it led to the establishment of a new governmental agency, the Massachusetts Water Resources Authority, that could take on the responsibility for the harbor's revitalization. And with innovative state and federal legislation and regulations relating to sewage treatment and discharge, this effort began the task of restoring the harbor's waters to full health.

Timing was crucial to the success of the litigation that began with *Quincy*. When the initial suit was filed in 1982, public dismay over the state of the environment was on the rise, and there was mounting impatience with the lax stewardship of government and the business community. What was lacking was a spark of leadership to ignite the widespread discontent, a spark that Judge Garrity and I sought to supply. What made the process especially gripping was that even as we were breaking new legal ground, we also built upon the oldest tools available—such as the law of nuisance, a time-honored category of English common law. After assiduous searches, we found various legal pathways toward achieving the harbor's renaissance, and in the process helped establish the role of our courts in assuring the attainment of society's goals and ideals.

Ultimately the *Quincy* lawsuit—and the determined response of the court—changed the course of Massachusetts history. The Boston Harbor case offers a model for legal responses to many pressing public dilemmas, and it reminds judges in complex public litigations that they are not merely arbiters; they can and must also be leaders.

The long road to the remediation of Boston Harbor's pollution, a massive undertaking that continues to this day, is a genuine triumph of environmental and legal activism over political inertia. This historic cleanup dispels the notion that environmental well-being is a luxury that governments can skimp on when times are hard. Instead, the conviction has taken hold that a healthy environment is a basic right and a cornerstone of a healthy polity. How an often fractious collection of activists, lawyers, legislators, and judges helped lead the public to that new understanding—and how the public, in turn, showed the way—is the story that this book tells.

THE HARBOR IN THE NATIONAL POLITICAL CAMPAIGN

George H. W. Bush's Landing

[Boston Harbor] was a stirring sight for us, who had been months on the ocean without seeing anything but two solitary sails. . . . Every sight was full of beauty and interest. . . . The high land of Cape Ann and the rocks and shore of Cohasset were full in sight, the lighthouses, standing like sentries in white before the harbor, and even the smoke from the chimneys on the plains of Hingham was seen rising slowly in the morning air.

—Richard Henry Dana, Jr.

George H. W. Bush chose a powerful symbol.

In September 1988, as the campaign to succeed Ronald Reagan as president was entering the home stretch, Vice President Bush carried the battle to the home base of his Democratic opponent, Massachusetts governor Michael S. Dukakis. The Republican candidate had not come to Boston bearing nuance. From the storied stage of Boston Harbor, Bush launched a daring daylight raid on the then-prevalent notion of the "Massachusetts Miracle"—a Dukakis-led economic revival whose epicenter was Boston.

The miracle's most visible emblem was the transformed Boston skyline. Throughout the city, ambitious urban development policies had attracted commercial and residential investors and developers. And at the geographic center of this reinvigorated metropolis lay the harbor. Large commercial container ships as well as small boats plied its waters, and with its estuaries and tidelands, its channels and wharves, its beaches and peninsulas, it glittered like a jewel in a sleek new setting. "Overall," wrote the authors of a report on Boston Harbor in 1984, "this mix of islands and sea, of buildings and vegetation, of commerce and recreation, of sky and water, creates a landscape that is never without new interest, that is never without a variety of recreational opportunities for the literally millions of people who live within a few miles of its shores."[1] Stirring as it was, this opening pronouncement by the Metropolitan District Commission, the agency largely responsible for controlling sewage flows into the harbor, bypassed the emergency that had prompted the report's commissioning in the first place: in the 1980s, as concerned citizens and environmental activists had warned for decades, the harbor was turning into a sink of pollution.

Bush shrewdly recognized that making an issue of the degradation of Boston Harbor in his opponent's backyard could serve a double purpose. The harbor's well-being touched intense feelings, and he exploited them masterfully. By pinning the harbor's deterioration on Dukakis, Bush could call the governor's entire record into question even as he deftly recast himself as an environmentalist concerned with the health of the planet, a person in touch with the concerns of the common man, a reformer instead of the incarnation of the governing elite. It was a capital move. He had chosen a timely topic, one that had grown in importance in the public mind in recent years, and a potent symbol of history and patriotism.

One hundred Dukakis supporters greeted the Republican candidate at the airport on that morning of September 1, 1988. They carried protest signs and chanted anti-Bush slogans as the vice president's party boarded the *Bay State* cruise vessel for a tour of the harbor.[2] Many of the Dukakis supporters followed the Bush cruise in a flotilla consisting of a rubber raft, a powerboat, a sailboat, and a small ferry. But this show of support for their home-state governor as the Democratic candidate for the presidency could not counteract that morning's *Boston Herald* headline, "Poll Shocker: Bush Ties Duke in Mass."[3] Nor would state Democratic Party support suffice to counteract Bush's characterization of Governor Dukakis as the person who had done nothing about the despoiling of a site that had once been host to the original Boston Tea Party. So the Democratic presidential nominee found himself playing defense on his own turf.

Speaking from an upper deck jammed with supporters and reporters, Bush told of a "sewage meter" on exhibit at Boston's New England Aquarium that measured pollution flow into the harbor: "That sewage meter is a measure of the cost of my opponent's neglect of the environment. While Michael Dukakis delayed, the harbor got dirtier and dirtier."[4] The amount of sewage dumped into the harbor in 1986, he went on, "would cover all of metropolitan Boston up to a depth of 17 feet."[5]

As of the beginning of September, neither candidate had received an endorsement from a major environmental group, but earlier in the year the League of Conservation Voters had given Bush a "D" on his performance and rewarded Dukakis with a "B" on his. Bush's grade was based on his role as the head of the President's Task Force on Regulatory Relief, which, not incidentally, led an effort to restrict the powers of the Environmental Protection Agency (EPA). Dukakis deserved his "B," the report said, because "when environmental and political leaders succeeded in getting him to focus on the environment, he produced."[6] An "A" eluded Dukakis because, for quite some time, he just did not fix his attention on environmental issues.

But on that morning the vice president charged ahead, noting that "[t]he current estimate of the cost of constructing the necessary [treatment] plants is six billion dollars. EPA estimates that if my opponent had gone ahead and built the plants in his first term, the cost would have been about one billion dollars." He then struck a theme of patriotism: "Two hundred years ago, tea was spilled into this harbor in the name of liberty. Now it's something else. We've got to do better."[7]

This theme of "doing better" was sounded again and again by the vice president on the campaign trail during the autumn as he distanced himself from the environmental program cutbacks of the Reagan administration. "I am an environmentalist," Bush declared repeatedly, adding, "That's not inconsistent with being a businessman, nor is it with being a conservative."[8] Dukakis and his aides, in an attempt at retaliation, tried to tie Bush to the anti-environmental policies of the Reagan administration in general and to specific cutbacks Bush had recommended as head of the Task Force on Regulatory Relief in particular.[9]

But the counterattack seemed half-hearted and tepid. To a question raised in an interview with the New York Times that appeared on October 9—"What our reporters and a lot of polls are finding is the things that people hold against you are things like . . . pollution of the Boston Harbor, why haven't you been able to get your side across . . . ?"—Dukakis lamely answered, "We will, we will. We've got a month to go."[10]

Throughout the 1988 campaign the Dukakis environmental program, like the rest of his platform, was presented in ways too diffuse and abstract to capture the public's imagination.[11] If there was any point in the Reagan-Bush record that afforded an obvious political target, it was that administration's selection of the nation's environmental policies as a prime object of its social revolution, reducing enforcement, slashing budgets, and opening public lands for private use.[12] To boot, this was an administration that had refused to recognize that there was such a problem as acid rain produced by industrial smokestacks. And George Bush himself was on record as saying that if elected president he would cut the funding of federal programs that paid for the construction of water treatment plants.

But Dukakis could not even make the EPA scandals—including indictments of top appointees in the Department of the Interior—and other Reagan environmental liabilities stick to his opponent. The legacy of the older environmental record receded as

a voter concern. Social memory is short. Ironically, a focus on
the future buried concern about the past; Bush's newly adopted
advocacy for faster action and more spending on cleaning up
pollution—"We've got to do better"—was what counted in the
voter's mind. And Bush effectively and with wit concentrated on
the Dukakis record, blaming his rival for the pollution that the
Reagan administration itself had done nothing to abate. "If you
tried to dump tea into Boston Harbor today, it would probably
bounce," he jested during his September cruise. "If tea were
spilled in the Boston Harbor today," he said on another occasion, "it would dissolve in the residue of my opponent's neglect
and delay."[13] And finally Bush mocked the so-called miracle of
economic revival under Dukakis: "The last miracle in Massachusetts was when they found a fish alive in Boston Harbor."[14]

DUKAKIS AND A REPUBLICAN EPA

Earlier on, Governor Dukakis had taken to the waters himself.
His excursion aboard the *Miss Belmar*, off the coast of Belmar,
New Jersey, at the end of May 1988, was intended to show his
support for an end to the ocean dumping that had closed New
Jersey beaches during the summer of 1987, when, to the public's
consternation, hospital waste, including syringes and needles,
washed ashore on more than one occasion.[15] To dramatize his
condemnation of dirty water, Dukakis left his pinstripe suit and
wingtips at home; dressed instead in a navy polo shirt sporting a
"Clean Ocean Action" button, khakis, and sneakers, he pronounced this environmental despoliation "disgusting."

Flanked by movie star and environmental advocate Robert
Redford, Dukakis framed himself as an environmental activ-
ist. At the same time he acknowledged that Massachusetts too
had water quality problems, admitting that the Boston Harbor cleanup "should have happened 50 years ago." But he emphasized the Reagan-Bush administration's frequent efforts to
weaken the EPA. "We have an administration who came into

office determined to destroy the EPA," he charged. Dukakis proposed instead to expand recycling and conservation programs, expressing support for biodegradable plastics made from corn and other crops. In sum, the governor pledged to be an energetic president who would work closely with business, labor, environmentalists, and state and local governments to clean up pollution.

Instead of setting the tone for the environmental battle of the campaign, however, this approach backfired badly, opening Dukakis to criticism of his handling of the Boston Harbor cleanup. Responding to Dukakis's Belmar cruise, Bush argued, "Why isn't he up there in Boston Harbor, doing something about the problem himself? . . . He can get his picture taken in New Jersey going after the administration. I'll get my picture taken in Boston Harbor going after him."[16] And, sure enough, in September he proved true to his word. The vice president recalled Dukakis's 1985 request to join New York and New Jersey in dumping Boston sludge off the New Jersey coast.[17] When the criticisms came, Dukakis tried to redirect attention, placing at least partial blame for the status of Boston Harbor on Reagan administration rollbacks of federal aid for water and sewer programs—but to little avail.

A telling episode illustrating the role of political partisanship in the national debate about the environment occurred after Dukakis's New Jersey cruise, in the wake of a groundbreaking ceremony in the Boston Harbor rehabilitation program on August 10, 1988—a moment that should have been a cause for celebration on all sides, and one that Dukakis could seize upon to demonstrate that Boston was indeed moving forward. The very next day, however, the chief of the EPA's New England office, Michael Deland, condemned Dukakis for six years of delay in cleaning up the harbor. In remarks that were at best impolitic and at worst opportunistic, he called the harbor neglect "the most expensive public policy mistake in the history of New England."[18] He cited the statistic that Bush would reemphasize three weeks later: what might have cost only $1 billion had Dukakis acted promptly was now going to run up to $6 billion.

The groundbreaking event for a cleanup that he had supported and for which he was partially responsible was an obvious opportunity for Dukakis to shine. But instead of enjoying the spotlight, the governor was forced to address a question for which there was no quick and easy answer. "Back in the 1970s," he attempted to explain, "we didn't even have the information to determine what to build and how to build it"—not an unreasonable excuse. But meanwhile the media highlighted Deland's accusation; it was more newsworthy for its shock effect than were the careful explanations issued by the Dukakis administration. Although Deland was a Republican appointee, the press and the general public never seemed to see his remarks as a partisan attack. "Dukakis and his aides were livid," the *Boston Globe* reported.[19] Not for the first time, political passions governed discussions of the harbor.

During his cruise of Boston Harbor, Bush simplified history considerably when he asked voters to remember that "the reason that Boston Harbor is not cleaner today is that the Dukakis administration twice sought to avoid making it cleaner." He asserted several times that Dukakis "missed the boat" and failed to lock in higher federal aid under an old formula. "He had a chance to get on board and he asked for an exemption from federal provisions." "That's too bad," the vice president concluded.[20]

That request for an exemption was a matter Dukakis found hard to explain. A major difficulty in resolving the harbor problem was posed by the political temptation to request an EPA waiver from secondary treatment requirements mandated by the Clean Water Act of 1977. Dukakis opted for the waiver in 1978. In 1979, Edward King, who served as governor between Dukakis's first and second terms, also sought the waiver. With

Dukakis back in office, Massachusetts officials then waited until 1983 to take further action when they learned the request had been denied. And even then, on the advice of their expert engineers and consultants, they asked the EPA to reconsider.

The distortions of the 1988 campaign were especially vexing because the complexities of the harbor pollution eluded easy answers. At the time I sought to correct exaggerations on both sides in an op-ed piece, though the *New York Times* tag-line put my position more starkly than I would have: "Bush Sinks the Truth in Boston Harbor."[21] The state as a whole had not lost any federal funding: other Massachusetts communities received the money allocated to the state by the federal government that might have gone into improving the harbor. Furthermore, it was not accurate to say that Dukakis had to be dragged by the court into taking action to clean up the harbor. While Dukakis had moved slowly at first, over the last two years of his first four-year administration he had begun to seek ways to combat the harbor pollution. It was Dukakis who had submitted the initial draft for establishing a water resources state agency early in 1984.

Moreover, it could be argued that seeking a waiver had been a reasonable decision.[22] Many of the experts who appeared during the *Quincy* hearings testified that the secondary treatment required by the EPA was ill advised. Indeed, secondary treatment produced additional quantities of sludge—for which, at the time, there was no acceptable means of disposal except ocean dumping. Such waivers were hardly uncommon on the East Coast. In 1985, for example, the EPA granted secondary treatment waivers to sixteen coastal communities in New England—including Kennebunkport, Maine, the location of Bush's summer residence.

In the Boston Harbor case, finally, the slow-moving national EPA bore its own responsibility for delay, taking years to process and eventually deny Massachusetts's waiver application. The Republican-led EPA's denial of a waiver to a Democratic state might have had more than a small dose of self-interest secreted within the interstices of a technological determination. At the end it was Dukakis, energized at last, who orchestrated agreement among the frequently contending groups concerned about the harbor and pushed through the Massachusetts Water Resources Authority program. But none of this was easy to explain in a campaign spot.

As the 1988 campaign continued, Bush burnished his image while he piloted his speedboat around Casco Bay, near Kennebunkport. Massachusetts Democratic senator Paul Tsongas's charge that Bush's presentation of himself as an environmentalist "is sort of akin to Bonnie and Clyde coming out for gun control" never caught on. Throughout the campaign, as part of the effort to wrest the issue of the environment from the hands of the Democrats, the vice president maintained that he truly was a Teddy Roosevelt Republican.

And in the crucial twenty-four hours after the first presidential debate, the vice president's campaign released the sharpest negative advertising yet to be shown on national television. In a thirty-second ad, broadcast on NBC during its coverage of the Olympics, Bush charged that Boston had the "dirtiest harbor in America." With brilliant tactics and quick remarks, Bush made a major issue out of the harbor.

On November 2, shortly before the election, the vice president delivered more pitches even though his lead seemed safe. The Bush campaign mailed one-ounce vials of what it claimed was genuine Boston Harbor water to reporters in California. "In Massachusetts this might pass for Perrier, but we suggest you don't drink it," said the Bush state campaign's letter. "We don't recommend it with fish. We don't recommend it with pasta. In fact, we simply don't recommend it." Meanwhile, Dukakis never found a theme or overcame the attacks. His unemotional responses produced negative ratings. "Dukakis is our single greatest ally," declared a Bush aide.

In short, the Republican nominee succeeded in securing the harbor issue for himself. It was a riverboat gamble that worked. Bush's tour of the polluted harbor put Dukakis on the defensive, responding to his opponent's accusations rather than taking the offensive, and doing so legalistically and half-heartedly. This failure to stake out the environmental issue was perhaps the single greatest missed opportunity in the Dukakis campaign. His campaign went adrift, and sank quietly.

These events underscored the fact that the degradation of Boston Harbor aroused intense emotions in Americans. The harbor was a potent symbol of history, national purpose, and patriotism. With the focus on the harbor, protection of the environment had become a widely discussed issue for the first time in a presidential campaign. Indeed, at least two conclusions regarding American attitudes to environmental issues can be extracted from the 1988 campaign. The pollution degrading the harbor was not a local or even a state concern alone; a national constituency was concerned about the outcome. Second, Boston Harbor had been and still was hostage to politics, which regrettably but inevitably intruded into what in essence was a complex scientific and technological problem.

A POLITICAL POSTSCRIPT

On May 19, 1989, the *Boston Globe* ran an article entitled "'Environmental President': A Slow Start." The article listed a series of environmental disappointments, but naturally, from the *Globe*'s perspective as a local newspaper, the most significant was Bush's opposition to federal funding for the Boston Harbor revitalization. Despite his campaign pledge, the newly elected President Bush refused to provide money to clean up Boston Harbor. In fact, he omitted from his 1989 budget the $59 million Congress had authorized for the harbor cleanup. And he cut in half Congress's $2.4 billion authorization for the national water cleanup program.

On September 4, 1991, three years after Bush's symbolic conquest of the harbor, twenty national, state, and local environmental groups gathered at the edge of Boston Harbor to denounce the president for abandoning the cleanup. His highly publicized 1988 visit was recalled. Candidate Bush "convinced us all that water quality problems would be a priority in his administration," lamented Sheila Lynch, president of the advocacy group Save the Harbor/Save the Bay. She charged that the federal government had provided only 3 percent of the $6.1 billion needed to build new sewage treatment facilities. Environmentalists felt that the public had been taken for a ride—or, in this case, a cruise.

On October 30, 1991, however, with the election year of 1992 moving into view, President Bush signed into law HR 2519, which included $100 million for the cleanup of Boston Harbor, as well as funds for the New York, San Diego, and Los Angeles harbors. The executive branch had proposed the law, and the Massachusetts delegation shepherded it through Congress, but the three years of delay caused environmentalists and Boston Harbor advocates to conclude they had been hoodwinked by the politics of the 1988 campaign.[23] In the end, Bush's $100 million came to only 1.6 percent of the expected total cost of the cleanup. The total federal contribution was estimated as saving each metropolitan area household $15 per year over the next thirty years.[24] Compared to the city's sewer rates, expected to be the highest in the nation, climbing from $500 per household in 1992 to a projected $2,000 per household by 2005, the federal contribution was truly just a drop in the harbor.

UNDER THE JUDICIAL LENS

The *Quincy* Case Is Launched

> If you are squeamish,
> Don't prod the beach rubble.
>
> —Sappho

In their more relaxed moments historians sometimes comment on how major events can be traced back to what appeared at the time to be minor happenings. This is true of the Boston Harbor cleanup, one of the largest and most successful environmental efforts in the nation's history.

For decades, experts and citizen advocacy groups alike pointed out how the pollution of the harbor was impairing the health and safety of the citizens of greater Boston, as well as the welfare of the state and region. One after another, public officials wrestled with the problem, to no avail. A familiar sequence of agitated public demands that something be done, followed by political furor and failed attempts to take action, played out again and again in different administrations and in successive legislative sessions. By the early 1980s the occasional speech that had found its way into the *Boston Globe,* together with a scattered series of environmental reports by various engineering firms filed away in the dustbin of history, remained the only marks of past efforts and abiding public concern.

And then one morning in the fall of 1982, William B. Golden, the city solicitor for Quincy and a representative of its district in the state legislature, went for a run on Wollaston Beach. The beach rests at the bottom end of the arc of land that begins to the north, at Winthrop, curves southwest through Boston, and then south and southeast to Nantasket, Quincy, and Hull to frame the inner portion of Massachusetts Bay that constitutes Boston Harbor. Enjoying the sight of the sky and the water in the early morning light just after sunrise, he was concentrating on his speed and breathing capacity—just out for a peaceful jaunt at low tide.

With the sudden emergence of the sun from the clouds, Golden saw a number of shiny objects gleaming on the shore. Newly arrived jellyfish, he thought, or some other treasures of the sea. He jogged over. To his consternation, he found instead the filth and garbage of an industrial metropolis: as far as the eye could see, a motley collection of human feces, rags, bandages, condoms, spoiled fruit, grease, decaying meat. The sight and smell nauseated him.

Golden's disturbing morning encounter prompted him to request a meeting with Governor Michael Dukakis, whom he counted as a friend, for an urgent conversation about steps that might be taken to improve conditions in the waters.

Soon thereafter, following a breakfast bagel in the governor's Brookline home, Dukakis and Golden spent a day together, debating strategies for yet another attempt to halt the pollution of the harbor. In response to Golden's suggestion that legal action be taken, Dukakis urged that the city of Quincy not file suit. He believed that his executive team, which had recently resumed power after four years of voter-imposed exile, could find a way to solve the problem—which he freely acknowledged to be a serious one.

The discussion between Dukakis and Golden took place at a time when the environment had emerged as a central concern for the general public, but political action lagged far behind political rhetoric. A growing recognition of the fragility of our planet— inspired by writings such as Rachel Carson's *The Silent Spring* (1962), spurred on by the findings of scientists and academicians, and symbolically captured by the Apollo space program's stunning photos of Earth from afar—had led to the establishment, in 1970, of Earth Day, an annual commemoration of national awareness of environmental issues. The Great Society initiatives of President Lyndon Johnson had paid considerable attention to the findings of his Task Force on Natural Beauty, including the importance of cleaning up the nation's rivers and harbors; Johnson's programs emphasized the contribution of national parks (and of vest-pocket parks in urban areas) to the public welfare, urged the preservation of undeveloped lands for future generations, and cited the need for coordination of policies at all levels.[1]

But as yet there was still little public appreciation of how environmentalism, which was regarded in many quarters as a conservation ideology most appropriate to the "wide open spaces" of the American West, could be applicable to the East Coast or to congested urban centers nationwide. Indeed, it was a lack of recognition of the importance of clean water and air, green spaces, and accessible recreation facilities to the quality of life of city residents that resulted in the failure of reform efforts in many metropolitan areas, especially in the East and including Boston. The idea of a vigorous environmental policy for coordinating the efforts of federal, state, and local entities was not in the political air. Action by government—including intervention by the judiciary—was simply not conceived of as a way to bring about better conditions on the beaches and in the waters surrounding cities.

Newly returned to office and a captive of his earlier political promises, including a commitment to the "Massachusetts Miracle" of economic growth, Governor Dukakis could not fully gauge the appeal that the growing environmental movement and a concern for "the quality of life" held for the public, especially the younger generation—even though he might be in basic sympathy with them.[2] He could do little more in that discussion with William Golden than reaffirm his concern for the health of the

harbor and express confidence in James Hoyte, his newly appointed state secretary of environmental affairs.

For his part, Golden was not persuaded that executive action
or influence would suffice. Citing the inertia of the past, he argued that only with the help of outside pressure could the governor secure the legislative consensus necessary to tackle the
mammoth task of regenerating Boston Harbor. Convinced that
conditions had reached an emergency state that required drastic
steps—especially as he thought of his own children walking or
swimming amidst the filth he had recently observed—Golden
advocated either a turn to the legislature to pass more stringent
environmental protection laws, or a move to a judicial decree
that would bring the pressure of a court sanction upon the relevant state agencies. The particular target was the Metropolitan
District Commission, which was in charge of the sewerage system of the Boston metropolitan area. It should be compelled,
Golden argued, to enforce current state and federal laws and
regulations mandating the proper treatment of sewage and the
protection of the environment.

While both men shared a commitment to the goal of cleaning
up the harbor, they could not agree as to which approach was
best. And so they parted.

Three months later, on December 17, 1982, the city of
Quincy, led by Golden, filed a complaint against the Metropolitan District Commission (MDC) and the Boston Water and
Sewer Commission (BWSC) that would break the political and
ideological logjam. Significantly, as part of its overall strategy, Quincy delayed pushing its suit to trial until Judge Paul
Garrity was on assignment to the relevant Superior Court of
Norfolk, the county in which the city is located. Under the Massachusetts judicial system, judges of the Superior Court continue
the grand tradition of the circuit courts of an earlier time in the
nation's history, rotating through each of the state's local dis-

tricts to hold trials in the neighborhood that is the site of the dispute.[3]

Quincy's trial lawyer, Peter Koff, an experienced environmental attorney, recalls that after the filing of the complaint, the parties engaged in discussions for several months, attempting to strike a compromise. In the interval, Koff patiently waited for Garrity to be assigned to the Norfolk court, which occurred in June 1983. Paul Garrity was widely regarded by Boston lawyers as a maverick ready to deploy the power of the court to address broad social problems and to overcome what he believed to be injustice. On the basis of his knowledge of Garrity's past decisions, Koff believed that this judge would not be afraid to take drastic and unprecedented steps in a case involving such a major issue as the befouling of Boston Harbor.

THE INITIAL COMPLAINT

Quincy's legal complaint was lengthy. At its heart it alleged that injuries had resulted and were continuing to occur from discharges of untreated and partially treated sewage from the Nut Island wastewater treatment plant in Quincy, and from the BWSC's Moon Island outfall, roughly in the middle of Boston Harbor, which discharged untreated sewage overflows that could not be handled by the MDC's Deer Island wastewater treatment plant, located further to the north in Winthrop. These discharges, the city argued, resulted in the continuous pollution of Boston Harbor and made the state defendants responsible for multiple violations of various state statutes.[4] Quincy sought injunctive, remedial, and declaratory relief, meaning that it wanted the chronic pollution of Boston Harbor, Quincy Bay, and adjacent waters stopped now and forever more.

More particularly, Quincy asserted five bases of liability:

- violations of the Massachusetts Clean Water Act, General Laws c.21, §§26–53 (prohibiting discharges of pollutants into coastal waters without, or contrary to, a joint federal-state permit);[5]

- violations of General Laws c.130, §25 (prohibiting discharges of pollutants into coastal waters) and c.91, §59 (prohibiting discharges into tidal waters or flats of any petroleum products or other refuse matter in such manner as to pollute or contaminate);[6]

- violations of General Laws c.92, §1 (requiring the MDC to maintain a system of sewage disposal for the towns it served);

- infringement of General Laws c.30, §61 (requiring the MDC to minimize environmental damage from Nut Island) and the Massachusetts Environmental Policy Act, General Laws c.30, §§61–62H (requiring environmental impact assessments);[7]

- violations of the common law of nuisance.

RAISING THE STAKES

In its answer of February 11, 1983, the Boston Water and Sewer Commission pointed the finger at the Metropolitan District Commission, claiming that discharges of untreated sewage from its Moon Island outfall were a direct result of the MDC's failure to properly operate the Deer Island plant. Furthermore, the BWSC argued, there was nothing in the record to support the contention that discharges from Moon Island had an adverse impact on Quincy Bay.

For its part, the MDC filed a counterclaim on April 20, 1983, alleging that Quincy routinely discharged pollution through storm drains at Wollaston Beach. The MDC, as owner and operator of the beach, alleged that it suffered injury from Quincy's disregard for environmental regulations in the city's failure to maintain its own storm drains—in other words, that the pollution alleged by Quincy was its own doing.

So far, the plaintiff and the defendants were engaged in the kind of narrowly adversarial accusations and responses, claims and counterclaims, that had stymied the effort to solve the problem of the pollution of the harbor for decades. That was about to change.

On June 9, 1983, without opposition, Judge Garrity granted the plaintiff's motion to amend its original complaint. The amended complaint joined three additional state parties as defendants: Thomas C. McMahon, director of the Division of Water Pollution Control in the state Department of Environmental Quality Engineering (DEQE); Anthony D. Cortese, commissioner of the DEQE; and James S. Hoyte, secretary of the state's Executive Office of Environmental Affairs. In addition, the plaintiff added a cause of action seeking a writ of mandamus based on these three defendants' failures to remedy the alleged violations of law.[8]

For all the parties involved, the state case was further complicated by another major lawsuit concerning Boston Harbor, this one brought in the federal district court by the Conservation Law Foundation (CLF). On June 7, 1983, the CLF filed suit against the MDC. Also joined as defendants were William Geary, in his capacity as chairman of the MDC, the U.S. Environmental Protection Agency (EPA), William Ruckelshaus, in his capacity as administrator of EPA, and Paul Keough, in his capacity as Region I EPA administrator. This lawsuit alleged that the MDC had systematically and illegally discharged billions of gallons of improperly treated or raw sewage into the harbor for more than a decade, and that the EPA had failed to perform its duties under the federal Clean Water Act to require compliance by the MDC with that act's requirements. Eventually, on March 27, 1984, Judge A. David Mazzone of the U.S. District Court in Boston stayed proceedings in the federal action in deference to the existence of the *Quincy* litigation in the state court.

Meanwhile, the action in Judge Garrity's court proceeded rapidly. On June 15, 1983, he held a hearing on three motions filed by the plaintiff: for a preliminary injunction; to refer the case to a special master under Massachusetts Civil Procedure Rule 53; and to order the MDC to give Quincy prompt notice of Nut Island sewage discharges. As part of its effort to broaden the scope of the case and bring pressure to bear on political leaders as well as the managers of the relevant state agencies, the city further requested that the court restrain the MDC from admitting any new communities to its system, allowing any major expansion of a municipal system connecting to the MDC system, or accepting for treatment more than 2,000 gallons of sewage per day resulting from any new connections to any municipal system constituting part of the MDC collection system. Quincy, in addition, asked that the court restrain the three newly added state defendants from approving any new sewer connection permits or financial grants for sewage collection systems that would expand the sewage loads at the MDC's treatment plants.

Although the nominal defendants in the case were state agencies and their administrators, the real albeit unnamed target, and the only body truly capable of solving the problem, was the state legislature. Years of underfunding and neglect of the MDC—including the legislature's taking advantage of an MDC fee assessment system that did not sequester collected monies for water treatment purposes but allowed them to go into the general treasury—had led to inadequate capacity and the failure to maintain and repair the agency's water and sewerage facilities. Therefore, it was the legislature's acts—or, rather, multiple failures to act—that formed the unstated bases for Quincy's complaint.

Further legal research soon led to further motions by the city of Quincy. In a letter to the court dated June 17, 1983, Quincy's counsel suggested an alternative remedy that would soon become the cry of the day: that the "[c]ourt order a system-wide reduction of two gallons/day in existing wastewater flow in the MDC sewerage system for every new gallon/day which would be added into the system by means of new connections, permits, expansions, new collection systems, or system expansion"—a proposal designed to capture the attention of anyone who had an economic stake in the Massachusetts Miracle.

PRELIMINARY RULINGS

Judge Garrity moved quickly to provide injunctive relief. On June 27, 1983, a mere ten days after the last in a series of motions for relief had been filed by Quincy, he issued a first round of "Findings, Rulings, and Orders on Plaintiff City of Quincy's Application for Preliminary Injunctive Relief," a dramatic harbinger of what would soon unfold. He found that the alleged violations cited in the complaint had more than likely occurred and concluded that the plaintiff had asserted "enforceable legal claims" under the applicable state statutes. He held that increased sewage loads (probably due to economic development in the metropolitan area), in combination with deteriorating conditions at Deer Island and Nut Island, had resulted in substantial amounts of untreated and inadequately treated sewage being discharged into Boston Harbor and adjoining waters. Consequently, Garrity ruled: "the damage to [Boston Harbor] and to the creatures who live in it may very well become irreversible unless measures are taken to control and at some point preclude the pollution and consequent destruction of that very valuable resource."

The court accordingly held that the MDC was indeed probably in violation of the Massachusetts Clean Water Act and other state environmental statutes by virtue of its discharging pollutants in violation of sewage permits issued to it jointly by the EPA and the state's Division of Water Pollution Control. In addition, Garrity concluded, the MDC actions (or, rather, inactions) presumptively violated the two other state statutes (General Laws c.130, §25, and General Laws c.91, §59) cited in Quincy's suit, because the discharges threatened both the public's health and valuable shellfish beds in the area.[9]

WHY QUINCY?

Looking back at these events, one question is particularly intriguing: Why was the city of Quincy willing to do battle in court, while other communities served by the MDC, including those similarly situated on the edge of the harbor, sat idle? A puzzling query, and one with important implications for citizen activism.

Undoubtedly the personalities and experiences of key individuals played a role, such as William Golden's run on Wollaston Beach and his determination to press the issue. Economic theory, too, may provide a clue, especially the notions of consumer surplus and the differential response to quality decline. Individuals or communities are essentially "free riders" when they benefit from "consumer surplus" and are able to enjoy more benefits than the average consumer from a given product or service and yet pay the same price for it. To the city of Quincy, the consumer surplus generated by adequate, effective pre-discharge sewage treatment—part of the service for which it was paying the MDC —was embodied in the opportunity to engage in fishing, sailing, swimming, and the aesthetic pleasures that accrue to a harborside community. That surplus had once been substantial, giving Quincy's residents more for their sewage treatment dollar than was enjoyed by their inland counterparts, who were also "customers" of the MDC but were further away from the harbor. However, as the harbor became increasingly fouled by inadequately treated sewage, the benefits enjoyed by the cities abutting the harbor were correspondingly reduced. Indeed, one could even argue that a "consumer deficit" had been created; it was the harborside cities that bore the environmental damage. This was one source of Quincy's incentive to take action.

If one envisions the city of Quincy as a customer faced with a decreasing consumer surplus, one can readily understand the city's willingness to expend resources in an effort to check the ongoing deterioration of the harbor's waters and its impact on Wollaston Beach. Since the consumers enjoying a surplus have the most to lose through a deterioration in the quality of a product or service, it is likely that they will be the ones who are most motivated to take action to prevent such a loss.[10]

But why did Quincy stand alone? Why didn't all or at least several of the cities along the harbor come together in a unified legal and extralegal front to take action against the pollution that grew more intolerable every year? To help answer that part of the query, an economist might point to the phenomenon of differential response to quality deterioration and its divisive effects.

Although all the members of a designated group of consumers may appear to hold virtually identical positions in a particular service market, a given deterioration in service quality may inflict quite different losses on each of them. In addition, customers' appreciation of quality varies, as does sensitivity to its decline. Consequently, even similarly situated communities do not necessarily react with strategic unity in selecting some point that represents an intolerable level of deterioration. Instead, individual actions will be staggered over time and will vary in both form and intensity, and these varied responses may have little or no effect on the larger situation.

As many of us who became involved in the *Quincy* litigation understood, the design and implementation of any comprehensive harbor revitalization plan would depend on creating a coalition large enough to unite the distinct interests of many different individuals and communities, agencies, and institutions in order to break through the differential response barrier.[11] This understanding shaped both the course of the litigation and the political and legislative action that followed upon it.

THE JUDGE

Just as Peter Koff had sensed, the personality and outlook of Judge Paul Garrity would dominate the *Quincy* litigation.

I had known the judge for many years before I became involved in this particular case. I enjoyed his humorous and tolerant outlook on life, and admired his strength of mind and dedication to public service. We had become close friends, able to talk directly and frankly about procedural and personal matters—and we shared an interest in Boston politics, the fairness of the legal system, and institutional reform.

We had first worked together at the Harvard Law School during the academic year 1970–1971, when Garrity studied for an LL.M. degree. At that time efforts were being made to change an establishment-oriented legal training (some labeled it a breeding ground for future mercenaries of capitalism) to encompass a broader, more humane, and more inclusionary legal vision. A grant from the Ford Foundation had initiated a program to support the newly emerging field of public interest law at Harvard. As part of this program Paul Garrity helped me to place students in firms and agencies that focused on addressing the physical, economic, and social deterioration of metropolitan areas that was then becoming pronounced throughout the country. Two important components of this work were fostering local community participation and finding ways to attract the private sector to join public agencies in meeting the need for affordable housing.

Three years later, Garrity was appointed by Governor Francis Sargent to the Massachusetts housing court, which was specifically designed to hear and resolve landlord-tenant disputes that had lingered too long in other venues. He threw himself into the endeavor with full force. During his tenure Garrity's special abilities to see problems afresh came to the fore. He introduced a new record-keeping system and novel guidelines for the presentation of cases; he endorsed videotapes and other technological means as admissible evidence of slum conditions; and he established criteria for compliance with building codes and housing laws. Through negotiation and mediation he used the power of the court to press for the settlement of difficult warranty-of-habitability disputes, and he pestered law firms to do pro bono work on behalf of tenants. All of this enormously creative work was aimed at eradicating slum housing and the racial discrimination that prevailed in the low-income housing sector. So outstanding was this work—unorthodox as it also was in many instances— that he was soon appointed by the governor as a general trial judge in the Superior Court.

Garrity's knowledge of the residential housing industry and his desire to improve living conditions for the poor were among the characteristics that made him the perfect choice to preside over litigation against the Boston Housing Authority (BHA) that arose several years later, in 1980. His judicial temperament did not tolerate excessive bureaucracy or unnecessary delay (paralleling, perhaps, his zeal in running each morning and participating in Boston marathons). Not only did he rail against unresponsive government in speeches and public forums, but he also came up with methods for applying the scissors to red tape, for shortening time for paperwork, and for seeking alternative remedies, thereby cutting through what seemed an impenetrable institutional hierarchy. In the same vein, he also pushed for consensus: "All right, if you need the participation of differing groups in order to have action, let's bring them together—now. Let's reason about it, and let's come to a conclusion—there's no justification for waiting months and months for matters to coalesce." He was experienced in sizing up a person's character, knew when to grasp and when to yield, and was always ready to argue, scold, and push for action.

Garrity's willingness to go beyond the confines of traditional judicial restraint disturbed some members of the bar who cast him as a self-aggrandizing cowboy breaking the rules. But while his unpredictability raised difficulties for those lawyers who were strongly wedded to rules and standard procedures, it was this very flexibility that enabled him to make reform possible.

The Boston Housing Authority case offered a striking example of Garrity's no-nonsense judicial approach. A group of tenants brought suit against the agency over the appalling condition of the public housing in which they lived. After a year of attempting to cajole and persuade the BHA (then under the dominance of Mayor Kevin White) to reform its ways, Garrity saw no option but to put it into receivership.[12] With his choice of a young, public service–oriented lawyer named Harry Spence as the receiver, he took the startling step of moving public housing units out of the hands of an inept administration and carving out a new path to improve the living conditions of 50,000 Boston citizens.

As a member of the advisory board put together to help with the transition, I attended regular meetings where alternative courses of action were analyzed and decided upon. I saw firsthand the extraordinary effort and ingenuity that Garrity and Spence applied to the task of improving conditions in the city's public housing projects, including heroic exertions to change the operation, outlook, and perceptions of managers and tenants alike on issues ranging from the bidding procedure for construction and repair jobs to the participation of tenants in managing the projects' affairs. By assuring the federal authorities in Washington and the regional office of the Department of Housing and Urban Development of the seriousness of their intent, and through direct intervention with congressional representatives, they were also able to secure increased federal funds for the BHA.

Later, working with Garrity in the Lincoln Institute Round Table on Land Policy, I witnessed his impressive combination of keen analytic ability and practical experience. His questions, observations, and conclusions about the role of law in environmental policy were insightful.

Finally, despite his elevation to Establishment status, Paul Garrity never lost sight of his roots, of his immigrant family's struggle to make it in America. He was proud of his father, a streetcar conductor in Yankee-dominated Boston, and a man who worked out his days as a shop foreman in a car barn in Jamaica Plain. "And why did I go to law school?" Garrity would ask rhetorically. "Irish insecurity. Boston Irish insecurity." Throughout his career he had been a fighter for the poor and abused, and he knew well how the legal system did not always act as responsibly as it should or as it presented itself as doing. The formative experiences and unique personality of the presiding judge would thus put their stamp on the *Quincy* litigation.

As was true for the BHA case, the lawsuit brought by the city of Quincy addressed a situation in which the breakdown of state institutions was causing direct harm to a large number of people and adversely affecting society as a whole. By their very nature such cases involve many parties, each with a different set of interests and a different stake in the outcome, resulting in an immense tangle of government agencies, laws, and regulations.

The *Quincy* litigation also posed a series of knotty scientific and technical questions. How could one determine which of several parties was responsible for the filth that had washed up on one particular beach? How did the condition of Quincy Bay relate to the pollution of the whole harbor? What action could be taken by the court that would provide a real remedy for the harm that had occurred and prevent further damage in the future?

No matter how brilliant and energetic, a judge is but a single individual. Cases of this scope present a huge challenge to a legal system designed, in essence, to resolve disputes between two contending parties based on the evidence and testimony offered by each. Hence the law provides for the appointment of a special master in complex litigations to aid the court in making findings of fact under the law—whether, for instance, an alleged violation of a statute has occurred—and preparing recommendations regarding judicial action. The activities of a special master, directed by the presiding judge, include taking testimony and affidavits relevant to the facts of the case at hand, soliciting the opinions of experts, and—in my view the most important—serving as an informal conduit for sharing information among the parties directly and indirectly involved.

On July 6, 1983, Judge Garrity convened a special hearing to consider the plaintiff's request for the appointment of a special master in the *Quincy* matter, "to come up with the most effective remedy and to prepare a comprehensive order with provisions for oversight and fine-tuning." I received a call from the judge one day later with an offer I could not refuse.

COPING WITH COMPLEXITIES 3
Signing On as Special Master

For the lawyers, they write . . . what is received law, and not
what ought to be law; for the wisdom of a lawmaker is one,
that of a lawyer is another. There are in nature certain fountains of justice, whence all civil laws are derived but as
streams; and like as waters do take tinctures and tastes from
the soils through which they run, so do civil laws vary according to the regions and governments where they are planted,
though they proceed from the same fountains.

—Francis Bacon

In the summer of 1983, on a trip to London that promised
to combine research on British and U.S. land planning laws
with evenings at the theater, I received an urgent phone call
from Paul Garrity. "When are you coming home?" he asked. "In
about two weeks," I told him. "Can you make it sooner? It's a
major case." We met a few days later at the Harvard faculty
club.

Our discussion over lunch was short and high-spirited. The
judge filled me in about the proceeding that was before him involving the city of Quincy's suit against various state agencies to
halt the pollution of Boston Harbor. This struck me at once as a
unique event with national ramifications. At the frontier of intellectual analysis, it was bound to prove critical for the ongoing
reformulation of environmental law and policy. Its results would
ripple through many ecological quandaries and require a close
examination of existing land-use and environmental rules and
the modifications necessary to adapt them to the conditions of
the modern world. For someone long involved with the law of
land planning, it was an irresistible opportunity.

When Judge Garrity asked me to serve as the special master in the *Quincy* case, I leapt at the invitation. But I needed to make quick decisions about other obligations. I had been active in public service before, notably as the first assistant secretary for metropolitan development of the newly formed U.S. Department of Housing and Urban Development (HUD) from 1965 to 1968. The Washington experience, which included working directly for President Lyndon Johnson on several of his task forces, had expanded my professional horizons. And it left me with the conviction that government action in the public interest can benefit people's lives.

Moreover, working on *Quincy* and striving to resolve conflicts among interest groups could benefit my teaching of the law. Experience with the world beyond academia, especially with what lawyers do on a day-to-day basis, is necessary for a law professor engaged in preparing people for actual practice. In my classes I have always tried to connect the course work to the realities of the society around us. Otherwise, an insulated perspective fosters an outlook too remote from the hard knocks of litigation and negotiation, the challenges of daily conflict and reconciliation that constitute the life of an active lawyer.

Moreover, my engagement in the harbor situation could be useful locally in showing that the Harvard Law School and its faculty were involved in community affairs and with their immediate neighborhoods. Town-gown relations might be improved by a member of the Harvard faculty working on practical issues confronting the Boston community.

As I learned from personal involvement, public service offers a residue of learning experiences and a sense of being challenged to the limit of one's capacities. As usual, Justice Holmes was right on point when he urged the lawyer to "wreak himself upon life" and engage in the passions and actions of his own time. And *Quincy* presented the rare opportunity to make a contribution to the general good: I knew that Paul Garrity was a fighter, possessed of outstanding capacity for personal loyalty and determined to use his office to the fullest, within the bounds of his authority, in the pursuit of social justice. As I learned, a relation of deep trust between the judge and the special master is absolutely essential when dealing with matters as contentious and strenuous as institutional breakdown litigations. Personal relations can become the deciding factor in situations that are unclear and unsettled, with no patterns or precedents to draw upon in a time of crisis.

At our first meeting a major concern was the pressure of time. Having just completed a new edition of a land-use planning casebook, I was eager to try it out in class, and I was committed to other research and committee work. Judge Garrity brushed these considerations off, saying that the stress of the litigation would not be unduly severe and it would all be manageable within the time constraints. I was not so sure, but the appeal of playing a part in this dramatic event was too strong.

In the end I was persuaded by the judge's assurances that the job would not be too taxing and that it would blend in with my normal professional activities. After all, I had found my three years of experience with HUD and at the White House riveting and satisfying despite all the demands and drains in terms of time and energy. After talking over the possibility with my family (being careful to emphasize the positive aspects of the work), I agreed to go ahead.

Based on his strongly worded preliminary findings, Judge Garrity announced his decision on July 8, 1983, to grant the plaintiff's motion for reference to a master, with me as appointee, charged first to resolve disputed issues of fact, to hear evidence, and to make findings thereon.[1] Turning to the remedy, as special master I was further ordered to make a report to the court with suggested injunctive relief, if any. It was clear that the judge wanted more than a narrow resolution of the case; he wanted a solution to the problems of Boston Harbor. "In sum," the judge concluded, "there is an urgency about this that the political branches of government just do not seem to be responding to appropriately."

Central to the outcome of the *Quincy* case was the court's appointment of Steven G. Horowitz, an attorney with the law firm of Hill & Barlow in Boston, as deputy special master. Steven had been a brilliant student at Harvard Law, serving as book review editor on the *Harvard Law Review*. He had also worked as special monitor for Judge Joseph L. Tauro of the federal district court in the highly publicized cases involving the state's treatment of the mentally retarded at the Fernald School. This experience had given him special insights into the role of a judge in complex institutional litigations, an awareness that proved indispensable as work on the *Quincy* case proceeded.

A superb analyst, Steven became a crucial counterweight to the more mercurial Judge Garrity and even to myself. He and I had worked together earlier, for Chief Judge Thomas Morse of the Massachusetts Superior Court, in a major Boston school system finance case in which we were successful in finding the money that enabled the public schools to continue to operate after the school budget ran out. This was accomplished over the objections of Mayor Kevin White, then engaged in a bitter running battle with the school board over its budget, and entailed dissecting the financials that concealed significant city assets. I admired Steven's capacity for grasping fine detail and his ability to stay open-minded and to analyze all sides of a case with careful deliberation. A lawyer's lawyer, he was bent on finding established legal principles to resolve situations rather than on inventing extrajudicial solutions. He asked probing questions of witnesses and would not be diverted from his pursuit. Of virtually the same generation as our student assistants, he brought out the best in them and coordinated their joint contribution to our efforts.

THE NATURE OF THE COMPLAINT:
ARGUMENTS MADE AND NOT MADE

After listing its charges of violation of five statutory rules, Quincy asked by way of remedy for preliminary and permanent injunctions. Well versed in the history of Judge Garrity's behavior in prior litigation, the city did not hesitate to take the rather extreme position of requesting that the court place the Metropolitan District Commission (MDC) in receivership. That would effectively take the agency out of executive and legislative control and put the judge in charge.

The shotgun approach of the complaint filed by the city thoroughly covered the statutory aspects of the case. But what about other claims not cited by Quincy that might be determinative, the arguments not made?

During one discussion, well past midnight, Steven Horowitz and I were speculating about what other causes of action, if any, might be raised. Part of our job was to consider pertinent claims not raised by the parties. Bolstering the Quincy complaint by raising constitutional issues, for instance, was an open possibility. We scoured that basic document—the constitution of the Commonwealth of Massachusetts—to ascertain whether its provisions supported or undercut the litigation. The general rule under which judges operate is that a court should confine itself to statutory provisions where possible to resolve a case, avoiding, where it can, the more fundamental provisions of the constitution, since their application may strain relations with the other branches of government. In addition, judges worry that bringing in the constitution too many times may dim its lustre. If one can resolve an issue on statutory grounds, only rarely is the constitution invoked as well.

On the other hand, a constitutional claim bears certain advantages. A breach of a constitutional provision is deemed a more serious flouting of fundamental rights than a statutory violation and therefore when properly invoked justifies a greater wielding of judicial power. Furthermore—and most important with respect to holding an exercise of executive or legislative power to be illegal—constitutional provisions are seen as the special terrain of judges, an area wherein their true competence resides and where they encounter the least difficulty about overstepping their judicial authority.

Our eyes fell on Article XCVII. It provided:

> The people shall have the right to clean air and water, freedom from excessive and unnecessary noise, and the natural, scenic, historic, and aesthetic qualities of their environment; and the protection of the people in their right to the conservation, development and utilization of the agricultural, mineral, forest, water, air and other natural resources is hereby declared to be a public purpose. The general court [that is, the legislature] shall have the power to enact legislation necessary or expedient to protect such rights. In the furtherance of the foregoing powers, the general court shall have the power to provide for the taking, upon payment of just compensation therefor, or for the acquisition by purchase or otherwise, of lands and easements or such other interests therein as may be deemed necessary to accomplish these purposes.[2]

Several themes and counterthemes play out in possible interpretations of this article. If the desire is to minimize its impact, it might be argued that Article XCVII was passed with the idea of supporting the ability of the commonwealth, through the exercise of eminent domain, to take land for environmental purposes. Therefore, its conferral of power should be interpreted narrowly as dealing only with the ability to exercise the power. This is plainly one meaning of the article. Yet conceivably its language, without much strain, could be construed broadly to include a right for every citizen of Massachusetts to a minimal level of environmental quality. If so, the plaintiff's case in *Quincy* would be strengthened considerably.

The constitutional issues presented an exciting potential as we explored the historic and legal background of the provision. But we realized that to find liability under Article XCVII would be to fashion a constitutional right that had not been recognized previously; under such circumstances there was risk in predicating the case on a theory that the state defendants would undoubtedly assert was a novel ground and therefore might not be accepted by Judge Garrity. Also, there was greater risk that if the judge did adopt the constitutional theory, such a bold ruling might not be affirmed on appeal. Was it too big a leap to argue that the state constitution, under Article XCVII, called for the cleanup of Boston Harbor? Could judicial action be justified by an expanded environmental right of a constitutional dimension?

If the answer was yes, we would be asking the judge to take a hazardous course of basing a decision on a previously unrecognized constitutional right. Furthermore, going the constitutional route might prove to be a distraction from the statutory claims that were so evidently relevant and well supported. In the end we put aside the temptation to ask Judge Garrity to make new law, while we kept Article XCVII's potential in mind as a constitutional basis for wider government powers for environmental issues in the future.

As for liability under the various state statutes cited in the complaint, a preliminary question arose that gave some pause. A general rule is that a legislature has no obligation to fund the programs it creates; the act to create a program and the act to appropriate money for its operation are independent of each other, and each action resides within the legislature's discretion. In Washington, for instance, it is common practice to distinguish between an "authorization Congress" and an "appropriation

Congress," for often the twain do not meet. If a legislative body creates a legal right but declines to appropriate sufficient revenue to carry it out, it has arguably repealed its own earlier mandate. Hence the applicable tenet of statutory interpretation, as one court has stated it, is that "a definite legislative intent as reflected in the general appropriation laws necessarily supersedes any previously expressed legislative desires at least for the duration of the particular appropriation act." As the opinion goes on by way of explanation, "[t]he earlier statutes cannot coexist with the enacted appropriation and, consequently, must be deemed to be suspended by adoption of the later appropriation acts."[3]

In the Boston Harbor dispute, therefore, even if actions or inactions of the MDC were found to violate state law, to the degree that this resulted from a failure of funding through lack of legislative appropriation, it could be argued, there was no "violation" at all. Instead, the legislature may be understood, by its choice of failing to appropriate, as having suspended the agency's obligation to conform with the authorizing provisions of the law.

An alternative possible ground for liability existed: the state court could hold that the Massachusetts legislature, by nonfunding or underfunding the MDC, was in violation of *federal* law. The legal relationship between the MDC and the EPA, the relevant federal agency, is governed in its specifics by the federal permit regulating the MDC's treatment of sewage rather than by the terms of a sweeping statute. In the past the EPA had repeatedly granted waivers to the MDC, excusing actions outlawed by the permit; hence the argument that the MDC was in violation of its permit was not available. Presumably the EPA should have enforced the original permit conditions and refused waivers, so that the city of Quincy could argue that in bringing suit, it was doing the work that the EPA should have undertaken.[4] Be that as it may, EPA's actions in not asserting powers over the violator emerged as an estoppel that weakened the possibility of basing judgment for the plaintiff on a federal claim.[5]

THE LAW OF NUISANCE

Another front for liability that Quincy had not pursued was the common law of nuisance. There always hovered in the background the possibility that the MDC and other defendants could be found liable for unlawfully polluting the city's beaches and surrounding waters under the common law theory of unreasonably interfering with the right of the citizens to the use and enjoyment of their property.

The black-letter statement is that the law of nuisance can be used to terminate a "noxious use" or avert a "public harm" that unreasonably interferes with the lives or property of the general public. These terms have come to encompass a miscellaneous group of offenses centering on interferences with the interests of the community at large. No better definition of a public nuisance, inconclusive though it may be, has emerged from the myriad of rulings dealing with disturbances of the welfare of the general public than that provided in a classic English text: "an act or omission which obstructs or causes inconvenience or damage to the public in the exercise of rights common to all Her Majesty's subjects."[6] Yet "there is perhaps no more impenetrable jungle in the entire law," one of the preeminent authorities in this field reminds us, "than that which surrounds the word 'nuisance,'" explaining that the term "has been applied indiscriminately to everything from an alarming advertisement to a cockroach baked in a pie."[7]

The doctrines of the law of nuisance go back to the twelfth century. And so the equitable remedy of an injunction against a public nuisance, one of the earliest milestones in English common law, has been used in a host of British and American judicial decisions. Owing to its amorphous parameters—and the flexibility it provides—defining the law of nuisance is a never-ending task for judges in state courts. There seem no anchors to be found once embarked upon the ship of nuisance. It has been applied with considerable openness to new uses and types of regulation. If in law the word "nuisance" comprehends a wide variety of conduct that can be held to represent unreasonable interference with the health, safety, morals, welfare, or comfort of the general public, why not add to the long and historic list the pollution of a harbor's waters?[8] This, it could be argued, represents a far more serious breach of the public good than cockroaches in one's pie.

At first glance, one answer to this question from the point of view of legal strategy is that the broad statutory schemes for environmental protection developed by the federal government in recent years preempt and supersede, to a large degree, the operation of the common law of nuisance. This interpretation, however, does not fit comfortably into our federalist system of the division of powers between the state and federal governments. Nuisance law is a matter of state, rather than federal, law. And as it has been developed by the states it is flexible and evolving, always subject to interpretation and expansion or contraction—with a consequent reluctance of courts to find it preempted by federal action. In any event, no federal statute has expressly stated that its purpose is to supersede state nuisance law. Therefore, since the usefulness of employing the hallowed nuisance concept in the interests of preventing environmental harm ought not be lost in a rush to bury the past, such federal preemption is unlikely to be found by the state court.

In a case such as that of Boston Harbor, where water pollution affects an interest common to the general public, the Massachusetts common law of nuisance—long-standing and applicable in a wide variety of resource settings—stands as a potent tool for environmental regulation or redress.[9] Certainly this approach received a boost after Justice Scalia's opinion in the U.S.

Supreme Court in *Lucas* in 1992, restoring nuisance to the everyday vocabulary of lawyers and judges.[10] There Justice Scalia happily allowed that nuisance law could trump a property owner's exercise of rights, as well as the owner's ability to receive compensation for a constitutional taking by land use or environmental regulations.

The truly exciting aspect of nuisance law is that it is not frozen in the concerns of a past period, but over the centuries has been reinterpreted in the light of contemporary learning and fresh understandings, reflecting technological advances, newly perceived hazards, and pressing societal changes.[11] It is thereby adaptable to newly arisen controversies and issues. Despite ancient lineage and origins in an agricultural and rural society, the value of the law of nuisance remains a factor to be taken into account in current litigations in the ongoing readjustments of doctrine to emerging needs.[12]

We decided to keep all our options open. As is apparent, there was a wide range of theories that environmental law could draw upon in the search for the regeneration of Boston Harbor. Choosing among the competing doctrinal possibilities—constitutional, statutory, and the common law of nuisance—would be a challenge for the lawyers and the court. The pleadings of the parties set the framework within which the report of the special master to Judge Garrity would be formulated. And with regard to strategies, motions, or procedures, it was the facts of the particular *Quincy* case that would be determinative of the end result.

But my reading of the complaint raised the question, why had the state not acted earlier? This was the query I put to the principals, their witnesses, and the experts during the *Quincy* trial. This issue cropped up as well in the interviews, the evaluations of technical and engineering reports, and the analyses of contemporary accounts. It was a puzzlement. Had the desire for economic growth obscured the undesirable technological by-products and pitfalls that threatened the vital natural resource of Boston Harbor? Was the dedication to economic progress so deeply embedded that the citizens persuaded themselves the pollution problems did not exist, and, even if they did, they could be solved later if and when a crisis arose? Had the visible dangers to the beauty of the city somehow failed to engage common perceptions? Were the business, educational, and political elites not aware of the impact of pollution in the harbor as it corroded the quality of life in Boston and the commonwealth as a whole? Were there powerful political and economic interests that simply wished the problem away?

THE SETTING
The Plants, Pipes, and Pumps of Boston Harbor

The sewer is the conscience of the city. All things converge
and confront one another there. In this ghastly place there are
shadows but there are no more secrets. Everything takes on
its true shape, or at least its definitive shape. One can say this
for the refuse heap—it is not a liar. . . . All the filthiness of civilization, once out of commission, falls into this pit of truth
where the immense social slippage ends up.

—Victor Hugo

Understanding the decline and fall of Boston Harbor calls
for a fuller description of the physical setting of the *Quincy*
case and of the sewerage facilities operated by the Metropolitan
District Commission.

Fed by three major tributaries—the Mystic, Charles, and Neponset Rivers—Boston Harbor encompasses an area of forty-
seven square miles and, depending on the tides, contains between 107,000 and 180,000 million gallons of water.[1] Tidal
flows circulate seawater between it and the larger Massachusetts
Bay and the ocean beyond; in addition, the rivers bring 500 million gallons of freshwater into the harbor basin each day. It is
one of the largest and best-situated natural harbors serving a
major city on the East Coast.

Geography, tidal flows, and shipping routes divide the harbor
into a northern half—consisting of the Inner Harbor, Dorchester
Bay, Winthrop Bay, and the portion of the outer harbor north of
Long Island—and a southern half, composed of Hingham Bay,
Quincy Bay, and the outer harbor south of Long Island.[2]

In addition to its practical uses, the beaches and islands of
Boston Harbor have been favorite recreation spots since the

days when President John Adams, a Quincy resident, enjoyed "the fishing frolick, the Water frolick" in the waters and islands of the bay.[3] "[T]here [are] no such pleasant Prospects of the Country as in Boston Harbour," he noted in his journal.[4]

The recognition of the area as a unique and distinctive combination of historical, commercial, and natural resources placed the participants in the *Quincy* case in the direct line of two hundred years of concern. "I hope that No Efforts, No Labour, or Expence will be spared in securing Boston Harbour against Enemies," Adams had written urgently in the crisis year of 1776.[5] Many engaged in the *Quincy* litigation felt that the current threat to the harbor was no less tangible than the one Adams had feared, and that the project of defeating the modern-day enemy of pollution was no less worthy of the most intense efforts.

HARBOR USES

When Quincy drafted its complaint in 1982, the port of Boston was the major seaport in New England, offering more than 156 piers, wharves, and terminals linked to its two primary shipping channels. It handled massive tonnages of petroleum and other energy products, and Boston and adjacent cities were home to important segments of the nation's shipbuilding and maritime shipping industries.

Since the 1970s the commercial and residential possibilities of an urban waterfront had drawn increased attention from planners, developers, and investors. There was renewed interest in attracting more marine-related uses as well as mixed commercial-residential development that would take advantage of the harbor's aesthetic, recreational, and tourist potential.

Recreational uses of the harbor included swimming, strolling, and sunbathing on more than thirty saltwater beaches—serving an estimated 160,000 people on an average summer day—in addition to sport fishing and pleasure boating of all kinds. Some

5,000 boats were moored in Boston Harbor, and another 30,000 vessels entered the harbor annually from the Charles and Mystic Rivers. The harbor's islands offered docking facilities, camping, fishing, hiking, and a host of historic sites.

Swimming in the harbor waters decades earlier, as a child and adolescent, remained a vivid memory for Judge Garrity and for many of his generation, a recollection triggered by sundry testimonies as the trial proceeded. The proximity of nearby city beaches such as Revere Beach, to the north of Boston, had always been a major boon for the people of the metropolitan area, especially the poor, who could not afford a car to travel to other recreational facilities farther away.

But despite the rosy vision of developers and planners, Boston, like many American cities, had turned its back on its harbor for too long. During the summer months the amount of sewage and other pollutants present in its waters often made the harbor's inner beaches—those most relied on by poor and working-class residents—unusable, a fact that rankled the judge as another deprivation imposed on the disadvantaged.

The increasing pollution of the harbor not only prevented swimming but also had a deleterious effect on local fisheries. For example, the harvesting of shellfish—especially of softshell clams—had been an important commercial use of Boston Harbor since time immemorial, but in recent years water quality deterioration had resulted in the loss of more than half of each year's potential shellfish harvest.

HISTORY OF BOSTON HARBOR POLLUTION

The pollution problem of Boston, however much it was worsening, was certainly not brand-new. Despite the cherished prospect it presented to President Adams, Boston Harbor had, in truth, been plagued by pollution ever since the colonization of the area by Europeans. And the disposal of sewage—"refuse liquids or waste matter" carried off by water through "an artificial, usually subterranean conduit"[6]—had proven to be the largest source of contamination throughout the harbor's history.

The wastes dumped directly into the harbor by the Puritans in the seventeenth century were limited primarily to garbage and the entrails of animals discarded by butchers (human waste went into privies). But as the town of Boston and the surrounding communities grew in size and sophistication in the eighteenth century, the townspeople built sewers to carry both the storm runoff and household and commercial wastes into nearby waters. Until the 1820s, upstream residents used the Mystic, Charles, and Neponset Rivers as arteries for carrying their waste out to the harbor. With greater Boston's emergence as a center of America's Industrial Revolution, the quantity and toxicity of the pollutants released into the harbor increased markedly, ranging from raw sewage discharged by the area's growing population to chemicals released by wool mills, dye works, and other industries.

At the same time, a series of landfill projects in Boston converted the coves and marshes that originally surrounded the Shawmut Peninsula into what are now the West End, Back Bay, and South End neighborhoods. The suburbs of Charlestown, Roxbury, and Dorchester were incorporated into the city. Not surprisingly, given the speed of growth, including waves of immigration and the advent of indoor plumbing, the approach to dealing with both the runoff from storms and sewage wastewater was disorganized, haphazard, and uncontrolled. Writing in 1885 about the beginnings of Boston's sewer system earlier in the century, Eliot C. Clarke observed,

> The way in which sewers were built at this time was, apparently, this. When some energetic householder on any street decided that a sewer was needed there, he persuaded such of his neighbors as he could to join him in building a street drain. Having obtained permission to open the street or perhaps ne-

glected this preliminary, they built such a structure as they thought necessary, on the shortest line to tide-water.

However, he went on,

> Such changes have taken place in the contours of the city, through operations for reclaiming and filling tidal areas bordering the old limits, that, from being an easy site to sewer, Boston became one presenting many obstacles to the construction of an efficient sewer system. . . . [As a consequence] the contents of the sewers were dammed back by the tide during the greater part of each twelve hours. The sewers were, in general, inadequately ventilated, and the rise of sewage in them compressed the foul air which they contained and tended to force it into the house connections. . . . Under certain conditions of the atmosphere, especially on summer evenings, a well-defined sewage odor would extend over the whole South and West Ends of the city proper.[7]

In 1820 the city installed storm sewers leading out from various neighborhoods to the nearest body of water and thence into the closest part of the harbor. This also allowed Bostonians to connect to the sewers and dispose of household sewage in what was then considered a quick and efficient manner. But the city soon learned, to its distress, that this system failed to carry the sewage far enough away. Complaints about stench and health problems due to the inadequacies of the storm sewers were commonplace. And in 1865 Boston suffered a cholera epidemic that killed many residents and compelled officials to deal anew with the city's sewage disposal problems.

In response to this crisis and other outbreaks of disease, the city constructed a new "Main Drainage" system, which included the use of pumping stations rather than simple gravity to move wastewater from one place to another. Completed in 1884, this system included interceptor sewers intended to divert sewage and stormwater to Moon Island, to the south of the city, where it could be held and expelled further out into the harbor twice a day on the outgoing tide.

In 1886 the Massachusetts Drainage Commission, appointed to consider the problem of sewage disposal from a wider perspective, endorsed the customary idea that "it is best to throw sewage into great quantities of free water." But in contradictory fashion, its report also pointed to the fact that the sheer volume of sewage produced by an industrial metropolis outstripped the capacity of natural processes alone to absorb and neutralize it:

> Human excrement, from its nature and consistency, is more difficult to handle [than solid waste], and it has been found that the easiest method of getting rid of it expeditiously, before it begins to decompose (that is within 24 hours), is to wash it away through pipes by the aid of flowing water. . . . By this method, called sewerage, it is easy to move the water and its contained filth away from the houses where it originates. It is not at all easy, however, to find places to put it where it can do no harm. . . . It is almost impossible to find places where crude sewage can be continuously emptied without doing harm.[8]

In an effort to respond to the increasing scope of the problem, in 1889 the commonwealth created the Metropolitan Sewerage District (MSD) to operate the area's sewage collection and discharge facilities. Not only did the MSD serve a burgeoning city, it was also intended to support the waste disposal needs of seventeen other cities and towns surrounding Boston proper. As a much-expanded system serving forty-three municipalities, it was later operated under the authority of the multiservice Metropolitan District Commission (MDC).[9] By the 1980s little of the system's ninety-year-old equipment had been replaced or updated. One of the main engines that powered the wastewater pumps on Deer Island, for example, was so antiquated that the Smithsonian Institution sought to obtain it as a historic relic for its hallowed halls. The request was turned down—because at the time the machine was still necessary for continued operations at the plant.

As both population and industrial production grew in the early part of the twentieth century, the commonwealth quickly found that dumping raw sewage off Moon Island was far more problematic than originally believed. During the first four decades of the 1900s, complaints induced the Massachusetts legislature to commission six separate investigations regarding the pollution of the harbor. These were careful technical surveys, but they almost invariably came down on the side of nonaction or its equivalent by way of tabling the matter for further study.

In 1936, with a limited knowledge of the pollution's implications for the well-being of local residents and with the wariness characteristic of their trade, researchers cautiously concluded that "the condition of Boston Harbor has not reached such a state as to be dangerous to public health, and the Special Commission cannot therefore recommend that treatment works be provided at this time." Nevertheless, their report went on to propose a specific sewage treatment construction plan since "the population residing in the vicinity of Boston Harbor will soon demand a change."[10] The comments of the 1936 investigators are typical of earlier evaluations: strictly speaking, no new treatment facilities were necessary from a public health standpoint, but warning flags were raised. The situation was acknowledged to be undesirable, but the will to remedy it—at considerable public expense in the midst of the Great Depression—was lacking.

THE THREE SCOURGES: EFFLUENT, SLUDGE, AND CSOs

A significant physical transformation of the MDC system began only in the early 1950s with the construction of new infrastructure aimed at finally satisfying the public "demand" for the "change" that had been foreseen in 1936. Following on the heels of yet another legislative investigation, the MDC was entrusted with the gargantuan task of designing and erecting treatment plants capable of processing all of the sewage and a portion of the stormwater of the metropolitan area. The idea was straightforward: divert wastewater from Boston and other towns and villages abutting the Charles, Neponset, and Mystic Rivers out and away to new and rebuilt facilities where it could be processed to reduce its harmful effects before being released into the harbor.

In 1952 the MDC built a plant on Nut Island—located close to the city of Quincy and now itself a peninsula due to landfill—to treat an average daily flow of 112 million gallons of sewage per day (mgd) and a peak flow of 280. In 1968 a second enormous treatment plant, occupying a considerable portion of Deer Island at the northern edge of the harbor, supplemented the Nut Island plant, which was already overextended. Deer Island was designed to routinely treat up to 343 mgd, with a peak flow of 848 mgd. After the construction of this second plant, the MDC split the metropolitan sewerage system into two distinct systems of community-run sewage collection and treatment networks—the southern system served by Nut Island and the northern by Deer Island—all under the ambit of its Metropolitan Sewerage Division.

The MDC's plants were built to provide only primary sewage treatment, a process by which raw sewage is separated into liquid effluent and solid sludge, then reduced and chlorinated. Screening and sedimentation removed debris and settleable solids (that is, those large enough to settle rapidly out of solution by gravity alone) and reduced the concentration of suspended solids.[11] Floating grease and scum were skimmed from the top of the sedimentation tanks while the heavier materials settled at the bottom. After chlorination, the sewage effluent and digested sludge were discharged to the harbor through submerged outfall pipes. At Deer Island two outfalls with a combined capacity of 400 mgd discharged the chlorinated effluent-sludge mixture to the President Roads shipping channel, near the Deer Island Light, at a depth of fifty feet. Three relief outfalls were utilized in cases of higher flow. The Nut Island plant had two main sixty-inch outfall pipes, each extending for a distance of about 6,000 feet from the shore, discharging effluent to the Nantasket Roads shipping channel. A short, 1,400-foot relief outfall and a 480-foot near-shore overflow outlet were also used for plant effluent when necessary. Sludge from Nut Island was carried along a 4.2-mile outfall across the harbor for release close to Deer Island's discharge point in President Roads.

Secondary treatment, in which the solids and liquids undergo further treatment to reduce the demand for oxygen generated by the decomposition of released waste, was not provided within either facility. Debate over its necessity went on for years between the commonwealth, represented by the MDC, and federal agencies, notably the EPA.

In 1983, as the *Quincy* litigation got underway, the 5,300 miles of local collection sewers owned and operated by the forty-three member municipalities disgorged their burdens into 228 miles of large MDC interceptor sewers. At the time the area served by the MDC exceeded 400 square miles with a total population of more than 2 million. In addition to the interceptor systems, the agency operated the two major sewage treatment plants, Nut Island and Deer Island, along with twenty-two pumping stations.[12]

The northern network collected sewage from twenty-two communities for treatment at Deer Island. The northern system included three headworks at Chelsea Creek, Columbus Park, and Ward Street, where large debris was screened out and grit removed before the wastewater plunged down vertical shafts into deep rock tunnels leading to Deer Island. The tunnel from the Chelsea Creek headworks was approximately four miles long and the one from Ward Street and Columbus Park headworks some seven miles long. A fourth headworks operation, the Winthrop Terminal facility, was sited at Deer Island. A large pumping station lifted all incoming sewage from the tunnels into the Deer Island plant.

Meanwhile, the southern system, serving twenty-one communities—notably Boston—directed sewage to the Nut Island treatment facility in a similar fashion. In the southern system a pumping station at Nut Island lifted the wastewater up from the High Level Sewer, which conducted all wastewater in the southern system from the MDC trunk sewers.

At both MDC sewage treatment plants the wastewater then went through a primary treatment, aeration of the influent for a ten-minute period (to provide oxygen and hasten the decomposition of organic material by bacteria), primary sedimentation (to allow remaining solids to settle out), and chlorination (to kill bacteria and other pathogens) of the treated wastewater prior to ocean discharge through submerged outfalls.

Well and good, but two crucial problems were not adequately addressed: what to do with the solids—aptly named sludge—left behind by the treatment process and regularly being dumped into the harbor, and how to reduce or eliminate the discharges from combined sewer overflows (CSOs) that dumped untreated sewage and rainwater into the harbor when storms overwhelmed the capacity of the collection system for the Nut Island and Deer Island plants.

One matter on which all sides in the *Quincy* case could agree was that a major source of the pollution afflicting Boston Harbor was CSO discharge. Approximately 50 percent of the population served by the MDC, and about 20 percent of the area in its northern sewerage system, utilized combined sewers, that is, sewers designed to carry both stormwater and sewage.[13] During heavy rainfalls, huge surges of stormwater flooded the networks, threatening backups of wastewater into the streets, homes, and businesses of local communities. To prevent this from happening, sixty-nine major combined sewer overflows and numerous minor overflow discharge points allowed wastewater, including sewage as well as stormwater, to flow directly into metropolitan waterways and the harbor.

There were two types of overflow incidents in Boston Harbor: storm-related overflows, which occurred for periods of several minutes to several hours from fifty to a hundred times a year, and dry-weather overflows, which involved continuous discharge of sewage. Dry-weather overflows occurred regularly at thirty-four locations, caused by a variety of factors, including sewer blockages, regulator malfunctions, and tide-gate failures.[14]

An awareness of the need to abate pollution from CSOs had resulted in the construction of three overflow treatment facilities. Nonetheless, as of April 1982 a total of 108 CSOs discharged into Boston Harbor and its tributary rivers and streams, including several in Quincy.[15]

As for sludge, serious study of the problem had not begun until 1973. In the years that followed, progress was stalled by what unfortunately turned out to be the usual public controversy and bureaucratic wrangling over how and where the sludge should be treated and disposed of. Shortly before the filing of the *Quincy* lawsuit, for instance, the secretary of environmental affairs had rejected as inadequate an environmental impact statement prepared by the MDC regarding its latest proposals for the disposal of sludge.

An August 1982 "Sludge Management Update" report examined the options of incineration, incineration with composting, or ocean dumping. But each of the possible treatments of the sludge turned out to be more or less undesirable, posing either scientific, economic, or environmental dilemmas. The MDC appeared unable to handle the sludge problem.

STUDIES AND SIGNPOSTS FOR ACTION

From 1965 on, a staggering amount of research was directed toward analyzing and solving the sewage problems of the greater

Boston area. Scores of studies were commissioned by federal, state, regional, and local authorities to determine precisely what needed to be done, how and when it should be undertaken, and what it would all cost. The study process itself even became the object of four case studies sponsored by the EPA.[16]

Concern with water conditions in the harbor was intensified by the release in 1968 of a report by the Federal Water Pollution Control Administration. It concluded that "[b]ased upon biological conditions about seven square miles, or 30 percent of the Harbor, were grossly polluted," citing restrictions on shellfish harvesting and recreational bathing, limited enjoyment of recreational boating and sport fishing, and reduced aesthetic values of the beaches, waters, and adjoining areas of the harbor. That study spoke in language by turns scientifically detached and refreshingly colloquial of "grossly polluted water." It also added that "excessive coliform bacteria in the northern portion of the harbor" posed potentially severe health risks to the public.[17]

The most comprehensive effort to draw up a remedial blueprint was represented by the "Wastewater Engineering and Management Plan for Boston Harbor—Eastern Massachusetts Metropolitan Area," familiarly known as the EMMA study. This effort, initiated in 1972, was researched and funded by the MDC and the U.S. Army Corps of Engineers, and involved the efforts of Metcalf & Eddy, an engineering consulting firm, a technical subcommittee with representatives drawn from several layers and agencies of government, and an eleven-person citizens' advisory committee. Nearly four years were required to complete its twenty-five volumes.

The EMMA study found relatively poor marine water and sediment quality, as well as meager species diversity in the Inner Harbor, with better but still substandard quality in many other areas moving out eastward and southward from the Inner Harbor.[18] Citing a 1972 survey by the New England Aquarium, it reported the highest water concentrations of trace metals in the

Inner Harbor, while outside of that area concentrations were highest near Deer Island's sludge outfall and lowest in the southern portion of the harbor.

During the summers of 1978 and 1979 the MDC conducted special sampling programs in connection with its application to the EPA for a waiver of federal secondary wastewater treatment requirements. The EPA's preliminary review of the MDC's waiver application data, which was not completed until June 1983—an indication of the density of the existing thickets of local, state, and federal regulations—suggested that the condition of the harbor had not improved since the release of the EMMA report in 1976.[19]

DOLLARS, DECISIONS, AND DELAYS

Environmental degradation of the harbor could be boiled down, from a managerial perspective, to a question of finances and of which groups within society should bear the costs and in what proportion. Building and maintaining an effective sewage system would carry an enormous cost. Modernizing the CSO systems, to take one example, would be extraordinarily expensive —well beyond the annual state budgetary appropriations for the MDC. Indeed, costs explain to a large degree the enduring reluctance to tackle the problem head on. At the time of the *Quincy* litigation, the consulting firm Camp Dresser & McKee gave high marks to the overall performance of the MDC's Dorchester Bay wastewater collection system, but also reported that $36.7 million in capital improvements were needed. In addition, the firm recommended the updating of miscellaneous management practices and proposed $485,000 in nonstructural improvements.

In 1982 an MDC study of the CSO problem in Boston Harbor as a whole reported that between twelve million and thirty million gallons of raw sewage had been discharged yearly during dry-weather periods, and in total it was estimated that during any given year six billion gallons of combined stormwater and sewage were discharged. This volume could be "substantially higher" when figures came in for the 1982 year, the director and chief engineer of the MDC's Sewerage Division stated in an affidavit submitted at the *Quincy* trial, because of the increase in rainfall that year. The MDC estimated remediation costs at $279 million. Operation and maintenance costs, furthermore, had to be taken into account, and these were projected at $4,130,000 per year.[20]

The EMMA study had recommended federal, state, and local spending of $1.2 billion over a twenty-five-year period for the planning, design, and construction of fifty-two separate projects. This included projected spending of more than $650 million to expand treatment facilities, $380 million to correct combined sewer overflows, and $150 million to improve sewer interceptors and pumping stations. Although modifications of several of the EMMA study's recommendations were negotiated among the affected agencies, and the timeframe for its implementation was stretched out, its call for massive public investments in the rehabilitation of the harbor was never seriously challenged. But only a fraction of the EMMA plan was carried out.

ORGANIZATIONAL PATHOLOGY

Virtually everyone who knew anything about the MDC's sewage collection and treatment system had no doubt that its inadequacies caused environmental damage. The warnings were in the air, and that psychological factor had to be taken into account when the *Quincy* litigation renewed the effort to improve the physical infrastructure of the harbor. Especially significant was its impact on the labor force of the MDC. For the public and the political establishment the situation was frustrating, even alarming, but for many of those who worked for the MDC it was positively corrosive. It produced a type of organizational pathology, virtually a law of mismanagement: how well-intentioned people produce perverse results.[21]

Faced with a daunting task and inadequate resources, the staff at Nut Island—the plant that served Quincy—performed difficult, dirty, even dangerous work without complaint, put in thousands of hours of unpaid overtime, and, on occasion, dipped into their own pockets to buy spare parts to keep the plant running. They also developed a cohesiveness that stemmed from a shared disdain for management headquarters; a main objective of the Nut Islanders was to stay off management's radar screen. The MDC management, concentrating on other issues, delegated total control over a portion of the wastewater treatment system to a team that managed itself. In any event, top management could not provide much inspirational leadership since the MDC had no fewer than ten commissioners in the eight years preceding the initiation of the *Quincy* litigation in 1982. Each camp twisted events to its liking: management did not want to hear of deficiencies; the workers disregarded plant breakdowns in their desire to fulfill their mission.

A situation developed in which machinists, technicians, and laborers, taking pride in their craftsmanship, developed a coping strategy to avoid the necessity of confronting the MDC higher-ups with the need to modernize the system. They grew accustomed (with scarcely a murmur) to pouring directly back into the harbor the sewage sludge they had just painstakingly extracted from the wastewater of the communities they served. Doing the best job they could under the circumstances, with limited funds and personnel, they were indifferent to advances in technology, never acknowledging problems even to insiders, and certainly not to management.

If a self-defeating coping strategy existed on Nut Island and throughout the MDC system, with professional zeal dedicated to an outmoded form of sewage treatment, no matter how poor the result, an additional explanation, perhaps even more relevant than senior management's default, may hinge on the MDC's relationship to state government. Political leaders in the legislature and the executive branch chose to overlook the deteriorating condition of Boston Harbor. Appropriated funds were insufficient for proper MDC operations or requisite staffing. Furthermore, the system as a whole had degenerated into a source of patronage jobs, a political resting place for many relatives of legislators.

"Flush and forget" was still the prevailing theme. Although it was the oldest metropolitan service district in the United States, the MDC was unable to muster adequate support, public or private, to effectively fulfill its mission.

The sanitary improvements driven by the public hygiene needs of the industrial city to overcome "the evil effects of its waste-products and excrement" were described by Lewis Mumford as "the most positive contribution to town planning during the 19th century."[22] In Victor Hugo's unforgettable description of underground Paris in *Les Miserables*, the old sewer's symbolic power had reflected the disintegration of society and the political chaos of a disordered universe. By contrast, in the modern Paris of Baron Haussmann's geometric and cleansed universe, the rebuilt sewers came to represent the progress of science and the triumph of modern technology, a manifestation of uniformity, control, and order imposed by a benevolent bureaucracy, indeed a literal triumph of enlightenment over darkness.[23]

In bringing suit against agencies of the state, those acting on behalf of the city of Quincy, more than coincidentally, were attempting to bring public attention to the larger problem of the ongoing pollution of Boston Harbor. And the remedies they sought were designed to put pressure on the executive and legislative branches of government to take action to halt that pollution and repair the damage to the environment. It was at this point that Judge Garrity and the special master entered the scene.

THE CAST OF CHARACTERS
Officials and Fish

It is an inevitable defect, that bureaucrats will care more for
routine than results.

—Walter Bagehot

As the *Quincy* case unfolded, finding the party or parties who
were responsible under the law for the inadequately treated
sewage and sludge that fouled Boston's beaches and adjacent
waters turned out to be extraordinarily difficult. Right at the
outset, in June of 1983, the court found probable state statutory violations attendant on the deplorable conditions in Boston
Harbor. But who or what bore ultimate responsibility for these
violations, in particular those that affected Quincy? Not only
did doubts emerge about salient scientific and technological details, but questions were raised as to what services the numerous
and overlapping agencies at the federal, state, regional, and local
levels were performing, what they were charged with achieving,
how they interacted, and what the outcomes of their interrelated
efforts had been or should be.

Not surprisingly, no one admitted even partial responsibility.
Instead, at trial the various governmental agencies pointed fin-
gers at each other. It was a classic version of the "pass it on"
theme in Leonard Bernstein's *Candide*. The Environmental Protection Agency's delays in ruling on the waiver from the requirement of secondary treatment were cited frequently by state agencies as the reason for uncertainties and delays in preparing their
own plans for improving the system. The Metropolitan District
Commission trained its sights on the Boston Water and Sewer
Commission as the party responsible for the Moon Island facil-

ity. In a quick pivot, the state agencies sought to pin overflow discharge problems on the managers of facilities owned by local communities. On another front, the MDC denied responsibility for the failure of the tide gates to prevent saltwater inflows to the system during high tide. At least no one blamed the sea, as Xerxes had.

Various agreements that divided turf and occasionally provided for coordination had been made, unmade, and remade between federal, state, and municipal agencies. Despite claims that changes were in the offing, much of the state defendants' testimony at trial conveyed a sense of business as usual. Preliminary, often hazy recommendations by consultants were introduced as if they had already been acted upon and completed. Future programs and strategies for the harbor's improvement were sketched out, but far more time and affidavit space were devoted to explanations of impediments already encountered, or difficulties likely to arise in implementation, or to predictions of inevitable snags and delays that would thwart performance.

How everything hung together required exploration and exegesis. The lines of authority were fuzzy. Often no one was in charge. At crucial decision points, jurisdictions overlapped. Nor was there any overall coordination of the many permitting, inspection, or enforcement activities by different agencies. Wherever one looked, there were either gaps in the machinery of pollution prevention and rehabilitation or there were too many mechanics, following contradictory plans and using their own favorite tools, working at cross-purposes.

And, in the background but looming large as the trial proceeded, was the fact that although politicians over the decades had voiced concern about the pollution of the harbor, in the end the legislature had always found it politically inexpedient to appropriate enough money for the "invisible" infrastructure that could have curtailed that pollution.

Government sovereignty over Boston Harbor and its wastewater facilities was spread out over a wide and disparate group of state executive branch authorities. It was crucially important to the *Quincy* case to understand their mandates under law—and the ways in which they interacted in practice.

STATE AGENCIES: EOEA, MDC, AND DEQE

The Executive Office of Environmental Affairs (EOEA), then and now, was responsible for carrying out Massachusetts environmental policy, and the state agencies involved in the Boston Harbor case operated under EOEA auspices. In effecting its environmental vision (to the extent it had one), the office had wide latitude to develop policies, plans, and programs for the management and preservation of air, water, and land resources as well as the protection of fish, wildlife, and endangered species. Tools available to the office include land-use and community development planning, management of marine and coastal fisheries, controls over natural wetlands and shorelines, regulation of solid and liquid wastes, and restoration of degraded environments.[1]

The Metropolitan District Commission (MDC), a multiservice regional agency operated under the EOEA, was the primary defendant in the city of Quincy's litigation.[2] Its Metropolitan Sewerage Division (MSD) provided sewage collection, treatment, and discharge services to forty-three cities and towns in the Boston metropolitan area, charging each city a yearly fee for the service. In addition, the MSD supervised a variety of short-term maintenance and long-term planning and construction projects intended to guarantee continued "reliable functioning" of its facilities.

The MDC granted a variety of powers to the MSD vis-à-vis the municipalities that were part of its system, including the power to mandate infiltration/inflow (I/I) control efforts and to set a baseline standard for local sewer-use ordinances. MDC sewage discharges were themselves governed by state and federal law.

The Department of Environmental Quality Engineering (DEQE), one of five subdivisions of EOEA, was responsible for the protection of environmental quality. Its Division of Water Pollution Control (DWPC) was the "state agency charged with the responsibility to clean up the rivers, streams, lakes, and coastal waters" of the commonwealth. It developed and enforced water quality standards, controlled the disposal of chemical and other hazardous wastes, and issued pollution discharge permits.

The DWPC oversaw the planning, construction, operation, and maintenance of the MDC facilities and also prepared and kept current a comprehensive plan for pollution abatement for Boston Harbor. Jointly with the EPA, it issued pollution discharge permits, and it also authorized financial assistance from the state, coordinated federal grant applications, and administered EPA/state construction grants to municipalities to assist them in the planning, design, and construction of water pollution control facilities, including correction of infiltration/inflow (I/I) and of combined sewer overflow (CSO) problems. One important function was its power to issue permits for extensions and connections to MDC community sewer systems or impose prohibitions, restrictions, or conditions on those connections.

The Boston Water and Sewer Commission (BWSC), overseen by a three-member board of commissioners appointed by the mayor with city council approval, operated and maintained Boston's water distribution and wastewater collection systems, including the Calf Pasture pumping station and the Moon Island outfall and tide gates, which came into use when the wastewater treatment capacity of MDC's Deer Island plant was exceeded.[3] The BWSC planned and constructed infrastructure improvements, established rates and charges for its services, and was authorized to issue general revenue bonds.

The Boston Redevelopment Authority (BRA) was mandated by the legislature to prepare and implement an overall urban development program for Boston and to serve as the city planning board, zoning commission, and economic development agency. Boston's mayor appointed BRA board members, except for one gubernatorial selection. Its role in Boston Harbor oversight consisted of its "harbor park plan" covering 2,100 acres of land, and its cooperation with the BWSC in the development of sewerage infrastructure. In general, the BRA attempted to guide harbor development in ways that improved opportunities for public access and enjoyment of the harbor.

ATTEMPTS AT COORDINATION

In the 1980s the Massachusetts executive branch recognized that the harbor-related responsibilities of these many agencies required both bureaucratic coordination and a unified public face. The Secretary of Environmental Affairs, James Hoyte, formed the Boston Harbor Interagency Coordinating Committee, composed of DEQE and MDC representatives and staffed by Coastal Zone Management personnel, to expedite the implementation of state policy and resolve interagency disputes. With limited powers, however, it had but slight impact.

The Boston Harbor Cleanup Committee, chaired by former Governor Francis Sargent, signified a more public effort to develop plans for combating the pollution of the harbor. Set up in 1983 by Governor Michael Dukakis after the commencement of the *Quincy* litigation, it was composed of distinguished Massachusetts citizens and officials, including Senator Edward Kennedy and Congressman Joseph Moakley, to help gain political credibility. One of its functions was to facilitate communication and coordination among federal and state agencies.[4] In accepting the task of cleaning up Boston's harbor, Sargent recognized the need for action. While nothing would happen overnight, he declared, "we're going to do something—I promise."[5]

It was never clear whether Governor Dukakis formed the group in order to improve the harbor or to outflank the *Quincy* litigation and keep control of policy within the executive branch where he believed it belonged. The MDC commissioner, William Geary, testified at the trial that he felt convinced that the *Quincy* litigation "is unlikely to solve the existing pollution problem, while it poses a serious danger to the Commonwealth's economic health."

At the trial and at various hearings held by the court, the state defendants repeatedly pointed to the Boston Harbor Cleanup Committee's detailed mandate as attesting to the seriousness of the current renewal effort. And they urged the court not to take jurisdiction over matters pertaining to the committee, expressing the pious hope that it would provide answers to the question of how to put an end to the pollution of the harbor. But as time passed and the litigation proceeded, the committee produced a few press conferences and little else. Although the staff of the court continued to send it news concerning the progress of the *Quincy* case and responded promptly to inquiries from its members, the committee's significance waned, and when chairman Sargent became seriously ill, it soon sank out of sight.

THE FEDERAL PRESENCE

The Environmental Protection Agency (EPA) was and continues to be the major federal agency with jurisdiction over water quality issues nationwide. In the *Quincy* litigation its first role was to act as an observer and friend of the state court, but the potential existed that it might become involved as a plaintiff in the federal district court.[6]

The EPA had been created in 1970 as a result of increasing public interest in the environment and growing awareness of the need for coordinated stewardship of environmental resources. Prior to that time, federal efforts to protect the environment were fragmented and poorly organized. No fewer than six distinct federal agencies carried out the kinds of fundamental environmental protection duties that were subsequently placed in EPA's hands. By and large these agencies had acquired authority over individual environmental problems on an ad hoc basis, with the consequence that decisions about closely interwoven environmental issues might be made separately by unrelated entities.

As pressure for federal action to protect the environment mounted, the EPA was created by executive order on December 2, 1970, and charged with implementing all federal laws pertaining to environmental protection. In other words, when Congress passed a law designed to protect the environment in some way, the EPA was to carry out the mandate by setting specific environmental standards, monitoring compliance, and applying sanctions to violators.[7]

As Congress passed more laws to protect the environment, the EPA's role grew, making it an important player in the Boston Harbor cleanup. In the field of water pollution control, the EPA had broad regulatory authority over discharges from publicly owned sewage treatment facilities. It approved receiving and effluent (what comes in and what goes out) water quality standards set by the states, and granted permits conditioned on compliance with those standards. It also provided funding. Under its construction grants program, it initially paid 75 percent of the cost of eligible sewage system improvement projects, though this was later reduced.

Controlling Legal Authorities

One key to understanding how these governing authorities interacted lay in the system of joint permits and administrative orders that had been adopted to try to inject discipline into the operations. No discharges into federal or state waters were allowed without a discharge permit, issued jointly by the EPA and DWPC, and complying with the terms of the National Pollution

Discharge Elimination System (NPDES). The permits regulated discharge volumes, pollutant concentrations, and conditions for releases, and imposed strict monitoring and reporting requirements.

The MDC's 1976 NPDES permit No. MA 0102351, for instance, authorized sewage discharges into Boston Harbor under specified conditions, allowing bypass of treatment facilities only "to prevent loss of life or severe property damage or where excessive storm drainage or runoff would damage facilities." The permit limited specified pollutants that could be discharged from the Boston treatment plants: biochemical oxygen demand (BOD), total suspended solids (TSS), settleable solids (SS), fecal coliform bacteria, and total coliform bacteria.[8] The BWSC's 1979 NPDES permit No. MA 0101192, which covered 113 CSO and stormwater discharge points, allowed wet-weather discharges, but provided that they be reduced or abated to the maximum extent possible. The MDC was responsible for monitoring the permitted discharges and notifying EPA of compliance or noncompliance. However, administrative requirements were complicated by a series of four administrative orders (AOs) issued by the EPA from 1980 to 1983 to deal with the MDC's failure to comply with a 1976 joint state and federal order requiring it to take major steps to end sewage discharges in the harbor. These AOs postponed compliance schedules, relaxed discharge conditions, and revised mechanical requirements, making allowances for what would otherwise be violations of the permits.

On paper, the NPDES system and the self-monitoring requirements established a straightforward and decisive enforcement system. Presented with alleged violations, the enforcer (or, later on, a reviewing court) need not launch an extensive investigation or engage in judgments concerning the appropriateness of the established effluent limits. The only question was to ascertain that a permit had been issued and had not been revoked or modified, and then compare the types and quantities of pollutants that were permitted with those listed in the monthly summary monitoring reports.[9] It was supposed to be simple and effective—but that is not how it worked out.

The Public

Clearly, the chronic lack of progress was the result of many factors, and in this connection we must introduce another player in our cast of characters. Local public opinion—over and above the customary grumblings of the typical taxpayer—was crucial in delaying many decisions relative to the siting of needed facilities. The prospect of having a sludge-burning operation as a neighbor was far more threatening to many of the citizens of the Boston metropolitan area than any broader image of the deterioration of Boston Harbor, even given the prospect of compensatory payments.

The chorus of public opposition—put facilities anywhere else, but "not in my backyard"—delayed, diverted, and destroyed many government proposals. Here are a few of many examples:

- The EMMA study's recommendation of 1976 that satellite treatment plants be built in outlying communities was ultimately rejected in large part because of intense local opposition in those communities.
- Likewise, the study's proposal that twenty-eight acres of Quincy Bay be filled in to provide the site for a secondary treatment facility at Nut Island was undermined by heated public protest. Indeed, the residents of Quincy and nearby communities prodded the state legislature to pass a bill expressly prohibiting the plan.[10]
- In 1979 the EPA released an environmental impact study on sludge incineration at various sites. Residents of Boston and Winthrop strongly opposed the plan's proposal for on-site sludge incineration at Deer Island.

But public opinion also could—and would—have a resounding impact on the affirmative side of the debate. Properly presented, the vision of a restoration of the waters of Boston Harbor was eventually able to stir the imagination of citizens, open their pocketbooks, and change the nature of the administrative and political process.

THE SETTING: BLUE WATERS OR BLACK MAYONNAISE?

The seafloor hosts an assortment of flora and fauna that, taken together, are referred to as the benthic ecosystem, or simply the benthos (Greek *benthos,* the depths of the sea). By the time of the *Quincy* case, the field of benthic ecology, devoted to studying marine organisms and the environment in which they live, was well developed. Among other forms of research, benthic ecologists collect sediment samples from the ocean (or coastal waters) floor and study the life within them, measuring such things as the number and types of species present and their distribution among the samples.

At some point early in its history, Boston Harbor's benthos was a vibrant, healthy place. Oysters and softshell clams lay on the sediments of the harbor floor, while lobsters and flounder scuttled about and smaller shrimp-like creatures floated in the waters above. Within the sediment lived small deposit-feeders and other creatures, many of which continually dug holes and built tubes, thereby aerating and regenerating the sediment layer.[11]

By the time benthic ecologists began to study Boston Harbor intensively, around the mid-twentieth century, the harbor was already severely polluted and its benthic ecosystem degraded. Many of the harbor's clam beds were so polluted that no shellfish could be taken for human consumption.[12] Larger, less sedentary organisms, such as shrimp and lobster populations in the harbor and bay, also showed the adverse effects of such damage, and the EPA concluded in 1983 that contaminated benthic fauna were passing toxins on to large fish, especially those that spend much of their lives near the harbor floor. This could partially account for the near universal "fin rot" disease observed in winter flounder.

Damage to epifauna, the organisms living on or just above the sediment layer, is striking and disturbing, but it is neither as well documented nor as drastic as the destruction that pollution wreaks on infauna, the organisms that live within the sediment layer.[13] Infauna are less mobile (as adults they cannot move away from pollution) and more diverse than epifauna. And their health and diversity—or lack of same—serve as an indication of the health of the larger ecosystem because they interact with organisms throughout the water column (from the sea or harbor floor to the surface of the water).

Benthic ecologists have coined a macabre term for sediments so contaminated by pollution that no infaunal life is possible: *black mayonnaise*. Black mayonnaise is a creamy, dark mud, rich in hydrogen sulfide and almost totally lacking in dissolved oxygen (D.O.), without which benthic fauna suffocate and die. It is created when the organic matter in sewage settles on the ocean floor and decays. At the other end of the spectrum from black mayonnaise is a fully healthy benthos, marked by high levels of species richness and evenness of distribution.[14]

What of the situation in Boston's waters? The fifty tons of sewage sludge discharged daily into Boston Harbor (contaminated with toxic metals, pesticides, oil, and polychlorinated biphenyls (PCBs)) had profound effects on harbor sediments. In the 1980s parts of the Inner Harbor, Fort Point Channel, and Savin Hill Cove were covered with black mayonnaise.[15] In the worst areas of the harbor and the bay, D.O. levels were far below 6 mg of oxygen per liter of water, the minimum that (according to the state's own standards) would support a healthy benthos. Only a few highly adaptive species of worm-like creatures could actually reproduce and maintain their populations in damaged environments such as the Inner Harbor and Savin Hill Cove.[16] Other organisms may hatch larvae in such areas, but the larvae never reach maturity or reproduce; some can complete their life cycle, but in ever-decreasing numbers.

No areas of Boston Harbor or Massachusetts Bay exhibited the typical characteristics of healthy benthic ecosystems, but it was hard to determine if pollution was the cause. Even models aimed at characterizing the effects of pollution by correlating variations in benthic degradation with distance from pollution sources were difficult to apply to Boston Harbor. This was the surprising and disconcerting conclusion drawn by the court-appointed experts. Boston Harbor and Massachusetts Bay have always had low levels of evenness in species distribution; even if they were perfectly healthy, only a small number of species would dominate benthic life in the area, those suited to handle the drastic seasonal changes in water temperature (up to 20° centigrade) that typify this region. Low evenness in a benthic sample from the harbor, therefore, is not always a sign of ecological degradation.[17]

The shallowness of the harbor and its complicated currents and topography break up the usual pollution gradient and serve to concentrate pollutants in the settling areas.[18] This complicated the task of determining the source of pollutants at any specific point in the harbor. But it also pointed to the central truth at hand: any piecemeal effort to clean up one corner of the harbor would be doomed to failure.

A STRATEGY FOR CHANGE OF ADMINISTRATIVE STRUCTURE

Even a cursory review of the administrative structure of governance showed how overlapping jurisdictions and fragmentation impeded solutions to the problem of the pollution of Boston

Harbor in the past and resulted in ongoing and systemic violations. Ultimately, it was this undisputed finding that led to the conclusion that responsibility for overseeing sewage treatment in the metropolitan region needed to come under the authority of a single, autonomous agency. While there was near-universal agreement that diffuse allocations of functions and powers exacerbated the environmental crisis, commentators on the *Quincy* litigation had yet to isolate the basic organizational premises that favor a single authority over a multiagency structure. As an analytical starting-point, in an effort to discern broad institutional truths amid the complexities of the Boston Harbor case, economic theory may provide some help in defining the causes of the problem.

A group of separate government agencies working toward a common goal can be said to operate as competing suppliers in a consumer market. When a number of independent agencies promise to deliver a similar service or to regulate the same sphere of activity, they offer potentially disgruntled consumers a choice of places to go in order to express dissatisfaction. Adopting this quasi-economic conception of interagency competition, one can readily perceive why a single government agency operating as a "monopoly" in a given regulatory sphere can be regarded as preferable to a "competitive" administrative structure, for there are many instances in which (contrary to the free-market theory that serves well in other arenas) competition among different agencies, far from counteracting managerial mediocrity and indolence, may indulge and bolster it.

In the sphere of public services and utilities, poorly served consumers complain to whomever seems the appropriate official, and should they receive an unsatisfactory response they will appeal to another bureaucratic office. The resulting administrative hopscotching can produce a situation in which all may be heard but no agency can be charged to effect positive change. And when bureaucratic competition has such a dilutive effect on complaints, an administrative monopoly may be a preferable alternative from the public interest standpoint.[19]

Consider the implications for the Boston Harbor case. The claims made by various competing government agencies that they were "dealing with the problem" prolonged institutional exploration by dissatisfied citizen-consumers—that is, rounds of complaints to a number of alternative agencies, none of which had the necessary power to resolve them. Such a situation prevented consumers from applying truly effective pressure on the multiple agencies that had to act together in order to deliver the sought-for "product": a cleaner Boston Harbor.

While it would be unfair to describe the behavior of the government agencies involved in the Boston Harbor sewage treatment system as collusive, they had little incentive to alter habitual ways of proceeding. For many of the managers of public agencies, the counterpart of "competition" among private firms becomes rival—and overlapping—jurisdiction. True, competition is the great leveler and protector of the public interest when it comes to privatization or partial deregulation of services that are not natural monopolies. But diversity of jurisdictions keeps consumers from uniting in coordinated complaint; this enables state agencies to maintain what is for them a comfortable state of affairs—business as usual rather than the potential disruption of change. Contrary to conventional expectations, under these circumstances, over and above the desire to preserve and enlarge their own specialized turfs, government agencies have a common interest in the maintenance rather than in the abridgement of this form of "competition." So they encourage the proliferation of separate agencies. Hence the impetus for establishing a monopolistic—or, as we might prefer to call it, a coordinated and effective—administrative structure as the driver of remedial action for Boston Harbor would not likely be generated internally, from within the state's governance structure.

To achieve such a unified structure that would combine both

the responsibility and the power to revitalize Boston Harbor, an outside force, be it the governor, legislature, court, or public opinion—or a combination of all—had to be introduced. And the move would have to be nuanced, for would it be reasonable to expect any single agency to willingly fall on its sword?

TURNING THE TIDE
Creating a Novel Trial Process

Dr. Stockmann: The miraculous springs that cost such a fortune to build, the whole Health Institute, is a pesthole. . . . You know the filth up in Windmill Valley? That stuff that has such a stinking smell? It comes down from the tannery up there, and the same damn poisonous mess comes right out into the blessed, miraculous water we're supposed to *cure* people with . . . actually where our beaches are. . . . I had a suspicion about it a long time ago—last year there were too many sick cases among the visitors, typhoid and gastric disturbances.

    —Henrik Ibsen, *An Enemy of the People* (Arthur Miller, trans.)

Throughout the month of July 1983, my colleagues and I consulted with a wide variety of experts and public officials, reviewed numerous documents and studies, and worked to assemble a report for the court that would provide an overall view of the condition of Boston Harbor as well as proposed remedies.

The purpose of this dawn-to-midnight marathon was to become as familiar as possible in a short time with an enormously complex problem and its many ramifications—environmental, social, and political. The subject was vast: the history and current operation of the metropolitan Boston sewerage system; the workings of its technical components; the administrative, financial, and regulatory context in which it operated; and its physical, biological, economic, and environmental impacts. The freedom we were granted by the court and the parties to craft our own investigation aided us immeasurably in achieving that goal.

From the outset it was clear to Judge Garrity and me that *Quincy* would not be an ordinary lawsuit. Sharp breaks with the routine course of litigation were necessary if results were to be achieved in the short period of time during which the window of opportunity for action would remain open.

This premise was challenged throughout the trial by the defendants' lead lawyer, Assistant Attorney General Michael Sloman, who considered *Quincy* "just another slip-and-fall tort case." He saw no need to suspend the normal rules governing an adversary proceeding, or to modify the way evidence was usually gathered and presented, or to expedite the conduct of the proceedings. As far as he was concerned, this case should be tried as a typical lawsuit, which meant as little stipulation of facts as possible and virtually no cooperation among the parties.

Such obliviousness to the novelty and urgency of the issues seemed strange to me. *Quincy* raised several unfamiliar legal questions and posed both a challenge and an opportunity as a model for lawsuits seeking redress against state agencies for harm to the environment. Indeed, the case clearly bore major implications for environmental policy and its implementation throughout the country. Its immediate outcome would affect more than two million people. Might the defendants' attitude be an instance of feigned nonchalance by lawyers eager to earn another notch in their collective belt of victories?

ARGUMENTS ABOUT A SPECIAL MASTER

Judge Garrity's resort to a special master to supervise the case proved highly controversial and quickly became a subject for objection and debate. The attorney general's office inveighed against it from the beginning. Years after the close of the case, Sloman, in an interview with a law student as he sat in his office in the Saltonstall Building, would still maintain, "The appointment of a master for the purposes of taking evidence and establishing remedies is not an acceptable process from my perspective."[1]

In his brief opposing the appointment of a master, Sloman argued that it was inappropriate for a judge to refer cases to a special master if the underlying controversy was of widespread public interest involving the official acts of elected officials. The complexity of the matter, he claimed, was not sufficient to offset the public policy objections to the use of a master. Rather, ran his argument, intricacy was a compelling reason for a trial before an experienced judge and no one other than that judge.[2]

Regarding litigation not brought before a jury, the theory of the common law is that a single trial judge, unaccompanied by partners or staff, runs the trial, listens to the testimony, rules on motions, sees the witnesses, notes their deportment, reads the briefs, hears out the arguments, and, unaided, decides the case and writes the opinion. Introducing a special master divides responsibility. Traditionalists regard this with deep suspicion. Sloman raised sharp and continuous objections to my appointment as constituting an unlawful delegation of judicial power.

Certainly there was scant support in precedent for a strong role for a special master in the *Quincy* litigation. Reluctance is typified in the warning voiced by the Massachusetts Supreme Judicial Court in *O'Brien v. Dwight,* that while the decision on whether to refer a particular case to a master is an exercise of judicial discretion, "the corresponding responsibility and consequences of a reference are such that the discretion should be exercised most discriminately and reasonably sparingly."[3] The assumption is that a special master will be appointed rarely and only when the court is faced with a situation that is "extraordinary."[4] The Boston Harbor litigation, it could be and was argued, was nothing if not extraordinary. On the other hand, reasonable interpretation of the rule might raise the bar higher, for use of masters remains the exception rather than standard practice. In cases where resort is made to them, lower courts often find themselves reversed.

Judge Garrity did not appoint as master a specialist on harbors or wastewater treatment—an individual who could supplement by training and expertise Garrity's own generalist skills as a judge. This contrasted with examples such as the *Mount Laurel* affordable housing cases in which the three trial judges charged with carrying out the court's mandate to make suburban land available for low-income housing appointed professional city planners as masters for monitoring the trials.[5] Instead, Garrity chose a lawyer. He later explained that a satisfactory solution to the *Quincy* litigation depended not on specialized knowledge but on an appreciation of the cultural setting of the case and the development of a general strategy to handle it. "Solving the harbor's pollution," he said, "is a matter of the will to do so, not of particular facts or technological skills."[6]

Part of the objection was that the judge cannot delegate authority that is inherently his alone to exercise; lawyers (and the parties they represent) are entitled to see *the judge* as the target of their arguments. The judge is the person, imbued with particular philosophies, proclivities, and prejudices, who is the decision maker; hence lawyers have—and ought to have—the opportunity to shape their arguments in line with their experience before that judge or according to the judge's general reputation in the world of legal practice.

It might well be that in a simpler agricultural society, an individual judge could be capable of dealing with all the sundry types of controversies that might come before the court. In modern societies, however, the complexity of the situations brought to trial—ranging from antitrust actions to intellectual property issues such as patents, to technical analyses of whether observed environmental pollution is attributable to factory X or municipality Y or individual Z—may involve issues that are beyond the professional capacity of a single individual, no matter how well trained in the law. Such a case cries out for the use of experts to gather and analyze information and advise the court. Resorting to other professions saves time and energy for the beleaguered judge, whose competence as a lawyer (which, after all, is what the person in judicial robes is) can hardly be expected to extend to highly technical nonlegal matters.

That said, critics cited a further significant risk of an improper delegation of a judge's powers when the master's findings of fact are subject to reversal only when clearly erroneous. This strict standard makes a successful appeal from a ruling by the master highly unlikely. In these cases the master's findings and authority can constitute a wall between the parties and the judge, with final authority in the realistic sense resting in the appointee.

Paul Garrity was of course well aware of these arguments. But in his judgment the scope and special nature of the Boston Harbor case outweighed the risks of appointing a master. In a situation so clearly involving a major institutional breakdown and an ongoing threat to a crucial public resource, he reasoned, a special master could be useful in both traditional and novel ways: by studying the site, gathering data, and securing information not otherwise available to the court; by reaching out into the community to tap public sentiments; and, in a break with the past, by mustering support for recommendations from the parties, interest groups, and the general public.

At times courts do use masters as fact-finders prior to a determination of liability, and in the pre-liability phase of complex cases they are often empowered to negotiate consent decrees. These are historical roles that existed at common law before they found their way into the Federal Rules of Civil Procedure.[7] My assigned fact-finder function, however, was unique: Judge Garrity appointed me after making his own determination that the law probably had been violated. The result of Garrity's redefinition of the role of the special master for *Quincy* was that I wore all of the masks in the master's kit, but not as they had been worn before. I would be a fact-finder and remedy creator, but my investigations would begin after the court's finding of legal violations—and would take advantage of ex parte communications prior to a finding of probable liability, and the remedies were to be for wrongs that had not yet been formally defined.

TIME PRESSURE

The thirty-day time limit set by Judge Garrity seemed astonishingly short. As the days flew by, I asked for more time to explore the situation, which had begun as a total terra incognita. But the judge insisted on keeping the August 9 deadline firm. He thought it necessary to seize the initiative in order to harness the momentum for change that the litigation had generated.

I understood the judge's motivation for wanting my report to come out in the middle of the summer—when people care if the beaches are closed. In Boston, summer is also shellfish season. It is a time for jogging or walking on the shore, and for leaving the windows open so that the breeze can come in—fresh sea air on a good day or the stench of polluted waters on a bad one.

In one respect the deadline worked to our advantage. Since we were willing to work as hard as necessary, often late into the night, to complete our report in thirty days, we felt freer to ask MDC or EPA staff to make similar efforts in order to provide the needed data and computer runs.

Counsel for the defendants, however, did not share our view on the deadline set by the judge. According to Assistant Attorney General Sloman, who stated his opinion in a later interview,

We had a very rigorous trial schedule, and briefing and so forth. The master, Professor Haar, did that very well, and I have no question about that. My question is more global in nature, and that is, there's a problem with the Harbor no doubt. It's been around for a considerable period of time; it is not the kind of thing that you can present all the evidence and make an informed judgment in a 30 day period. It just can't be done, and . . . some of the evidence that was put on during the two and a half days of trial was interesting, but largely irrelevant. There are points that should have been addressed that were not because of the time constraints.[8]

In any event, the deadline enhanced the sense of excitement of being participants in a momentous public event. This pressure also affected observers and the media. It lent a sense of drama to the course of the litigation that kept the public's concentration focused on the harbor.

AN UNCONVENTIONAL PROCEEDING

Judge Garrity deemed the problems of Boston Harbor to be urgent, and had expressed in open court his belief that no effective solution would be forthcoming anytime soon from local political leaders in either the executive or legislative branches of government. He had directed me to deliver a report no later than thirty days from the date of direction (July 8), and to include in that report recommendations for proposed injunctive relief for remedying the harbor problem. To carry out the charge of the court, I was forced to implement a radically different dispute resolution procedure than is typical in ordinary litigation.

In a standard civil lawsuit, discovery—the process whereby information is gathered and culled through the production of papers and depositions—may continue for a long period, as much as several years, during which massive accumulations of documents are pared down to provide key exhibits for presentation at trial. The typical trial is heard by a judge, or by a jury under the watchful eye of a neutral and largely passive judge, who makes rulings on evidentiary issues, guards against procedural infirmities, and shepherds the case to conclusion. Parties begin by presenting their versions of the "story" leading up to the suit and by laying out the legal foundation upon which they base their claim or defense. Following opening statements, each side in turn calls witnesses and furnishes exhibits in an attempt to prove essential elements of the case. Finally, with all the evidence presented, each side lays out closing arguments, attempting to piece together a coherent picture of that evidence, one that is favorable to the presenter's side. The judge or the jury comes to a decision, and the court enters judgment accordingly. On the whole, this process is painstakingly precise but oftentimes duplicative; as in a game of chess, each side counters the opponent's move with another countervailing measure, played out to finality in a series of intricate steps.

In the *Quincy* case, none of the participants were able to indulge in a leisurely back-and-forth exchange of intermediate motions. I consulted with the attorneys for both sides and with Judge Garrity, after which all parties agreed to employ a procedural model (resembling, in part, the structure of European law courts) that allowed the special master to employ an active and independent approach to fact-finding. We fixed on a system of "hearings on the record," a process in which direct testimony would be submitted by affidavits simultaneously by both parties. In order to streamline the process, all the witnesses were encouraged to restrict the ambit of their testimony to the essential facts as they saw them, to state as precisely as possible their views on the causes and effects of the pollution of the harbor waters, and to pare down adversarial rhetoric. Once the affidavits and counter-affidavits were exchanged, we proceeded to an intensive trial phase in which the special master cross-examined witnesses in person. During the latter part of the month of July 1983, the testimony of thirteen witnesses was heard over two-and-a-half days of the trial.

This streamlined process enabled us to narrow the inquiry to focus on essential factual issues and the weighing of determinative value judgments. Each side presented the affidavits of its own experts and witnesses. Laying the documents side by side, we could see where there was agreement and where there were disputes that had to be resolved, where matters were clear and where they required further elaboration. The hearings served as follow-up sessions to the affidavit process in which the lawyers and I tested the judgments of experts. Differing theories of causation could be compared, contrasted, and appraised in the context of an ever-growing body of information, and we were able to probe inconsistencies or lacunae in reported facts.

Although attorneys for both sides were free to ask questions of opposing witnesses or experts, we were careful to limit the scope of questioning to matters in dispute. Moreover, representing the judge, I actively engaged in the fact-finding process, asking witnesses and experts alike to clarify their opinions in light of contradictory evidence, or to resolve conflicts or inconsistencies in the testimony.

Conducted without the rigid evidentiary rules of the usual court proceeding, the trial was fashioned for a more informal and flexible process. James Hoyte, the Dukakis administration's secretary of environmental affairs, felt that my team showed an appropriate mix of being cooperative and ready to work hand in hand, at the same time being prepared to raise a little Cain if things were not moving in the right direction.[9]

As the *Quincy* litigation proceeded, it became clearer that it did not fit the mold of traditional civil adjudication. The parties—including those few who were formally joined in the action and the many that had a stake in the outcome—were sprawling and amorphous. Reading the titles on the complaint, those that had an immediate interest in the suit could be specified as the city of Quincy as plaintiff and the MDC and BSWC as defendants. But whole other groups also had compelling interests at stake: communities and residents who would have to pay for the cleanup of the harbor, localities that might become the sites of expanded sewerage facilities, towns and factories whose sewage was the source of the pollution, industries whose operations might be curtailed, fishermen who stood to benefit from the cleanup, abutting landowners whose property values varied with the condition of the harbor, the governor and legislators who might be called on to appropriate large amounts of money and, in doing so, expend political capital, and an endless number of other individuals and groups. Again this emphasized how deeply interconnected the harbor environment was—also why environmental and social change is so difficult. For the same reasons that this plethora of parties could not be rendered bipolar, the suit itself was not self-contained. The court could not render judgment in regard to this litigation without creating significant consequences for others who were not named as parties to the suit but had a stake in its outcome.[10] Representatives of these other groups joined the proceedings from time to time at their own behest or under compulsion. Notice of proposed actions was at times haphazard, but word spread well enough through the grapevine so that no party later complained of being excluded from the proceedings.

Finally, the *Quincy* suit was not retrospective in nature, as is the typical civil adjudication, in that the plaintiff did not seek damages for past wrongs. Instead, the city of Quincy sought injunctions that were prospective in nature, to prevent future wrongdoing. One of the functions of the fact-finding duties assigned to the special master was an assessment of causes of past pollution, but this mandate and the court's request for recommendations regarding remedies were made for the larger purpose of helping shape the future.

A DOUBLE-AGENT DEFENSE?

The *Quincy* litigation became a surprisingly non-adversarial process. Even the defendants' representatives (with the possible exception of the attorney general's office) conceded that poor planning and implementation by government agencies responsible for the harbor had resulted in a failure of statutory mission. There was enough blame to go around. On the goal of regenerating the harbor, all could agree. And all shared a sense that time was of the essence: this was an emergency, and for once in the long history of efforts to clean up Boston Harbor, forces had come together that might switch on a light at the end of the tunnel.

A spirit of camaraderie and a deeper understanding of each other's positions and sensitivities came into being among the contenders before the court. From time to time Steven Horowitz and I had what we lightly termed "power breakfasts" at the Wursthaus Restaurant in Harvard Square with James Hoyte, the Massachusetts secretary of environmental affairs. Plain, old-fashioned gossip accompanied the scrambled eggs as we discussed the course of the litigation and explored various agendas for resuscitating the harbor as quickly as possible. Secretary Hoyte, who coordinated the defense for the state agencies, was eager to settle the litigation and get on to the necessary remedies. From the outset, he later stated, the governor's administration had determined that it was going to cooperate with the city of Quincy to find a way to solve the Boston Harbor pollution problem.[11]

As the evidence about the deterioration of the harbor accumulated, press coverage of the lawsuit increased the public's knowledge as well as its impatience with executive and legislative inaction. With a shared recognition of the dangerous condition of the harbor it was possible to weave diverse interests into an alliance for constructive action. Even the defendants wanted to go beyond the past and begin to envisage a more vibrant harbor.

Bill Geary, the commissioner of the MDC and a man experienced in Massachusetts politics, quite openly admitted the agency's fault in the pollution of the harbor and was consistently deferential to the court. In private one-on-one conversations with me, he was most reassuring of the commission's desire to cooperate at trial and, later on, to implement any resultant judicial orders or recommendations.

Noel Baratta, the MDC's chief engineer and the main witness

for the defense at the trial, was helpful throughout the proceedings. (I was glad to see a familiar face, as he had been a classmate of my son.) He explained clearly the operation of the Deer and Nut Island plants, traced the course of the sewage that runs under the pavements of Boston, and aided us in understanding the technical drawings and specialized terms of his profession.

As became clear during his testimony and later in the inspection of plants and pumping stations under the guidance of the MDC staff, the "defendants" actually welcomed the litigation. Again and again, even during the most technical expositions on the operation of the plants, along with an understandable defensiveness about standard procedures, one could note support for the litigation as a way to effect needed change. The case publicized the lack of funding and support. The legislative neglect and log-rolling, gubernatorial indifference, and the low priority that had been accorded to the agency workers' sweat and toil were now brought to the light of day. The litigation was featured in the newspapers, and the attention, however controversial, lifted the MDC staff's spirits. The *Quincy* litigation was bringing to the surface the importance to the life of a modern metropolis of the concealed sewer and water infrastructure—a system to which few citizens ever give much thought, but upon which all depend.

Furthermore, the proceedings of the public trial provided a mechanism for institutionalizing and legitimating dissent from within the MDC agency. Channels of communication were fashioned to encourage potential dissenters among the agency's staff (and others) to provide the information and commentary essential for the analysis of a failing organizational structure. My highly visible position served to amplify and enhance expressions of diverse views, granting them solidity beyond the faint and scattered rumblings of a dissatisfied citizenry or workforce.

The staff was no mere passive sounding board. Rather, we actively pursued an ongoing dialogue with knowledgeable informants so as to fulfill the larger objectives of finding remedies for the problems of the harbor. We sought, synthesized, and used information that would have lacked persuasive power in a more diffuse form. This added significantly to the number of citizens who were willing to participate in the process of institutional reconstruction and in the revitalization of Boston Harbor.

GOING OUTSIDE THE COURTROOM

It is unusual, although not unheard of, for judges to view the site relevant to a case. But given our mandate as finders of fact, the Deer Island, Nut Island, and Moon Island plants obviously warranted visits. Several trips to Wollaston Beach also proved instructive. Above all, the visits were important for keeping the public abreast of what was transpiring.

On our drop-ins to the MDC and BWSC sites, we were often accompanied by representatives of the parties to the *Quincy* lawsuit, the media, and interested citizens. The informality of the boat rides to the facilities, the walks around the plants, the inspection of machinery and operations, and our conversations with workers and supervisors led to fruitful questions and illuminating answers.

The visits allowed us a freer mode of communication than would have been permitted in a courtroom. Proud of their plants and desiring to succeed in their missions, the superintendents of the facilities spoke bluntly and informally about their operations. The experts from the MDC who came along gave us explanations about the machinery that we could see endlessly sorting, munching, skimming, digesting, and purifying the waste spewed out by the population of a major metropolitan area. The visits drove home the importance of effectively communicating the factual underpinnings of the need for institutional change in the management of the harbor.

At the various facilities the managers also presented in lucid and often forceful language how the conditions of the harbor appeared to the front-line workers. Interestingly, employees at the two major plants differed in personal style: Nut Island workers were a smaller, more cohesive group with an intense personal attachment to their plant and its successful operation; their counterparts at Deer Island seemed to be less spontaneous and more reserved or inhibited.

Whatever their differences, the plants spoke for themselves. They presented, collectively, an imposing, almost overwhelming, picture of industrial muscle. The cavernous interior of the Deer Island plant, the blasting noise, the enveloping blackness of the open space surrounding the internal unenclosed iron staircase that spiraled up twelve stories in height—all would have provided an apt setting for a Hitchcock film or a modern-day techno thriller. The plant's digesters were huge and imposing— blocks long, chewing and churning the sewer waters as if they were live beings, feeding and breathing—not to mention the smells they gave off, or the distinct odor of the chlorination plant nearby. The journalists, especially the photographers, were intrigued by the sheer physical realities of the island purification factories.

EX PARTE COMMUNICATIONS

Employment of outside experts was another major break with judicial custom. From the very beginning, the court approved the special master's intention to consult independently with environmental experts and to employ research assistants to help gather information to supplement the affidavits and testimony provided by either the plaintiff or the defendants. With the court's permission, and with the advice of professional colleagues at the American Academy of Arts and Sciences, I sought out the assistance of Professor E. Eric Adams, Principal Research Engineer at MIT; Joseph J. Harrington, Gordon McKay Professor of Environmental Engineering and chairman of the Department of Environmental Science and Physiology at Harvard's School of Public Health; and Allan R. Robinson, professor of oceanography at Harvard's Center for Earth and Planetary Physics and chairman of the Committee on Oceanography. These consultants provided guidance in deciphering the technical aspects of the affidavits, appraised the testimony of the contending experts, and worked independently to gather information about the causes of the pollution of Boston Harbor and the efficacy of proposed remedies.

In a provocative way, this use of experts transformed the role of the special master from a slightly specialized temporary judge into a miniature administrative agency.[12] What would ordinarily have been a lengthy adversarial process became an expeditious and efficient mechanism for uncovering crucial facts and proposing workable solutions.

How did this approach differ from the traditional role, expressed in the Latin phrase *lis inter partes?* In theory, under this rule the judge is not supposed to seek information outside the courtroom or the lawyers' papers and arguments. *Lis inter partes* also bars the judge from discussing or consulting with others about a case except in the presence of legal representatives from both sides. With the approval of the court and at Steven Horowitz's insistence (based on his experience as monitor with U.S. District Court Judge Tauro on the Fernald School case), I asked the assembled lawyers at our first meeting for their permission to consult independently with experts and other individuals and groups. I wanted to be able to seek out information that was not presented in their briefs or arguments, and to make private contacts with the parties or witnesses.

This request for an ex parte approach troubled the defendants. But I soon learned the great power wielded by a judge, even a temporary one. It didn't take long to convince the lawyers that it would be acceptable for me and the deputy master and staff to undertake ex parte contacts and review documents not strictly introduced as evidence; I suspect they believed they had little choice in the matter. I was experiencing yet another advantage, albeit an uncomfortable one, of my role as master: being treated like a judge.

It was this ex parte agreement that freed up the pursuit of information. On our own, my staff and I met with the parties, their lawyers, and their witnesses, as well as with Judge Garrity, the court-appointed experts, and several important "outside" actors, including the Conservation Law Foundation lawyers who were working on the parallel case in the federal court, EPA representatives, and public finance specialists.

We assured the lawyers that all findings of fact and conclusions of law in the special master's report would be based on evidence and documents appearing in the record of the trial proceedings, with the testimonial or paper sources carefully noted. The parties' right of appeal to Judge Garrity, or to a higher court, would thus be preserved; the trial court could hold a hearing on objections to the master's report when it was issued, and make final rulings and determinations.

The strategy of informal hearings and ex parte contacts had another purpose: it could facilitate compromise and encourage the parties to come to a settlement. With an ex parte policy in place, and with a master rather than a judge presiding, the emphasis would be on mediation and coming to an agreement rather than on one side "winning" and the other "losing."

When devising my approach to the case, I fervently wished to avoid the fate of Professor Curtis Berger, who had been appointed special master in a New York school desegregation case by Judge Jack Weinstein, a former colleague of Berger's at Columbia Law School. No ex parte contacts were allowed, and an unscalable wall was built between the master and the judge. After extensive examination of facts and months of intensive work with neighborhood groups and federal, state, and local officials, Berger was able to hammer out an elaborate and potentially useful settlement.[13] However, the judge, who had no inkling of the course Berger was pursuing, rejected the proposed remedy out of hand when the special master presented it to the court. The lesson from that case was the vital importance of communication between judge and master at all stages.

Undeniably, the ex parte meetings that played such an important role in the *Quincy* trial did raise ethical considerations. Relying upon ex parte communications meant relying on evidence untested in the crucible of the adversary process. "The master knew things that I didn't know, and I don't know how he knew them," Assistant Attorney General Sloman later complained. "He knew things before I did . . . and so I was always catching up."[14]

Ex parte contact is an awkward business for no other reason than it may increase the tendency to trust one's own judgment—not subject to challenge or direct countervailing evidence—more than one should. Yet it is often the only way to extract vital information, to get people to speak frankly and feel free to reveal their real intentions and goals. It can lead to more open and fruitful negotiation. As long as the lawyers agree in advance to the use of ex parte contacts, and they are cautiously employed, the benefits seem to outweigh the risks. Even in the most traditional procedure, few judges can compartmentalize their minds to the extent that they rely only on the evidence produced for the record. All judges bring into the courtroom previous experiences, earlier decisions and cases, and personal values. The ex parte agreement at least brought some of this into the open.

Finally, experience imposes some bounds on the uses of evidence produced ex parte. As I had learned in Washington, life in the public sphere is life in a goldfish bowl; if people say something "off the record," or if a conversation is deemed to be in complete confidence, the recurring actuality is that the information will still leak out. This is the practical limitation on potential abuse of discretion. While this vulnerability lessens the potential usefulness of the ex parte procedures, it pushes the dissemination of information in the direction of prudence and care.

DAVID AND GOLIATH: THE IMBALANCE OF POWER

Another memorable aspect of the *Quincy* litigation was its direct recognition of what is commonplace in environmental cases in which a government agency is a party: we might call it the David-and-Goliath scenario.

That the legal outcome must depend on expert knowledge of the relevant science and technology—on knowledge of the complicated interactions of tides and winds, on the reaction of toxic chemicals, solid wastes, and trace metals to natural processes and different forms of purification—means there must be calculations beyond the resources of ordinary citizens. Much of the case relied on testimony of experts and specialists. This brings another rule into play: the greater the expertise, the greater the expense. Time needed for surveys, examinations, and evaluations stretches out trial time, which is also costly.

Quincy was a small city, with a modest expert staff and a limited budget. On the other side, the MDC was a state agency with the resources to assemble a strong group of experts to support its defense in court. Compared to Quincy, the state was Goliath.

As the case progressed, I found myself relying increasingly on the court-appointed experts for their judgments and evaluations, at times asking them to fill in the lacunae left by the consultant enlisted by the plaintiffs. The independent experts provided me with questions to raise with both sides' experts, aimed at clarifying testimony or highlighting inconsistencies and conflicts.

We were careful to keep an open mind, for there was much to learn from all the parties. But it was clear that Quincy just did not have the resources to analyze the voluminous data and copious expert opinion submitted by the defendants. To compensate for this imbalance, I adopted a posture of "creative impartiality" on the city's behalf. The advice of the three court-appointed experts was shared with the parties in the case. And we sought to clarify positions in open court when it seemed necessary to do so. The aim was not to take sides, but to elicit the facts and arrive at the fairest and most promising remedies. We also took initiatives concerning the strategy of the case. In one crucial instance a plaintiff's lawyer proposed bringing in the EPA as a defendant—whereupon, no doubt, the EPA would then invoke its absolute right to remove the proceedings to the federal court, thus ending Judge Garrity's jurisdiction over the case. When the lawyer kept on this tack, I called a recess, trying to divert the line of reasoning away from this dead end. During the break Steven Horowitz pointed out to the lawyer the likely response to this motion: a takeover by the federal courts and an end to the state case. The plaintiff withdrew the motion.[15]

LOOKING FORWARD: WHO HAS THE POWER?

The breadth of the *Quincy* litigation and the scope of its remedies did not fit into existing categories. Quincy's claim was limited to the effects of pollution on its own shores, most particularly on Wollaston Beach. Wollaston, however, was only one link in the chain. Meanwhile, the plaintiffs lacked the resources to investigate causes or to devise remedies, while the named defendants lacked the legal authority to tackle the pollution of the entire harbor even if they were both liable and repentant. The lack of legislative support for a cleanup had resulted in inadequate budgets. Therefore, even if liability were to be found and relief decreed against the MDC, that outcome would amount to an exercise in futility since, despite the will to improve, the agency lacked resources and skills to do so.

This combination of circumstances, if taken to another courtroom, could have ended in yet another stalemate. But under Paul Garrity's determined leadership, the scope of the case was widened, especially by his subsequent "procedural order" issued on September 9, 1983.[16] The judge's actions pulled the condition of the entire harbor into the ambit of the court's concern, and enlisted the abutters, state and local governments, and individual actors as de facto, if not de jure, participants in the litigation. Expanding the scope of the *Quincy* suit encouraged the consensus building that would be critical to a workable remedy, but by itself it would not resolve the dispute. By general agreement of the parties, the court was enabled to confront the broader issue of the degradation of Boston Harbor as a whole. But what remedy could it fashion? Obviously, the court did not have the resources itself to solve the pollution problem, and it could provide little relief by ordering the defendants to do what they were unable to do. Receivership of the state agencies, used so powerfully to mitigate tenants' miseries in the Boston Housing Authority case, was a possibility, but that path was littered with stumbling blocks both legal and practical.

As the trial and investigations proceeded, a solution slowly emerged: a new state agency with independent funding capacity. It became clear that without the creation of an independent institution with the power to act decisively, the harbor might never be cleaned and restored. But only the legislature and the governor could create such an agency. As a result attention shifted to them, although neither was a party to the case.

In enlisting these branches of the state government, we sought means to point the way while avoiding overt judicial interference. Although Judge Garrity did not have the power to create a new regional water resources authority directly, he was not without influence. He could order injunctive relief and perhaps even impose a form of receivership on the MDC and the BWSC. Even if these drastic measures could not bring about an immediate solution, the court could apply them as leverage to move the political branches of government into action.

And there was always the power of public opinion. The role of the media has not normally been part of a court's conscious strategy, but in this case both Judge Garrity and I resorted to interviews, press releases, and public forums as a means of calling the public's attention to the defendants' actions—or, rather, inactions.

It turned out that the defendants within the Dukakis administration did not need much prodding. Neither the governor nor individual legislators wanted to be on the wrong side of the issue. At no time, with few exceptions, did anyone indicate that the current state of affairs was satisfactory; the main argument in defense rested on the conviction that the political branches of government should be left to do the job of regenerating Boston Harbor without the intervention of the courts. But even on that point, the defendants' protests weakened as the court applied judicial pressures.

All three bodies—the court, the legislature, and the executive—benefited from political triangulation. Although the state administration would not have chosen to go to court to resolve the pollution issue, once it found itself there it seemed willing to take advantage of the additional momentum the court added in support of setting up an independent regional sewer authority. The governor's appeal to the legislature was direct: it was better for the problem to be solved by legislators than by the court, better to halt the continuous intervention by the judiciary into further aspects of state and local governance, better to retain control as much as possible. And the governor's willingness to use the court to generate increased political pressure allowed Judge Garrity to expand the scope of his remedial powers.[17]

This phenomenon produced the seemingly contradictory result of enhancing the state defendants' political muscle: with the backing of the court and the public, the defendants now had the means to remedy wholesale the problems that the *Quincy* lawsuit, at its outset, could not have adequately addressed.[18] In the end, I believe, Governor Dukakis actually was happy to have Judge Garrity and the *Quincy* case as allies.

A DYING HARBOR?

The Battle of the Experts

7

I believe that in this age of science we must build legal foundations that are sound in science as well as in law. Scientists have offered their help. We in the legal community should accept that offer, and we are in the process of doing so. The result, in my view, will further not only the interests of truth but also those of justice.

—Stephen G. Breyer

Throughout the investigation of the condition of Boston Harbor, the task of ascertaining the causes, extent, and consequences of pollution lay in the hands of professional experts who specialized in the nature and movements of coastal waters and the treatment and disposal of sewage. Obviously this is not a field in which graduates of a law school are knowledgeable. Yet the legal system calls for lawyers to familiarize themselves with technological issues, to communicate with experts, to examine and cross-examine scientific reports and testimonies—indeed, even to "prepare" the experts engaged by their side in order to present the best possible case to a busy judge charged with the responsibility for deciding the matter.

Those involved in the *Quincy* case struggled with this ordinary reality. We had the unusual advantage of the assistance of court-appointed experts from the university world, in a sense representing the public interest, entrusted as they were with the same pursuit of justice as was the judge. Not only did the professional contributions surrounding the special master's activities set a tone for subsequent dialogue, they also sharpened the testimony of the experts for both sides who realized that they were presenting arguments not to an unenlightened generalist but to a team that included professional peers whom they respected. The experts knew their opinions would be tested by highly experienced people familiar with the latest theories and technological innovations. At the same time, by the rules of the game, the evidence had to be directed at issues framed by the legal profession; the lawyers' way of thinking about the world and the processes by which they arrived at conclusions influenced what the experts said and how they testified. In order to keep the issues clear, the court's informal proceedings permitted interventions by the special master and the court-appointed consultants or at times by opposing counsel and their experts. Through these means we tried to avoid the sorts of misunderstandings that can easily arise out of the diverse approaches of such different professions.

The special master's hearings began on July 14, 1983. Over the course of three days, the city of Quincy and the attorney general's office, representing the defendants, made their arguments and presented witnesses and exhibits. With the participation and assistance of Steven Horowitz, I was an active judge conducting the hearings and gathering information.[1]

TECHNICAL QUESTIONS WITH VARYING ANSWERS

Among the fundamental issues facing the court were the causes of increased sewage flows that overwhelmed the existing capacities of the Metropolitan District Commission (MDC) treatment plants, and the potential for reducing the amount or toxicity of the flows. The various parties to the suit offered widely differing explanations, culprits, and approaches to solving the problems.

The divergence of views allowed Noel Baratta, director and chief engineer of the MDC's Metropolitan Sewerage Division, to dispute Quincy's estimate that two billion gallons of raw sewage a year was discharged from the Nut Island treatment plant. Labeling this approximation "misleading," Baratta pointed out that "1.3 billion of this figure is directly attributable to rainfall conditions," and, he contended, that stormwater overflow had minimal bacterial counts.[2] Furthermore, he claimed that David Standley, the city's primary expert, had overlooked such sources of harbor pollution as six billion gallons of raw, untreated wastewater flowing annually into the harbor from combined sewer overflow (CSO) outfalls, which were beyond the control of the MDC.

Standley countered that Baratta's argument artfully dodged the true issue, which he maintained was "the flux of contaminants and not the entering concentration." In an illustrative example he calculated that a rainfall that doubled the volume of flow entering the system would more than double the volume of pollutants entering the bay, even though nothing but fresh, clean rainwater had been added to the flow.[3]

"So," the plaintiff's expert concluded, "it is not 'just rainwater' that is bypassed." In addition, he went on, the increased sewage flows were caused by factors such as population growth in the Boston metropolitan area and recent connections and extensions to the sewerage system, not just wet-weather conditions that were in any case an occurrence that should be part of the MDC's planning. "The volume and strength of this 'base-flow' wastewater," he contended, "varies in a limited and roughly predictable way with diurnal, weekly, and to a lesser extent seasonal cycles."[4]

The suggested remedies were equally divergent. Quincy had proposed a plan for system-wide prohibition of new connections or extensions having capacities of more than 2,000 gallons per day. Quite a different approach was urged by William Gaughan, of the state's Department of Environmental Quality Engineering (DEQE). He denounced Quincy's proposal as socially irresponsible. To begin with, Gaughan observed, it would effectively impose a moratorium on all new construction in the communities serviced by the MDC. Furthermore, he maintained, a 2:1 reduction of inflow for every gallon allowed in new connections, as some others had suggested, would not be an equitable solution for Boston-area citizens since it would unfairly penalize municipalities that had conscientiously maintained their sewer systems. Instead, Gaughan recommended a case-by-case approach to evaluate narrowly defined problems and to tailor narrow remedies for them, which might or might not include outright prohibitions or restrictions on additional connections and extensions.[5]

Glenn Haas, supervising sanitary engineer for the DEQE, took an absolutist position. He also disliked the plan presented by Standley, if for no other reason than that he believed the MDC had already outlined plans to address the problem of pollution in Boston Harbor. The MDC, he stressed, was "actively participating in efforts to develop and implement immediate, short and long term solutions to the inadequacies of the MDC sewer system."[6]

Another issue that the special master requested all the parties to address was the consequences arising when sewage flows exceeded the treatment capacity of the plants. What, in fact, were the resulting water quality impacts?

Not unexpectedly, the responses differed significantly. Whereas the city of Quincy put forth a veritable compendium of environmental, sanitary, commercial, and recreational repercussions due to Nut Island overflows—all negative—the MDC in its affidavits acknowledged no serious consequences. In the "State Defendants' Proposed Findings of Fact and Conclusions of Law," the MDC forswore any causal connection between its operations and the pollution that afflicted Quincy's shores. Indeed, the commission requested that the special master find, as a conclusion of law, that "[t]he sewage treatment operations of the MDC do not pose any threat of immediate and irreparable injury to Quincy or to the environment in or near Quincy."[7]

In making these arguments the MDC offered the affidavits of several employees and environmental engineers familiar with its operations. Deborah McKechnie, a principal sanitary engineer with the DEQE, had conducted two water quality surveys of Boston Harbor from an MDC police boat during the summer of 1982. She testified that the tests performed on samples from four sampling locations in Quincy Bay proved its water quality to be "excellent." On no occasion when she herself had ventured onto those waters had she ever noticed any debris or sewage particles in the water. In short, she volunteered, "nothing I observed on all of the days of sampling, or this sampling data I have reviewed, would indicate permanent or irreversible impairment of the water quality in this area of Boston Harbor."

Robert Holthaus, director of treatment in the sewerage division of the MDC, minimized the impact of the discharge of excess flows from the plants even during heavy rainfalls. The discharges "are very dilute to begin with," he argued, and the combination of chlorination with the high degree of turbulence occurring behind the spillway and in the sluiceway at the entrance to the outfall pipes "results in complete mixing and thorough disinfection prior to discharge even in the short outfall." Bacterial counts of samples taken directly over the outfalls, he claimed, showed complete disinfection.[8]

To the extent that it did acknowledge a problem of sewage discharge in Quincy Bay or Boston Harbor, the MDC placed the responsibility for it squarely on individual local communities and on other state agencies. The MDC pointed to community-owned combined sewer overflows, over which the MDC had no control, as the likely culprits responsible for the discharge of raw sewage into nearby waters. Likewise, the defense contended that chloride analyses on sewage at the Deer Island plant yielded evidence that approximately 10 percent of the total flow to that facility was attributable to saltwater intrusion from tide-gate malfunctions, which were, as it happened, also the responsibility of local communities.

Contradicting the MDC's assertion that Boston Harbor and Quincy Bay were not suffering from any action of the commission's treatment plants, the city of Quincy offered a panoply of affidavits from individuals from all walks of life, both expert and amateur, testifying to the degradation of water and health conditions as a result of Nut Island discharges. According to these observers, the repercussions of excess flow fell into three categories: environmental and marine consequences, health and sanitary effects, and loss of recreational opportunities. The city of Quincy's "Proposed Findings of Fact" cited numerous statistics to support its contentions:

> On a day of average flow, the Nut Island Treatment Plant dumps into Quincy Bay and Hingham Bay 48,000 pounds of suspended solids; 38,000 pounds of grease and petroleum ethyl solids; 6,232 pounds of settleable solids; 7,900 pounds of chlorine and chlorine byproducts; 20 cubic feet of grit and screenings; and an undeterminable amount of trace metals and PCBs.

The city also blamed Nut Island and Moon Island outfalls for polluting large portions of Quincy coastlines and beaches, and for contaminating substantial portions of the bottom of Quincy Bay with thick black mucky ooze—"black mayonnaise"—that stymied marine growth.

In terms of marine life, Quincy's proposed findings asserted that MDC sewage flows were causing fin rot in flounder and other fish, contaminating clam beds, and radically altering the balance of marine life in waters near the treatment plants so that pollution-tolerant species were thriving to the detriment of pollution-sensitive species, such as dolphins.

The harm to human health that the city alleged was even more alarming. The plaintiff cited high levels of fecal coliform and other water-borne pathogens in untreated sewage being discharged by the MDC's plants, pathogens that can cause illness in humans who come into direct contact with them or who eat contaminated shellfish and finfish.

Public health specialists supported these contentions. Dr. Grace Hussey, commissioner of public health for the city of Quincy, testified that she had become concerned when routine water samples taken during the swimming season repeatedly revealed *e. coli* levels far in excess of state standards, posing risks of salmonellosis and hepatitis A for swimmers and shellfish consumers. Likewise, Hull's officials were often forced to close its beaches and shellfish areas because of "bacterial levels indicative of contamination by sewage and exceeding state standards for public safety," which also inflicted severe economic damage on business in the town.

Thomas Gecewicz, the director of public health for the town of Braintree, Quincy's inland neighbor to the south, detailed the tough decision, one that often faces public health officials, between releasing raw sewage into surrounding waters or allowing it to back up into residents' homes. He testified that he always regretted having to decide to release excess flows, but experience had taught him that the alternative was worse, since sewage backups rendered homes uninhabitable.

More poignant than the recitations of statistics and opinions by experts were personal stories about how the pollution of the harbor had impaired the lives of individual citizens of Quincy. Peter Mahoney, a commercial fisherman for over twenty years, offered the following statement:

> I have noted obvious and identifiable debris floating in these various waters. Such debris includes the following: human wastes, birth control devices, sanitary pads, and plastic applicators. An odor is also extremely noticeable from these waters on occasion. I have also noted that sea strain[er]s, behind Peddocks Island, are clogged by greaseballs. Periodically, I must clean my boat's one-and-a-half-inch (1½") sea intake screen. On these occasions, I find so much debris and foreign objects that it is comparable to cleaning out a sewer. When I

pull up some of my lobster traps and gill nets, I find that a horrible odor is present, as if they had been sitting at the bottom of a sewer. I have on occasion noticed that discharges from the Nut Island area turn the surrounding water to a milky-brown or silver-gray color. . . . I have noticed the line between the clean incoming water and the cloudy, milky, filthy, outgoing water. The stench of the outgoing water is terrible. The odor and sight of these waters resembles a sewer.

Jim Walker, the assistant dive chief of the Quincy Underwater Recovery Unit, observed that in areas up to one-half mile away from the Nut Island outfalls there was no trace of animal life or vegetation at the bottom of Quincy Bay. He described the seafloor there as seemingly covered by "a thick coat of material which looks like pine needles and consists of a thick mucky substance," a phenomenon he said he had never encountered elsewhere.

The connection between conditions out on the water and the MDC plant was stated with much authority by another witness, boat owner Robert Daylor:

[D]ischarges [from Nut Island] leave a visible boil on the surface of the water and on incoming (flood) tides; the gray-brown discolored plume is easily visible curling around Pig Rock. . . . There is an obvious, visible degradation of water quality in an area designated as a State Park and used for boating and fishing. It is my opinion that the degradation in this particular part of the harbor is most directly related to the MDC Nut Island treatment plant.

In sum, the city denounced the ongoing mismanagement of the treatment plants as rendering the bay unfit for swimming, boating, and fishing by polluting it with "discolored water, floatables, grease, fecal matter, foul odors and various birth control and sanitary devices."

One area in which expert opinions diverged concerned the effects of Quincy's own storm drains on the condition of Wollaston Beach. In a penultimate effort to disclaim liability, the MDC argued that the Quincy storm drains themselves were the only significant source of contamination on Wollaston Beach. The MDC put forth several scientifically based affidavits to support this broad contention. To cover all bases, the MDC volunteered to show that not only was the city of Quincy responsible for any increased rainfall flow from its connections to the MDC system, but it was causing the Wollaston Beach pollution more directly. To shore up this argument, the MDC offered analyses by environmental engineers Jekabs P. Vittands and C. F. MacKinnon showing significantly more contamination in water taken from points immediately adjacent to Quincy storm culverts than in samples taken further out in Quincy Bay. Conducted during the summer of 1983, these tests revealed that fecal coliform levels recorded around Wollaston Beach were indeed alarmingly high.[9]

With David Standley taking the lead, the city responded, hypothesizing that any increased levels of fecal coliform in its storm drains were directly attributable to the backup of bay water contaminated by bacteria from Nut Island effluent. Severely criticizing the methodology employed by the MDC in its testing, Standley maintained that the MDC's failure to take samples anywhere but in the immediate vicinity of the storm drains cast significant doubt on the veracity of its results. Pointing to the absence of testing done at points fairly distant from the culverts, Standley claimed that there was no evidence to suggest that the Quincy storm drains had anything but an ephemeral and highly local impact.[10]

Lending support to Standley's rebuttal, the city offered into evidence a study conducted by the Carr Research Laboratory during July 1983.[11] The Carr study argued that the Quincy storm drains were, at most, only partially responsible for the damage at Wollaston Beach, postulating that much of the bacterial load found in the Quincy storm drains, particularly that of human origin, was attributable to contaminated bay water backing into the storm drains at high tide.[12]

THE QUEST FOR A REMEDY

The conflicting affidavits and testimonies of the experts, taken as a whole, clarified the nature of the pollution of Quincy Bay and (by implication) Boston Harbor. The wide divergences of opinion about causes and effects, however, reflected the paucity of scientific knowledge and the difficulty of securing sound empirical data. This presented the court with a dilemma in seeking to fashion a remedy: it was difficult to fix blame or prescribe solutions when there was such dispute about even the most basic questions of conditions and contamination sources.

Conflicting testimony in both the general writings and specific oral statements of the experts revealed the difficulty of measuring environmental damage. Scientists and specialists with the best of professional qualifications often differ considerably in their judgments and evaluations about what, exactly, the problem is and what its solution might entail. And almost inevitably politics and economics creep into the perspectives of all parties. The independent, court-appointed experts, who provided more objective and neutral evaluations of the evidence, helped the special master and court come to their conclusions about the responsibility of the MDC for the condition of the harbor, which was a precondition for mandating remedial action. Their evaluation of the minimal effects of fixing Quincy's storm drains within the context of the harbor conditions as a whole was but one example.

Temporal and spatial factors complicated the task. Time lags between human actions and their consequences for the natural world cloak the origins of pollution. It can take years to determine the causes and extent of environmental degradation. With regard to Boston Harbor, for instance, much of the deterioration of the benthic environment had been caused by toxins dumped into the waters in previous decades, and the complex effects of the changing winds and currents made any attempt to identify their sources exceptionally difficult, if not impossible. Moreover, the cumulative impact of countless small insults to the harbor system can do unforeseeable damage, as the pollutants accumulate and interact, so that individual blame becomes essentially immaterial.

In such a complex system, a court's usual question requiring the affixing of blame and assignment of damages becomes almost irrelevant. The traditional orientation toward correction asks how the world would have evolved absent the defendant's wrongful practice, and seeks to bring about that state of affairs. But part of Judge Garrity's decree would also need to deal with prevention, and there the orientation of the parties turns to the predictive: it imagines a continuing probability of wrongdoing and puts forth measures to ensure that the practice is mitigated and, generally, that misconduct and harm will come to an end. The burden of proof for a judicial decision is higher than that for a public report or speech, since it has a direct impact on the lives and property rights of many persons, but complex adjudication cannot follow a single line of social causation forever, just as the court should not lose itself too deeply in multiple causal analyses. If the case was to move forward toward a solution, then somehow, relying on a judgment of the general situation, a determinate causal responsibility would have to be attributed to the given practices of the MDC.

The state continued to deny that sort of culpability. Running as leitmotifs through the state defendants' affidavits were four arguments: First, the state was not solely or even partly responsible for the pollution problem on Quincy's beaches. Second, matters were proceeding well on course to correct any operational deficiencies in the metropolitan sewerage system in a manner that ensured the future reliable functioning of treatment facilities. Third, the court lacked the authority to intervene in the spheres of governance properly allocated to the executive and legislative branches. And fourth, the relief requested by the city of Quincy—especially prohibition of new sewage connections for systems generating more than 2,000 gallons of sewage per day—would have a catastrophic impact on the economic well-being of the citizens of the commonwealth.

So far as Quincy was concerned, the cause of the poor condition of the harbor's waters seemed obvious and the MDC denials were simply untrue and insulting. Both laboratory tests and personal accounts bore this out, it claimed. The eyes and noses of many witnesses were telling them that the harbor was near death, perhaps beyond resuscitation. And the state agencies were a contributing cause, with their promises that proved to be but empty talk, their plans and programs subject to delays, their abundant catalogs of unexplained misfortunes, and, overall, their lack of will and purpose.

The public, alerted by media reports about the *Quincy* hearings that included candid admissions by several officials about troubling facts, was becoming alarmed at the increasing frequency and volume of bypasses of the sewage treatment facilities. Perhaps more disturbing was the apparent inaction by the state. Discharges of hundreds of millions of gallons of untreated sewage violated federal and state laws, rules, and regulations; they breached legal duties; they indicated beyond question a sustained risk of irreparable harm; they posed immediate threats to human health and safety. Dolphins and porpoises no longer cavorted in the waters. Finally, photographs illustrating the chronic fin rot in flounder, a major link in the food chain, focused public attention on the serious threat of continued pollution to marine life and to the ecosystem of the entire harbor.

Public concern forced the political and economic leaders of Boston to acknowledge the pitiful state of what had once been the city's greatest asset.

Despite the difficulty in tracing the precise causes of the harbor's troubles, it became clear to all, laymen and experts alike, that the problem could be boiled down to one simple proposition: more waste was coming into the metropolitan sewage system than the current system could handle. In the end this was the common denominator underlying the analysis of the environmental degradation of Boston Harbor.

How could the court synthesize and reconcile the work of experts, each in specialized and separate scientific and engineering niches? Virtually all the technical advisers, no matter by whom employed, acknowledged—without attempting to exhaustively catalog—that Boston Harbor was dangerously polluted. In consequence the testimony of the contending experts and the voluminous technical literature introduced at the trial pointed in but one direction: no matter who funded the research and quite apart from their views on the wisdom of government intervention, the scientists and engineers agreed that major public investments were necessary and appropriate.

The special master's report (which is discussed in the next two chapters) therefore concluded, and the judge concurred, that although it might be desirable to have more precise data extracted by further research and analysis, the existing scientific conclusions, the testimony at trial, and the conclusions derived from the court-appointed experts supported a finding that discharge of raw and inadequately treated sewage into Boston Harbor provided a sufficient legal predicate for remedial action. The judicial search for scientific precision was at best a limited one. A continuation of business as usual would pose a risk of irreparable harm to the environment and attendant jeopardy to human health, safety, and welfare. Looking beyond the claims and counterclaims and the grandiloquence of arguments that enter into adversarial proceedings, the need for major improvements in the Boston sewerage system could not be denied. Billions of gallons of raw and undertreated sewage poured into Boston Harbor—and this was so even if the responsible party or parties could not be precisely and completely determined. It was enough that the named defendants contributed to the problem. This was a finding a court could act on, and Judge Garrity was willing and able to act.

Two further observations about the trial experience itself. One dimension of the case was unexpected: the eloquence of the average person speaking of a subject close to the heart, the beauty of the great harbor, the role it played in daily activities, the play of light upon water, the fate of fish, dolphins, seals, and seafloor life, the deleterious repercussions of pollution and the "plumes," the dangers to health—all came out in personal terms, often vivid, that brought ordinary life into the courtroom.[13] The people at large are the patient makers of our treasured inheritance.

Another phenomenon, of more general applicability, is the need to utilize the power of scientific knowledge in court proceedings, while simultaneously recognizing and dealing with the limits of the scientific method. Explaining the conditions of Boston Harbor were experienced people—on both sides—who had dedicated their lives to garnering knowledge about complex coastal marine systems, yet in their testimony disagreed on causes and consequences, and when pushed to the limits by sometimes naïve queries, conceded lack of knowledge or analytical capacities or undone research that might provide better answers to the questions raised in court. There were but few certain or uniform views among the experts—even among the independent ones appointed by the court. In light of such uncertainty, unsupported values and subjective individual judgments were difficult to screen out of presentations of scientific conclusions. Approximate understanding of the state of scientific

knowledge of the condition of the harbor was all that could be
achieved, and it had to suffice for dealing with the legal questions.[14] Courts cannot be held hostage to the standard of an unattainable certainty.

In the Boston Harbor case, what remained clear after reviewing the public record was the existence of a firm factual foundation, as well as a general concurrence among the experts, regarding the seriousness of the existing pollution in the harbor and the hazards it posed to the health, safety, and enjoyment of the citizens of the metropolitan area. Plainly, the potential of the resource represented by a healthy Boston Harbor for enhancing the quality of life was diminished by a perennial unwillingness or inability to take actions that would counteract ongoing pollution. All the costly studies that had been undertaken, all the expensive facilities proposed for the harborside, would be for naught if the historic trend of inattention and inaction could not be reversed.

REPORT OF THE
SPECIAL MASTER
Findings of Fact

8

Like I said, these things are all fact driven: you push too hard,
it tilts; you don't push hard enough, you lose. . . . Most cases
are not won, they're lost.

—Joseph H. Flom

Getting to the bottom of highly technical issues about Boston Harbor was a vital part of my instructions from Judge
Garrity. The mandate to make "findings of fact" required probing, expert evaluation, interviews, and close reading of documents in order to piece together a mosaic of the complex operations of the metropolitan sewerage system and how they affected
the harbor. Facts are never inert; they need collection, sifting,
and interpretation before they can be said to be legally alive and
proper subjects of judicial investigation.

That was one function of the report that I prepared and submitted to Judge Garrity on August 9, 1983.[1] A further question
was how to get this information across to the most important
actor in this drama—the public. The report was meant to present the findings of fact both to the judge and to the court of
public opinion. Potentially, the findings and recommendations
of the special master's report represented the coming to an end
of decades of stalling, malaise, and indifference to one of the
most serious environmental tragedies in Massachusetts history.

In retrospect, the ability of the court and the legislature to
take effective action in this instance was based on one pivotal
factor: the crisis of the harbor tapped deep and shared sources

of attachment and sentiment among the people of the metropolitan area. The city of Quincy's formal complaint and the media coverage of the court proceedings that followed provoked a swell of collective opinion, a reaction that made it clear to political leaders that the redemption of Boston Harbor was a social good for which the public was willing to pay. Repairing the damaged environment, it seemed, was now a higher community priority than any of the pundits or political leaders had realized.

The special master's report was intended to serve as a basis for actions to be taken by the trial court and as a source of support for its determinations in the event of an appeal; in addition, its findings of facts provided a legal record for later review and evaluations of actions proposed or taken. Equally important—and this was constantly in mind—was presenting the findings to the public. In constructing the master's report, therefore, a delicate line had to be drawn between two somewhat contradictory objectives: first, to present the technical details necessary to clarify the operation of the sewerage system but not strain the patience of a general audience; and second, to satisfy public questions about the legal process, yet not overwhelm with intricacies. And the richness of materials invited detailed attention and elaboration. The more we waded through the unfamiliar technicalities, the more we became fascinated by the strange and mysterious underworld of pipes and technology that underlay the Boston metropolitan area.

With these considerations in mind, the report's findings of fact clustered around the question of how a modern metropolis could find itself in the position of dumping raw sewage directly into a major harbor, thereby threatening the health of its citizens. To understand why this malfeasance had proceeded unchecked involved the unraveling of the skein of human activities of the entire metropolitan sewerage system.

THE LEVELS OF SEWAGE FLOW

The special master's report started with two major findings. The first was the more obvious but also the more crucial: excess flows in an antiquated system caused significant discharges of untreated or partially treated human and industrial waste into the seriously polluted harbor. Each and every day 450 million gallons of wastewater and 50,000 pounds of sludge entered the harbor. On rainy days more than one hundred shoreline overflow ports dumped additional raw sewage and stormwater runoff into the harbor's tributaries and waters. This situation, already deplorable, was getting worse.

The second central finding was that infiltration/inflow (I/I) of water from outside the sewerage system was the primary cause of excess flows in the system. This condition was exacerbated by inaction: the state defendants had done little to address this situation beyond commissioning a series of studies.

Population Figures and Projections

Conditions in the harbor had to be set against the underlying population pattern, for trends in growth and composition are major determinants of sewage flow volume. At the time of the *Quincy* litigation, the south metropolitan area served by the Nut Island plant had a total population of 750,000 and a contributing population of 630,000. (Contributing population—the number of persons adding wastewater to the system—was the lesser figure because parts of the area were not sewered and relied instead on such means as septic tanks.) In the much larger north metropolitan area served by the Deer Island plant there existed a population of 1,306,500 and a contributing population of 1,246,500.[2]

Based on the population and sewer extension projections, the report sided with those experts who projected that the average sewage flow in 1990 would be 151 million gallons per day (mgd) in the Deer Island service area and 61 mgd in the Nut Island service area; corresponding peak flows in 1990 were projected at 310 mgd for the Deer Island service area and 118 mgd for Nut Island.[3]

This led to the conclusion that these factors would cause only marginal increases in system influent. This in turn led the report to focus on other factors affecting flow. It also meant that population growth and new connections, relatively immune as they are from any governmental influences in the short or medium term, certainly were not the issues that required the most attention; other components, fortunately more susceptible to public or private action or a combination of the two, were identified and emphasized by the report.

Infiltration/Inflow

Engineers use the term "infiltration/inflow" to refer to the total quantity of water that enters a sewer network from outside its formal collection system. These "extraneous flows" are subject to varying technical definitions, but there is a common understanding about their major components. *Infiltration* is the surface or ground water that enters a sewer system through defective pipes, joints, connections, and manhole walls. *Inflow* is the water fed into a sewer system from roof leaders, foundation and surface drains, streams, catch basins, and tidal overflow weirs, but the term also covers water that enters sewer systems— sometimes in large quantities—through illegal connections to sanitary sewers.[4]

Thanks to the work of the court-appointed scientists, one startling conclusion emerged at trial: wastewater directly collected by the system's sanitary sewers contributed only 41 percent (110 mgd) of the peak flow in the Nut Island service area; I/I accounted for the rest, fully 59 percent (161 mgd) of that facility's peak flow.[5] The proportions for Deer Island were similar.[6]

This was truly a remarkable revelation of where corrective energies should go, and it prompted us to investigate the costs and history of attempts to remedy the I/I problem. Experts testified that the cost of reducing inflow was, on the average, roughly constant per unit of inflow since it required the removal of illegal connections, which could be accomplished through physical inspections. In combined sewerage systems, inflow removal may also be accomplished by the separation of storm sewers from sanitary sewers. By contrast, reduction of infiltration required discovering and fixing leaks in the system, and since finding large leaks was easiest and least expensive per unit, the cost of removing the last gallon of infiltration incurred a greater cost than removing the first gallon.[7]

The *Quincy* trial and subsequent investigations revealed that despite a multitude of studies of the I/I problems, little reduction in their levels had been achieved. MDC status reports on I/I reduction revealed that most member communities had not progressed beyond the initial stages of analysis or sewer system evaluation surveys. Why?

An Assessment of I/I Remediation Efforts as of 1983

In a sharply critical analysis, my report found that it would be quite feasible, financially and technologically, to remove much of the I/I flow into Boston's metropolitan sewerage system, and that this alone would prove a major step toward improving conditions in the harbor. The root of the problem, as elsewhere, was the tangle of overlapping jurisdictions of municipal and state agencies, along with their connections to federal agencies.

The cast of characters responsible for I/I regulation included two divisions of the Massachusetts Executive Office of Environmental Affairs: the Metropolitan District Commission (MDC) and the Division of Water Pollution Control (DWPC).[8] In addition, by virtue of its programs offering funding for I/I removal and sewage system improvements, the federal government was also an important player. The EPA specifically prescribed a process for state and local agencies to follow in order to receive federal funding for the identification and removal of excessive I/I in a sewer system, and all applicants for grants to support new treatment facilities had to first show that the existing sewer system discharging to the proposed plant did not contain excessive I/I.[9] Ironically, the complexity of the funding guidelines had the unintended consequence of further delaying specific programs for I/I removal.

The state agencies clearly had sufficient power to remedy the situation. The MDC had authority to approve or deny member communities' applications for connections to the interceptor system, which could be conditioned on the reduction of I/I, and the DWPC issued permits to developers for extensions and connections to the MDC sewer systems, which could also be conditional.[10]

The DWPC had used this power sporadically, with some effect. DWPC records from the period January 1982 to May 1983, introduced at the trial, listed fifty-four sewer extension or connection applications from the twenty-one communities within the south metropolitan service area. In particular cases DWPC had imposed restrictions on sewer extensions or new connections, most commonly requirements to remove two gpd (gallons per day) of I/I for every new gpd allowed.[11] Two local responses became common: in many cases the town initiated I/I removal projects and established a "banking" system with DWPC whereby developers could acquire rights to add one unit of flow to that town's total for every two units of I/I removed. In other instances, where the town did not initiate I/I removal projects, developers—either individually or collectively—undertook sewer rehabilitation programs and then applied for credit to the DWPC. The evidence at trial disclosed no case where development in a community ceased as a result of the 2:1 reduction requirement—I/I reduction work had been undertaken in all of them.

Additional findings of fact were damning in their documentation of the lack of proactive implementation and enforcement of policies and regulations by the state agencies. Despite MDC studies that indicated the cost-effectiveness of I/I removal in the south system service area, the only program instituted by the MDC in the 1970s that actually reduced the total volume of flow into the Nut Island plant was a waste pretreatment program, which reduced flows by four to six mgd. According to the MDC studies, 30 percent of infiltration and 50 percent of inflow could be cost-effectively removed from the flows generated by the south system service area.[12] As the report pointed out, if only 15 percent of I/I were removed from the south system service area, approximately 57 mgd of flow would be eliminated, a result that would significantly decrease discharges of inadequately treated sewage into the southern portion of the harbor.

THE TREATMENT PLANTS

The evidence presented regarding operations at the MDC's Nut Island and Deer Island treatment plants led to one inescapable conclusion: their performance was woeful. Findings of fact in the report went into detail as to their failings, focusing on Nut Island as most immediately relevant to the *Quincy* case, but including what had been learned about the Deer and Moon Island facilities as well.

Foremost among concerns, the Nut Island facility could process only limited volumes, an average of 250 mgd of flow, 60 mgd less than the High Level Sewer interceptor could deliver to it. True, it was capable of accepting up to 280 mgd, but the quality of treatment it could provide for the higher level of flow was significantly poorer. Thus, as of 1983, the actual average daily flow greatly exceeded the capacity of the plant.

Inadequate operations budgets and poor maintenance at the Nut Island plant further reduced functional capacity. The plant was thirty years old and badly in need of major rehabilitation. Testimony at the trial showed that over the years successive MDC administrations had neglected preventive maintenance and equipment replacement to the extent that nearly all upkeep was done only in response to emergencies. As a result, key components of the plant were frequently out of service for extended periods of time.[13]

Equally disturbing was insufficient staffing: in 1982 an average of only 86 persons filled an authorized 112 positions at the Nut Island plant; on more than one occasion so few people showed up for work that the plant could not be operated at all.

During this time, moreover, the Nut Island and Deer Island treatment plants continued to suffer crisis after crisis, often failing to provide even basic primary treatment before dumping raw sewage into the harbor. Indeed, within eighteen months of the filing of the *Quincy* litigation, both the Nut Island and Deer Island treatment facilities experienced major breakdowns.

On one particularly ill-fated occasion, on Mother's Day of 1983, a pipe coupling in the Deer Island treatment plant broke due to lack of maintenance. Because a backup system was not in place, raw sewage began to spill onto the plant floor, ultimately covering the bottom two stories of the plant and enveloping the engines that sent treated sewage out to sea. The MDC found itself poorly equipped for such an emergency; it was forced to send teams of MDC police frogmen to make repeated dives into the sewage in an attempt to locate the source of the problem.

After fumbling in the malodorous darkness for three days, the team was able to find the broken coupling two tunnels away, beneath a grate and among a jumble of machines. In the end, the workers were able to replace the coupling, allowing the plant to resume pumping. In the meantime, however, 153 million gallons of raw untreated sewage were discharged into the waters around

Moon Island, the divers suffered from dysentery and other infections for weeks after the nightmarish assignment, and the taxpayers faced a bill for $1.5 million to repair the engines.

Because of both design flaws and mechanical and personnel problems, Nut Island simply could not handle either average daily flows or peak flows of sewage. First, peak flows increased the velocity of influent and reduced the efficiency of treatment equipment such as grinders, grit removal screens, detention tanks (for oxygen transfer), and chlorinators. Second, the encrustation of the primary outfalls, as well as high wet-weather flows, led to the increased use of emergency outfall 104, which was located close to Boston shores.[14] Third, excess flows caused influent sewage to bypass treatment at any one of four points.[15] During 1982 and the first half of 1983, approximately 2.1 billion gallons of influent bypassed primary treatment at the Nut Island plant.[16] Consequently, the plant regularly discharged untreated or undertreated sewage into the surrounding waters, often quite close to shore. Witnesses described "plumes," visible flows of sewage that were decried by citizens and experts alike. They were often seen near the Nut Island outfalls, producing objectionable colors, odors, and turbidity, significantly impairing the uses of harbor waters for boating, fishing, swimming, and other recreation.[17]

This situation revealed a startling example of a difference in perceptions between bureaucracy, indeed, the professional classes, and the general public: of all the many pollutants carried onto Quincy's beaches, only high coliform counts were deemed by the regulatory agencies to be grounds for beach closings; thus, by administrative fiat, beaches remained open despite the presence of grease, oil, tampon applicators, scum, and other sewage particles in adjacent waters. Yet plumes clearly violated the public's standards for bay and harbor waters, as well as the standards of the EPA.[18]

In sum, the report found that Nut Island effluent visibly degraded the water quality of Quincy and Hingham Bays; that the plumes from its outfalls carried unacceptable amounts of sewage matter, debris, grit, and sludge; and that the Nut Island plant contributed significantly to the pollution of Quincy's beaches.

Wind and Tidal Patterns

The question of how tidal patterns affected the dispersal of pollutants in Boston Harbor evoked considerable controversy. Tidal charts showed a weak and variable flow between Moon Island and Long Island, but a strong one along the south side of both islands.[19] At certain times the currents of this tidal regime captured any raw sewage discharged from Moon Island that passed south of the Long Island Bridge, several experts testified, and carried it into Quincy Bay.

Most of the Moon Island effluent, being composed of non-saline liquids that were generally warmer than bay water, tended to rise to the surface after exiting the outlet.[20] This had three significant effects: it decreased the rate of dilution; it amplified the effect of wind direction and velocity on the flow of the discharge; and it increased the likelihood of swimmers or boaters coming into contact with highly contaminated slicks of raw sewage floating on top of the water.[21] Of course it was this part of Quincy Bay's waters, the top layer, that was most enjoyed and appreciated—when it was clean—by users of the bay and its beaches for swimming, boating, or fishing. Obviously, as pointed out at trial, even when people did not come into physical contact with it, the sight and smell of raw sewage floating in the water impaired their enjoyment of the bay.[22]

Flow Levels and Bypasses

As a result of inadequate design, Nut Island was unable to offer optimal primary treatment to the member communities of the southern half of the metropolitan sewage district. First, the plant's insufficient treatment capacity for both daily and peak or wet-weather sewage flows resulted in frequent bypasses.[23] Second, the shorter Nut Island outfalls, 103 and 104, much closer to the nearby shores than other outfalls, provided insufficient chlorine contact time for effective disinfection of effluent that was allowed to bypass primary treatment.[24] Third, all of the plant's four outfalls either lacked functional diffusers or had no diffusers at all to disperse and dilute discharges.[25]

Effect on Marine Life

Discharges from Nut Island contributed to a degradation of marine life, including the benthic communities near its outfalls, shellfish inhabiting the flats of Quincy Bay, and finfish throughout the harbor. Shellfish flats were closed automatically when a Nut Island bypass was reported as well as whenever local coliform counts exceeded 70 per 100 ml of water.

Studies indicated that benthic flora and fauna, organisms inhabiting the bottom of the harbor, were altered from their natural state. Since the benthos had a reduced assimilative capacity, even small amounts of organic pollution, such as human wastes, reduced oxygen levels. Water quality analyses showed relatively high concentrations of toxic pollutants, including heavy metals, near Nut Island discharges. This pollution resulted in a benthic population dominated by pollution-tolerant species, which in turn decreased the food supply for fish.[26]

DEER ISLAND AND MOON ISLAND FACILITIES

Matters were no better, we reported, in the northern division of the metropolitan sewerage district. The Deer Island plant suffered from an equally inauspicious history of breakdown and neglect. Although its equipment was somewhat more modern than that at Nut Island, its operations were crippled by chronic problems related to its diesel engines, which were used for pumping up the sewage running through a tunnel 300 feet beneath the harbor. Due to a design flaw, the engines never worked properly. Still more unfortunate was the circumstance that the engines were manufactured by the Nordberg Company, which went into bankruptcy soon after the equipment was purchased, foreclosing any possibility of obtaining replacement parts. As early as 1973 a consultant concluded that the Deer Island engines, installed just five years before, functioned on average only half of the time. In 1976 a task force found that on occasion the plant had been down to two, out of eight, working engines. On April 28, 1981, a situation that had been a chronic source of worry came to the boiling point: when six of the plant's engines failed, sewage that could not be pumped into the plant for treatment was simply released into the harbor and its tributaries.

Whenever its Deer Island treatment plant could not handle the amount of flow it was receiving, one action the MDC took in response was to shut off altogether the BWSC's ability to feed into Deer Island. This was accomplished by closing gates at its Columbus Park headworks on Carson Beach. Sewage and stormwater were forced back up the system into house connections and basements in the many low-lying sections of Boston. In essence, the Calf Pasture pumping station and Moon Island acted as an overflow valve for the MDC's Deer Island treatment plant. As much as 180 mgd of raw sewage were discharged, wholly untreated, through the Moon Island outfall during storms.

The four Moon Island sewage storage tanks, as originally constructed, had a total capacity of 45 million gallons. Their purpose was simply to hold effluent until it could be discharged on the outgoing tides; indeed, Moon Island was originally referred to as a "detention facility."[27] The study undertaken prior to its construction indicated that effluent released with the outgoing tides would travel out four miles into Massachusetts Bay, return two miles on the incoming tides, and then, during the next tidal cycle, be washed further out toward the ocean. By the time of the *Quincy* trial, however, the BWSC and its predecessors had allowed the holding tanks at Moon Island to fall into a state of complete inoperability.[28] Consequently, Moon Island merely released incoming sewage at whatever time it received it, whether the tide was going out or coming in. According to BWSC's witnesses, the cost of putting the four holding tanks at Moon Island back in service would be only $250,000, but, incredibly, the work had not been done.

Design and Capacity
The Deer Island treatment plant was designed to treat an average daily flow of 343 mgd and a peak flow of 848 mgd. The majority of the influent was conveyed by gravity to the plant via two independent tunnel systems, terminating a hundred feet below the main pumping station, which pumped the influent up into the plant.[29]

Our report found that as a result of equipment limitations and failures, as well as staffing inadequacies, the functional capacity of Deer Island was considerably below its design capacity. Furthermore, the frequent inability of the main pumping station to handle the total volume of influent it received was a principal cause of consistently low performance. This finding required considerable digging into documents and oral testimonies. It proved essential for public understanding of harbor pollution as well as for the credibility of the report.

The engines that drove the wastewater pumps, housed in the main pumping station, had proven extremely unreliable since installation. They broke down constantly. Since spare parts were unavailable from the defunct manufacturer, replacement parts had to be fabricated by a machinist on the plant site. In addition, several engines were cannibalized to provide spare parts for the others; by 1983 there were not enough parts to keep more than five engines running at any one time. This cut the plant's capacity by almost half.[30]

The smokestacks connected to the engines that drove the

pumps posed a significant maintenance problem as well as being a serious safety hazard. Owing to the accumulation of oil and carbon from the pumping system engines, the stacks often caught fire. During the fires the engines could not be switched off due to fear that the flames would travel down the stacks and ignite the entire pumping station, a structure that was literally drenched in oil. Therefore no efforts were made to extinguish the fires—they were simply allowed to burn. The Winthrop fire department continually raised objections to this situation and the hazards it presented, but the practice continued.[31]

By the time of the *Quincy* litigation, the report concluded, large volumes of raw sewage that should have been treated at Deer Island were being routinely dumped into Boston Harbor. Much of the system that fed the plant consisted of combined sewers, so that during wet weather the quantity of influent directed to Deer Island was significantly increased by stormwater mixing with the normal influent of sanitary sewage, thus overwhelming the plant's capacity. And during dry weather, when the Deer Island influent consisted only of raw sewage, either equipment breakdowns or staff failure frequently reduced the pumping and treatment capacity of the plant to a point where influent was diverted to Moon Island and released untreated through that facility's outfall.[32]

In addition to the design and technical problems of the Nut Island and Deer Island facilities, inadequate funding led to the MDC's inability to carry out preventive maintenance and to complete necessary repairs effectively. Over time, proud shiny plants turned into collections of outmoded equipment subject to wear and tear that crippled their performance. By 1983 most of the equipment installed at Nut Island was deemed antiquated by outside investigators, yet the MDC was not able to provide for a comprehensive preventive maintenance program, let alone stock an inventory of spare parts.

These problems came to a most embarrassing head in January

of 1976, when every generator at the Nut Island plant broke down simultaneously. As a result, millions of gallons of sewage had to be dumped, untreated, into the harbor. Nonetheless, little was done to rectify the situation. A second complete shutdown of the facility occurred six years later, at the end of February 1982. This time the disruption lasted for three days, and even after the plant's directors finally managed to bring a rented generator on line, the spillage amounted to several hundred million gallons of raw sewage. The plant's generators were not repaired until mid-October.

On a much-debated point at the trial—the bacterial contamination of Wollaston Beach itself—the evidence turned out to be inconclusive. Quincy's system of stormwater drainage serviced an area of approximately 798 acres and included eight storm drains that emptied onto Wollaston Beach; these were the drains that the MDC cited in its counterclaim alleging that the city itself was the cause of the pollution at the beach.

With respect to Wollaston Beach in particular, Nut Island discharges appeared to be the origin of bacterial contamination under adverse wind and tide conditions. But data presented by the state defendants indicated that these discharges were not the sole source of such contamination. Accordingly, the report concluded that although Nut Island caused significant pollution of Quincy's waters, including the defiling of beaches close to the discharge points of its outfalls, it did not appear to be the primary cause of bacterial contamination on Wollaston Beach; the Quincy storm drains did contribute to the contamination in immediately adjacent areas. It was a complicated matter, but fortunately under the time-limit constraints one not calling for complete resolution immediately.

SPECIFIC HARMS

Boston Harbor had come a far cry indeed from the days when Nut Island was a favorite landmark for sailors who enjoyed the refreshment of what an early settler described as its "divers arematicall [that is, aromatic] herbes and plants." A seventeenth-century sailor could write that "Shipps have come from Virginia where there have bin scarce five men able to hale [haul] a rope until they come near Nut Island and smell the sweet airs of the shore, where they have suddenly recovered."[33] What would the sailor or colonial settler say to the stench of the contemporary harbor? How could the commonwealth begin to reverse over two centuries of environmental carelessness and abuse? The court could start with the facts and go on from there.

We found from the studies and testimony that wastewater flows included or resulted in the following specific harms:

- visual and olfactory pollution caused by large solids, floating matter, and aquatic plant overgrowth stimulated by waste nutrients;
- organic pollution straining the harbor's dissolved oxygen resources and inhibiting aquatic life;
- eutrophication caused by excessive nutrients in the water that overstimulated aquatic plant growth, thereby strangling other life forms and reducing species diversity and overall aesthetic quality;
- accumulation of toxic substances, including DDT or PCBs in bottom sediments, pollutants that move up the food chain causing health problems and inhibiting aquatic life; and
- potentially dangerous concentrations of disease-producing bacteria and viruses that required the closing of numerous beaches and restrictions on shellfishing (the risks included human diseases ranging from gastrointestinal disorders to hepatitis and typhoid fever).

Under Judge Garrity's order of reference, the preliminary stage of the *Quincy* litigation focused on the level of sewage flow to the MDC's treatment plants and on the primary sewage treatment processes at Nut and Deer Islands as they affected Quincy Bay and adjacent waters. After we had held evidentiary hearings, viewed the facilities, and reviewed numerous studies, our report provided three major findings of fact, each of which pointed the way for future action.

First, reducing the amount of sewage piped to the treatment plants at Nut and Deer Islands would reduce the frequency and volume of overflows that discharged raw or partially treated sewage into the harbor. A way of accomplishing the goal would be to decrease the amount of I/I to the system by repairing leaks in pipes and monitoring illegal hookups. While more than $4.3 million had been granted for I/I work, little had been accomplished beyond studies and plans; this was so even though it was in fact feasible to remove much of the I/I. The state defendants admitted that 30 percent of infiltration and 50 percent of inflow could be removed cost-effectively—a reduction that would have a dramatic effect on the volume and frequency of overflows, and therefore on subsequent discharges of inadequately treated sewage into the harbor.

Second, due to its age, insufficient capacity, inadequate maintenance, and breakdowns, the Nut Island plant was unable to treat influent sewage to meet primary treatment standards. Consequently, raw or partially treated sewage was regularly discharged through the primary outfalls, and in wet weather partially treated sewage flows were pumped out through the plant's shorter outfalls and released even closer to shore. The resultant sewage "plumes" degraded the waters, especially when bypasses occurred, and contained contaminants that threatened marine life and pathogens known to cause disease in humans.

Third, as a result of equipment breakdowns and staff failures at Deer Island, as well as the inability of the plant to handle wet-weather flows, enormous amounts of untreated, raw sewage were periodically diverted and discharged into the waters off Moon Island. This effluent rose to the surface and was swept into Quincy Bay by tides and wind. It affected the shellfish flats and the beaches within the arms of Quincy Bay, including Wollaston Beach. Its presence posed an environmental affront and a grave public health hazard to swimmers, boaters, fishermen, and others who sought to enjoy the natural beauty and bounty of Quincy Bay.

Although in theory the MDC's sewerage division was self-supporting through the user assessments procedure, it was nonetheless dependent on appropriations by the legislature—and just as vulnerable as other state agencies to its decisions. The legislature set an annual operating budget for the MDC, but this was far less than the need and often well below what the agency actually brought in through user fees, which went into the state treasury rather than the agency's funding. Year after year, politicians voiced concern about the harbor pollution problem, but in the end they proved unwilling to dedicate extra funds to address it because they found it politically unwise to appropriate money for an infrastructure that was mostly invisible to the public.

But they had not reckoned with the fish. What turned out to be a key to rousing public opinion concerning Boston Harbor was our finding about the health of fish. Discharges from Nut Island, the report concluded, contributed to fin erosion in winter flounder. Fin erosion may result from contact with toxic metals; the flounders' liver cancer, which affected as much as 12 percent of that population, was related to organochlorides such as pesticides and PCBs. Furthermore, at high concentrations, many common pollutants kill off local fish populations.

The flounder findings received wide publicity. The city of Winthrop—"the world's capital of flounder" according to its welcoming sign at the entrance to the city—was particularly sensitive to this threat and expressed intense concern. The health of the flounder made the danger to the harbor seem immediate in a way that the plight of a lowly, anonymous benthic creature or even the degradation of the harbor's shellfish did not. Like

Boston's legendary cod, the flounder was both a valued resource and a symbol of local pride, and this threat to it became a source of public outrage.

The general unease felt in many circles about the deteriorated condition of the harbor now had the very public backing of the latest carefully sifted scientific examinations and technical analyses, reinforced by stories from witnesses who lived by the sea. Through the media reports and other revelations as the *Quincy* litigation unfolded, the facts were now available and the citizens of the metropolitan Boston area began to respond.

The findings of fact in the special master's report on the extent of the pollution of the harbor and on the causes for the breach of federal and state laws would prove indispensable for developing a fresh public consensus. This consensus could turn outrage into action.

REPORT OF THE
SPECIAL MASTER
Remedies and Recommendations

But the fountain sprang up and the bird sang. . . .
Redeem the time, redeem the dream.

—T. S. Eliot

In addition to reporting the facts on the pollution of the harbor and the operations of the metropolitan sewerage system, the charge to the special master included submitting "conclusions of law" as recommendations to the court. In this connection we were empowered to hold hearings on legal arguments as well as collect oral testimony and affidavits from the parties to the case and outside experts. Throughout this process we kept in close contact with Judge Garrity, apprising him of our findings. At its end we submitted both the facts and the conclusions of law in the "Report of the Special Master Regarding Findings of Fact and Proposed Remedies."[1]

The 197-page report to the Superior Court represented an intense effort on the part of many people to clarify the Boston Harbor situation by exploring the physical, social, legal, and economic causes of the environmental degradation of the harbor's waters and to present the findings in an objective and persuasive manner. The assumption throughout was that substantial problems existed—Judge Garrity had decided as early as June 1983 that violations had occurred—but that they were solvable, that reason could be applied and that it would prevail. Above all, we had faith that once the record was completed and presented to the people of the commonwealth they would come to understand the serious implications of the evidence—and would support and adopt the proposed reforms.

The remedies presented in the report were meant to incorporate a comprehensive rather than piecemeal approach. They were responses to specific deficiencies at the Nut Island, Deer Island, and Moon Island facilities, to specific practices, and to specific harms, but they also were designed as an interrelated whole, whose effect would be synergistic. Since Boston Harbor is an environmental system with an organic unity, even short-term remedies needed to fit into a pattern of coordinated relief. As when a stone is dropped in water, the implications of the *Quincy* case rippled outward, and the court took on the challenge of a coordinated approach to the larger problems of the pollution of the harbor as a whole.

The report addressed, and for the most part dismissed, the main arguments in the "Proposed Findings of Fact and Conclusions of Law" submitted by the attorney general's office, acting for the state defendants. The attorney general argued against ordering immediate remedial actions on the ground of potential interference with the existing plans of the Metropolitan District Commission (MDC) to address the problems of combined sewer overflow discharges and treatment plant bypasses. He also contended that the Environmental Protection Agency (EPA) was a necessary party to the litigation since otherwise the defendants would be subject to the risk of incurring multiple conflicting obligations. Furthermore, the attorney general asserted, Quincy did not have a private right of action or standing to enforce the statutes that it alleged were being violated, and the trial court lacked the authority to compel the legislature to appropriate funds or to require the executive branch to modify its operations except as necessary to correct or prevent narrowly defined violations of law.

Clearly the attorney general and his staff failed to recognize

Judge Garrity's willingness to exercise the court's discretionary powers.

DENIAL OF A MORATORIUM ON MDC SEWER CONNECTIONS

Economic concerns were central elements of the remedies section of the report. In its motion for a preliminary injunction, Quincy had requested that a moratorium be placed on all new sewer connections, extensions, and construction grants in the MDC system until the problems with respect to Deer Island, Nut Island, and Moon Island were corrected.[2] While this proposal for a halt to all new development reflected an understandable frustration with the tedious processes of fragmented government bureaucracies, and while the dangers to the health and safety of the citizens of Quincy and the commonwealth were evidenced on a daily basis, such a drastic course of action nevertheless was deemed inappropriate.

The reason was straightforward. For one thing, new buildings requiring connection to sewer outlets were not the main sources of environmental degradation.[3] Adopting such a ban, furthermore, would be unfair to developers and to potential system users, who, by not being allowed entry, would be called on to bear the whole burden of a problem that had been created by many parties. In addition, given the urgency of the ongoing economic revitalization of the Boston metropolitan area, stopping development would put a halt to many positive benefits, including increased government revenues that could help pay for the upgrading of the wastewater infrastructure on which, arguably, all economic activity depended. Granting the requested moratorium would destroy these benefits, cutting off the societal nose to spite its face.

Our report therefore concluded that other remedial measures proposed after the filing of the original complaint, some of which the state defendants indicated a willingness to implement, would be adequate for the present time.[4] Of course, the report went on to suggest, should the court's orders not be carried out fully, thereby causing further hazard to the public health and continued violations of law, the court would then reconsider the option of imposing more severe remedies such as a complete sewer moratorium.

PROPOSALS FOR REDUCING FLOW WITHIN THE MDC SYSTEM

In sharp contrast to the denial of the moratorium request, the report smiled upon Quincy's proposals for reducing excessive flows within the MDC system as a whole. The city proposed two general remedies to address excessive influent to the treatment plants: a carefully planned system-wide infiltration/inflow reduction program, and a "2:1 program" making the granting of new sewer extension or connection permits conditional on the elimination of at least two gpd of extraneous flow into the MDC system for every new gpd of flow to be added.[5] Furthermore, the report recommended a conservation inducement via a restructuring of sewer charges to the users of the system. Together, these approaches could form the basis for a comprehensive plan for reducing the load on the metropolitan system.

Infiltration/Inflow Removal

As negotiations on remedies proceeded, the subject of I/I reduction aroused particularly sharp divisions among the parties. Initially, the state defendants proposed to undertake an I/I reduction program for the southern service area that would begin with a series of assessments and legislative proposals. Historically, however, the ratio of actual removal of I/I to the performance of research on that subject was far too low. The report, therefore, called for hard and fast deadlines, approved by the court, for the completion of any further research by the Division of Water Pollution Control (DWPC) and the Metropolitan District Commission and, most crucially, for the design and implementation of those I/I removal projects that were determined to be cost-effective. Similarly, the MDC was to be called upon to implement a conservation incentive scheme by a given date to be established by the court.

Quincy and the state defendants disagreed about the extent of I/I removal that would be possible even under the most ideal circumstances. Quincy advocated a reduction of roughly 33 percent of the current peak of stormwater flows in the sewer systems of member communities, which it asserted would bring the MDC's overall system flows within the design capacity of the upgraded treatment plants.

Although the state defendants initially argued that a 33 percent reduction was simply not feasible,[6] they ultimately acknowledged that it would be cost-effective to remove 30 percent of I/I from tributary sewer systems.[7] They also allowed that it might be advisable for the commonwealth, albeit not cost-effective under the federal guidelines, to remove an additional 15 percent of infiltration, paying for this effort with supplementary funds authorized by the state legislature.[8]

In the last analysis, the time it would take to reduce I/I so that bypasses would no longer be necessary at Nut Island—or at the interconnected Deer and Moon Island facilities—depended primarily on the funding available for the purpose. The EPA had stated its willingness to cooperate with state officials to improve Boston Harbor, and the report emphasized the expectation that the EPA would help expedite federal grants in the immediate future, speeding up what was often a long and tedious process. In addition, the use of follow-up reviews and incentive mechanisms could hasten the process of I/I removal in all of the communities served by the MDC.

The report therefore recommended that the court order the immediate initiation of a system-wide I/I reduction program, one that went beyond the defendants' proposal by enlarging its scope and inviting the participation of the state's Division of Water Pollution Control. (See "Summary of Recommendations," section I-A, p. 311.) This proposal combined a number of techniques designed to use the resources and the regulatory authority of the two existing agencies, the MDC and the DWPC, that were the closest to the *Quincy* case. It did not rely on voluntary implementation by these agencies, instead recommending specific, court-mandated implementation schedules. The report predicted that a cost-effective I/I removal program could bring total peak flow in the MDC's south system down to levels that were within the treatment capacity of the Nut Island plant.

The 2:1 Reduction Program
The second approach to flow reduction advanced by Quincy proposed a 2:1 system-wide requirement under which two gallons of untreated sewage would have to be removed from the system before one new gallon of sewage would be allowed into new sewer connections.

The state defendants objected strenuously, contending that the reduction program would penalize municipalities that had conscientiously maintained and replaced sewer lines or had newer sewer systems, while rewarding municipalities that had failed to maintain or replace sewer lines as needed; the conscientious cities would be hard put to make further reductions, while the negligent ones could do so easily. The defendants also argued that removing I/I from separate sewer systems would get no more credit than removing I/I from combined systems, though the benefits differed.[9] Furthermore, they asserted, the 2:1 reduction requirement could not be enforced because the MDC had no statutory authority to deny, or even to review, local communities' connection requests and was not always notified of their existence.[10]

The state defendants' argument did not persuade me. The report addressed each of these arguments, discussing the fairness claim at particular length before concluding that an equitable result could be reached.

Concerned with designing an evenhanded system for remedy, I took very seriously the defendants' arguments against penalizing municipalities that had conscientiously maintained sewer lines while rewarding those that had not. But the evidence before the court indicated that these problems would be rare occurrences, and so they could be handled fairly on a case-by-case basis. Moreover, it seemed that the possibility of unequal regulation could be forestalled by using fresh administrative techniques, such as a system-wide "banking/trading" system. Under such a disposition, verifiable removal of a unit of extraneous flow to the system would become a marketable commodity, one that could be entered in a central registry and sold or traded under appropriate terms to other communities or developers who were seeking to add new flows to the system.[11] Such an arrangement would eliminate the inequities caused by past efforts to reduce I/I by granting credits for the past improvements. Municipalities that did not have I/I that could be cost-effectively removed would be able to purchase the connection rights they needed.[12]

For such a program to operate effectively, the report stressed, it would be essential for the DWPC to heighten the municipalities' awareness of the statutory and regulatory requirements for sewer connection permits, and for it to substantially improve its enforcement of those laws and regulations, including sound engineering for all new facilities in order to minimize future infiltration. The report recommended that special attention be paid to employing a system of rewards and incentives to motivate individual cities and towns. Admittedly, the 2:1 reduction program would be an interim rather than a cure-all remedy for the problem of the pollution of Boston Harbor, serving to keep new connections from exacerbating the current failures of the system and only slowly reducing the entry of untreated sewage. However, a 2:1 program—or even a 3:1 or 4:1 program—could be initiated immediately while a longer-term remedy was designed and implemented.

Our report therefore recommended that the court order the immediate initiation of a system-wide 2:1 I/I reduction program covering all permits for new connections to or extensions of community sewer systems. It suggested that the court order the establishment of a "banking/trading" program, and that other education and enforcement measures be taken by the DWPC and MDC. (See "Summary of Recommendations," section I-B.)

Conservation
The report then shifted attention to conservation as another means of alleviating environmental harms. Conservation may not be a glamorous or dramatic solution, but it can be cost-effective, and it does not entail complex technology or large capital expenditures. While the testimony, affidavits, and other evidence of the *Quincy* litigation focused primarily on specific engineering and management remedies, scant attention was paid to the realm of prevention measures as a way of reducing overflows and bypasses at Nut and Moon Islands. Wielding MDC municipal assessments as a conservation device had been strongly urged upon the court and the parties by several experts. The report therefore recommended a two-part conservation program for the harbor, consisting of a project to inform and educate the public about the value and ease of water conservation, and, on a more materialist level, a pricing strategy that would encourage and reward reduction of wastewater output and diminution of peak flow.[13] As a final recommendation for reducing total flow to the system, the report asked the court to order the MDC, jointly with the Executive Office of Environmental Affairs, to submit a report by January 1, 1984, on how and to what extent

the MDC municipal assessment system could be utilized to encourage conservation and voluntary lessening of sewage influent ("Summary of Recommendations," section I-C, pp. 311–312).

Maintenance at Deer and Moon Islands
The testimony at the hearings, combined with site visits to the Deer Island plant, vividly confirmed the deteriorated, even dangerous, state of much of its equipment. If the most serious problem was the chronic failure of the engines in the facility's main pumping station, which repeatedly caused the dumping of raw sewage into the bay and harbor via Moon Island, its most dramatic emblem was the recurrent bursting into flame of the smokestacks that vented exhaust from those engines. Upgrading and improved maintenance of the facilities at Deer Island were urgently needed.

As a first step toward improving the condition and operation of the Deer Island facility, the report recommended that the court order the MDC to develop a plan for the physical improvements to Deer Island that were necessary to reduce Moon Island discharges. The commission was to submit the plan by January 1, 1984, along with a supplementary budget request to the legislature for the funds needed to complete the transformation.

The report did not suggest ordering any specific project for the Deer Island facility, and it was equally restrained in its recommendations regarding Moon Island, although specific measures for improving their operations were known to be feasible and clearly necessary. However, since these facilities were part of the northern metropolitan service area, their deficiencies were less immediately relevant to the *Quincy* case. At least in this respect, the report embodied an attitude of restraint in fashioning proposed remedies.

Because any upgrading of the MDC's Deer Island plant would

take years to complete even under the best of circumstances, the report looked for short-term actions to lessen the impact of Moon Island discharges in the interim. Two measures seemed feasible and cost-effective vis-à-vis their environmental benefits. First, the Moon Island storage tanks could be renovated for only $250,000, and the work could begin within a year; this would enable the BWSC to hold the wastewater it received until it could be released during outgoing tides. Second, chlorinating Moon Island's discharges would reduce the bacterial content of the effluent, and chlorinating facilities could be constructed by the summer of 1984 at a cost of only $20,000. The situation was complicated, however, by the fact that the BWSC, not the MDC, owned the Moon Island facility, although the MDC controlled the conditions that resulted in Moon Island discharges.[14] And, somewhat disconcertingly, the parties resisted proposals for chlorination and the rehabilitation of the storage tanks at Moon Island.

Measures such as I/I removal in the north system, the MDC argued, or improvements at Columbus Park and Deer Island, or perhaps other programs not yet formulated, would be more cost-effective than large-scale chlorination of discharges.[15] The state defendants focused on construction projects listed in the MDC's study of combined sewer overflows that would reduce wastewater overflows from member communities in the north service area, notwithstanding the defendants' own assertions that, unfortunately, reductions in federal funding might jeopardize their completion.[16] Further hindering the proposals was strong local political opposition, especially in the Dorchester Bay area just to the north of Quincy.

All in all, it appeared that under current economic and political circumstances, the MDC had not yet begun to develop, let alone implement, any remedy for its diversion of raw sewage to Moon Island. Even if the MDC's overflow treatment proposals and other improvements to its north metropolitan system were completed, its own testimony at trial showed that discharges from Moon Island were expected to continue.

As for the BWSC, at the time of the *Quincy* litigation, that agency had already requested bids for the construction of chlorination facilities for dry-weather discharges from Moon Island. However, its officials and experts testified against reconstruction of the holding tanks, although the idea had been considered for some time. They also expressed serious doubts about the advisability of chlorinating wet-weather discharges. Another argument made against even exploring the upgrading of Moon Island's facilities was a specious one that it would necessitate an inspection of the Dorchester Bay Tunnel (which led from Deer Island to Moon Island) that could cause the tunnel to collapse.[17] This argument was not convincing, since no one had suggested that its condition was precarious. Furthermore, the BWSC testified that it expected to continue to use the Moon Island outfall for some time into the future.

In the end, the court had to strike a balance. The uncertain funding and implementation schedules for other remedial measures, combined with the relatively low cost and short timeframe that would be required to introduce chlorination at Calf Pasture and renovate the holding tanks at Moon Island, provided a strong rationale for recommending immediate adoption of the two measures. Nevertheless, exercising caution, the report did not ask Judge Garrity for such a ruling (however much I might be inclined to do so today given the circumstances). Instead, the final recommendation to the court was that by January 1, 1984, the defendants MDC and BWSC present to the court a plan and schedule for minimizing the volume and environmental impact of Moon Island's discharges[18] ("Summary of Recommendations," sections II-B and III, pp. 312–313).

However, the report went on, "if no solution is forthcoming, the court should not hesitate to insist on implementation of a known remedy. The state defendants and the BWSC cannot be allowed to continue the unacceptable dumping of raw sewage because those solutions which are deemed cost-effective remain stalled for political reasons."[19]

UPGRADING THE NUT ISLAND FACILITIES

The next section of the report moved on to recommendations that could be implemented at the treatment plants. It urged completion of a planned Nut Island upgrade, maintenance and upgrading of the Deer Island plant, and reduction and treatment of discharges from Moon Island.

After finding substantial problems with sewage treatment at the Nut Island plant, the report, rather than asking for the adoption of new technologies or radical innovations, sought first to force action on a plan the MDC had already designed but so far failed to actualize. Successful completion of the existing plan for upgrading the facility (which the defendants contended could be completed by 1984) would improve the plant's effectiveness in treating peak flows, reduce the likelihood of operational failures, and curtail the use of outfalls 103 and 104. According to affidavits, the MDC was also undertaking another $4.5 million in repairs and improvements to the Nut Island plant.[20]

The report also suggested that the court require the MDC to evaluate and report on the feasibility of a number of existing proposals put forward by the MDC itself. The most important of these was the cleaning and relining of outfalls 101 and 102 in order to increase their capacity and thus reduce the use of outfalls 103 and 104. If this was found not to be feasible, the report requested that a plan and timetable for replacement of the outfalls be presented to the court by March 1, 1984. No excuses for delay would be allowed. The record at trial indicated that with the timely approval of MDC's plans, reconstruction of the outfalls could be completed in as little as one-and-a-half years or three years at most.[21]

Other reviews requested in the report dealt with pumping facilities for outfalls 101 and 102, improved diffusers at the outfalls, and lengthening outfalls to permit discharges farther from shore. Also, the report recommended that the MDC resolve ambiguities in its replies to other requests by the plaintiff regarding Nut Island improvements—including a list describing which proposed improvements the MDC would agree to undertake along with a proposed time schedule, and which it would not undertake and why not—and provide an analysis of the remaining twenty-five individual projects included in its own immediate upgrade plans ("Summary of Recommendations," section II-A, p. 312).

QUINCY'S STORM DRAINS

As noted in the report's findings of fact, the evidence was conflicting and ultimately inconclusive regarding an aspect of the case that was minor in relation to the pollution of Boston Harbor as a whole but major in a jurisprudential sense: this was the state defendants' counterclaim that Quincy itself was responsible for the pollution of its beaches. The court-appointed engineering consultant, Dr. E. Eric Adams, who had been uncertain at the outset, became convinced from the proceedings and further reviews that Quincy's storm drains were the primary cause of this local pollution. (An investigation conducted later in the year revealed that surreptitious chlorination and other concealing tactics may have been deployed by Quincy workers in order to influence the findings of investigators employed by the court.) And, taken together, the testimony of other experts indicated that Quincy's storm drains were in fact responsible for at least some pollution in the immediately adjacent areas of Wollaston Beach.

The state defendants indicated a willingness to work with the city of Quincy in correcting any sewage infiltration problems in the city's storm drains. In light of this posture, the report urged that the state defendants and the city jointly implement a new testing program to identify the volume of pollutants coming out of the drains, supplemented by studies to determine "the extent of the corrective action taken on Quincy's storm drains between 1978 and 1980, and to develop a program to identify and eliminate the remaining sources of pollution."

Once the results of these investigations were received, it was recommended that the parties develop a timetable for corrective measures for presentation to the court, with the final resolution directed toward making the beach safe for continuing public use ("Summary of Recommendations," section IV, p. 313).

ADDRESSING STAFFING PROBLEMS

In the fashioning of remedies to ameliorate the environmental degradation of the harbor, attention was continually directed to staffing issues that had arisen at trial.

Although faulty machinery and recurring breakdowns created severe problems for the MDC, many insiders—including the superintendents of the Deer Island and Nut Island facilities—also believed that a major problem with the MDC was its inability to retain an adequate and well-trained staff. Inflexible promotion and seniority schemes that prevented managers from rewarding top performers made employee retention difficult and led to serious morale problems. Compounding this issue were the opportunities in private industry and elsewhere in government, often at higher wages, for the most experienced and hardworking members on staff.

At the time of the filing of the *Quincy* lawsuit, Nut Island was 21 percent short of its staff authorization. In January 1981, the EPA noted with alarm that approximately 50 million gallons of raw sewage had been allowed to overflow on Christmas Day of 1980 because there were no qualified employees available to work that day. A subsequent EPA report related the agency's concern that "lack of adequate staffing results in inadequate maintenance and lab testing."

Statements by the superintendents of the Deer Island and Nut Island facilities, along with my on-site inspections, confirmed that these facilities remained woefully understaffed. While authorized positions remained unfilled, work by inadequately trained people caused repeated discharges of untreated sewage. The MDC also lacked the staff at the managerial level to apply for and administer federal and state construction grant funds.

The MDC informed the court that reports on the staffing needs of the Deer Island and Nut Island treatment plants were expected to be completed by January 1, 1984. In view of the seriousness of the situation, which had the potential to lead to breakdowns at the plants and to jeopardize any and all court-ordered remedial measures, the report proposed that a supplemental budget be submitted forthwith to the state legislature by the MDC, in cooperation with the Executive Office of Environmental Affairs, to provide funds to address staffing needs. It was further recommended that the MDC present to the court and the legislature a summary of the MDC's overall staffing needs, including any additional personnel required to comply with the orders of the court ("Summary of Recommendations," section V-A, 1–3, p. 313).

EDUCATION, MONITORING, COORDINATION, AND ENFORCEMENT

Quincy had requested changes to the MDC's and BWSC's National Pollution Discharge Elimination System (NPDES) permits that the EPA had granted under the federal Clean Water Act. These permits regulated the amount, timing, and location of discharges, as well as monitoring and notification of bypasses. I found that such changes were not needed for implementation of the most cost-effective remedial measures that were recommended, and that altering the NPDES permits would require a conclusion that these permits were themselves in violation of the commonwealth's own Clean Water Act.

One legal question in the case turned on which effluent standard—the EPA-Massachusetts 1976 NPDES Permit or the 1980 EPA Administrative Order—governed the discharges into Boston Harbor, and on whether the AO's language should be interpreted as lessening the requirements of the 1976 permit or as a design to enforce it. While the state defendants argued that the AO had amended the MDC obligations regarding effluent in a way that meant the MDC satisfied the less stringent limits of primary treatment, an AO could not alter a permittee's duties without going through extensive regulatory procedures—which had never been undertaken. For these reasons, among others, it seemed that the more demanding effluent standards set by the 1976 permit controlled.

A further, more particular question arose as to whether the 1980 AO modified the 1976 permit requirement on the treatment of sludge. The AO provided that digested sludge could continue to be discharged into Boston Harbor during high tide until sludge disposal facilities were completed. Did this language lessen the permit's requirements and, as the defendants argued, confer a blanket license to discharge unlimited quantities of sludge for an indefinite period of time? Anyway, could such a broad power of modification reside in an AO?

In addition, interpretation of the permit-AO interrelation was affected by the state's application to the EPA for a waiver from secondary treatment, since the state might later be excused altogether from secondary treatment requirements. But this contention went only to the choice of remedy, not to whether the federal Clean Water Act (and the permit's limits) had been violated. The claim could be stated simply: the community had a guaranteed right to a clean harbor, the terms of sewage disposal were set out by a joint federal-state permit system, the MDC had

discharged pollutants and sludge into the harbor, and the discharges went beyond the authorized limits of the permit.

In light of the EPA's stated position that it would take appropriate enforcement action with regard to repairs and modifications of outfall 104, and that it would continue to act as a friend
of the court in the litigation, the report suggested that no particular action concerning sludge treatment be ordered by the court
other than the stipulation that the court and the plaintiff be kept
informed of EPA's enforcement efforts. In fact, I was pleased by
the EPA's presence and by its willingness to undertake the inspection and enforcement actions. By their nature, these are activities
more suited to administrative agencies than courts, and the fact
that this was a national agency with the cumulative experience
of many and varied pollution sites was reassuring.[22]

Despite the best individual efforts of the parties involved, a
chronic lack of communication among the various state agencies
charged with duties relating to Boston Harbor, the member municipalities in the MDC's Metropolitan Sewerage Division, and
the state and local levels of government hindered the implementation of a coordinated strategy for managing the huge task with
which they were collectively charged. The free exchange and discussion of information and plans and the meshing together of
their separately conceived programs would be essential for successful efforts. The report therefore recommended that the court
order a series of actions aimed at increasing transparency and
communication ("Summary of Recommendations," sections
V-B, 1–3, pp. 313–314).

Quincy also sought increased enforcement of DWPC's sewer
extension and connection permit program, as well as a public
education program on the permit requirements. The state defendants agreed. In addition, the report noted that any plans for
permit enforcement should be developed in conjunction with
enforcement of the recommended 2:1 I/I reduction program
("Summary of Recommendations," section V-B, 4–5, p. 314).

It came out at the trial that the MDC's sewerage operations were plagued by dissension and lack of coordination among its subdivisions, leading to institutional inertia and an inability to accomplish relatively simple tasks. For instance, an electric engine purchased in the late 1970s to replace one of Deer Island's diesel engines, which had been dismantled for parts, was not installed until six years later, due to disagreements between the MDC engineering and sewerage divisions.

Reports of such incidents had begun to attract the attention of local and state governmental agencies, and were galvanizing public support for a comprehensive harbor cleanup effort. Federal officials were also placing pressure on the Massachusetts legislature to reform the MDC system. With all of this in mind, the report recommended that within sixty days the DWPC undertake an extensive educational program—aimed at public and city officials, chambers of commerce, the construction industry, and especially at law firms, lending institutions, and mortgage companies—that would emphasize the existence and scope of the sewer extension and connection regulations, the potential penalties that might result from disregarding them, and the incentives available for compliance ("Summary of Recommendations," section V-B, 5, p. 314).

THE DISCIPLINE AND DIRECTION OF A FINANCIAL PLAN

Amid all the plans, schemes, consultants' reports, and agency recommendations over the decades for dealing with the problems of Boston Harbor, one vital link remained unforged: a realistic financial program, without which no plan for the future could be enacted or carried out. Considerable experience has persuaded me—revising the old maxim—that "to plan is human, to implement divine." Following through on a bright idea isn't easy—or cheap.

Accordingly, the report advised that the court order the defendants MDC and DWPC to present a comprehensive financial plan, following a procedure that involved both the court and well-qualified financial experts, for obtaining the funds necessary to carry out the recommended construction, rehabilitation, and maintenance programs. Since the fee charged by consultants for this kind of work is normally contingent upon final enactment of the financial program, the costs would not be overburdensome.

As an integral part of the financial plan, a legal program was also called for in order to ensure the proper drafting of the necessary votes, referenda, amendments, and approvals upon which various stages of the financing of public works are dependent.

In the course of the investigation and trial, a number of substantive issues directly related to the financing of the MDC sewerage system loomed as major considerations. The report strongly urged that the possibility of creating an independent sewerage authority, with its own financing, should be addressed. The financial report was to examine the mechanisms for capital financing, the legislative budgeting process, and the system of local sewerage charges ("Summary of Recommendations," section VI-B, p. 314).

In raising these questions the intent was not to require the affected agencies to undertake any particular measure. Instead, the proposals were designed to force the defendants to face issues squarely and make financial determinations themselves. The court could and should force the local and state authorities to act, but those authorities would determine just what actions to take—and then implement them. The authority of the court served as a catalyst; the local and state governments would continue to bear the final responsibility.

An active judicial role was mandated by the complex nature and towering scope of the problem at hand. Every day that raw or undertreated sewage continued to be dumped into Boston's waters would mean a lowered quality of life for people, a threat to public health, the destruction of marine life and the benthic environment, and economic losses both direct and indirect. The remedies proposed at this stage were acknowledged to be only first steps in an extensive cleanup effort. Whatever remedies the court chose to fashion, the report concluded, it would be to the benefit of the people of the commonwealth if the parties now began to consider the means by which the long-term maintenance and improvement of the sewerage system could be undertaken.

For as President John Adams, a neighbor of the harbor in days long past, would surely have urged, no efforts, labor, or expense should be spared to restore once again the clean waters that are our birthright.

THE JUDGE LAYS DOWN THE LAW

The Procedural Order for the Rehabilitation of the Harbor

10

The great tides and currents which engulf the rest of men do not turn aside in their course and pass judges by.

—Benjamin N. Cardozo

My report as special master constituted a stinging condemnation of the practices that had led to the degradation of Boston Harbor. To begin the rehabilitation of the harbor, it included specific proposals for immediate action to reduce flows to the Metropolitan District Commission's antiquated sewer and sewage treatment system, to upgrade existing plants and pipes, to repair broken machinery, and to provide for adequate staffing and maintenance. But even if each and every one of these projects were to be undertaken right away, backed by proper funding, and pursued vigorously and in good faith—none of which was certain—this reforming of the MDC system nevertheless embodied at best a bandage rather than a true remedy for the harbor. Behind the scenes a consensus was growing that an effective cleanup effort would require a totally new regime. Hoping to build upon this consensus, the report concluded with a series of questions that pointed in this direction, and in court I ended our presentation with a challenge: "We know how to fix the problems, and the financial mechanisms exist, but we lack the political will to merge the two."[1]

How did the court get from this point to the creation of a new institution, the Massachusetts Water Resources Authority, that would ultimately fulfill the promise of an unpolluted Boston

Harbor? The report's major recommendation to Judge Garrity stressed the need for implementation. What the situation required was a dramatic intervention, a different structure for administering the complexities of Boston Harbor. Faced with the overwhelming task of constructing, rehabilitating, and maintaining complicated technologies and facilities, such a new entity would have to be endowed with significant power and financial capabilities as well as administrative expertise. Public interest groups, environmental and financial experts, and MDC managers and regulatory officials all played their parts in moving from proposed remedies to achievement. But decades of inertia could never have been overcome without the participation of the media to rally public support and put political pressure on the governor and the legislature—and without the willingness of the court, in the person of Paul Garrity, to take the risk of acting as catalyst.

REACTIONS AND RESISTANCE

A barrage of media coverage accompanied the unveiling of the special master's report on August 9, 1983, and the media kept its attention on the issue throughout the month that elapsed before Judge Garrity made his ruling. Early press coverage emphasized the various elements of our proposals for immediate reform and rehabilitation of the MDC, but reporters and commentators also noted that nothing would happen unless the court adopted and backed the report's recommendations. "If you don't have a court order," I was quoted as saying in a telephone interview, "you can kiss this report goodbye."[2] The same *Boston Globe* front-page article concluded that the pollution brought about by the dumping of raw and partially treated waste into the harbor threatened the health, safety, and welfare of those frequenting the area, was harmful to economic and tourist activities, had already endangered beaches and shellfish flats, and curtailed commercial and recreational fishing.

Almost immediately following the report's issuance, parties from both sides threw their support behind its proposals, as did the representatives of numerous public agencies, turning an adversarial process into a collaborative, problem-solving one. Spokesmen for the city of Quincy, the state Executive Office of Environmental Affairs (EOEA), and the MDC expressed strong enthusiasm for the report, praised its recommendations as "good stuff," and vowed to implement them regardless of whether or not Judge Garrity issued a court order.

Likewise, editorial reaction in the press was encouraging. Opinion ranged from the *Boston Herald*'s acknowledgment of the report's recommendations as "a starting point"[3] to the *Globe*'s vision of a "positive and constructive process that holds the promise of a cleaner harbor."[4] Massachusetts lawmakers, according to the *Christian Science Monitor,* "now may have little choice but to face up to the pollution problem."[5] The *Globe* stressed that "the court suit over pollution of Boston Harbor has turned out better than could have been expected."[6] So far as the *Quincy Patriot Ledger* was concerned, "If such proposals are adopted by Judge Garrity, the years of much talk and little action on harbor pollution would appear to be past."[7] Throughout August and early September, the media kept the harbor pollution story alive and vivid, citing the report, interviewing the parties, posing questions to legislators about the inaction of the past, presenting the views of the person on the street, and asking questions of the judge and the special master.

During the next phase of the proceedings, most of the state defendants were quite cooperative. EOEA Secretary James Hoyte commented several years later that one of the reasons why the special master was able to get things done quickly was that Hoyte's department was trying to facilitate the work. He explained that the parties naturally felt the report captured the essence of the situation because they provided a lot of input for it.[8]

By contrast, the state's attorney general's office remained adamantly against sacrificing any portion of the commonwealth's legal position, arguing "that, in view of the willingness of [the] administration as a whole to address the question of pollution of the harbor, why do you also need a court order?"[9] Publicly stated, that approach rallied those opposed to change and fueled the many arguments about the details.

In mid-August of 1983, Judge Garrity began issuing a series of orders, negotiated among and agreed to by all parties, that closely followed the special master's recommendations as to which specific efforts the defendants (and the plaintiff) would be obliged to undertake in the near future. However, despite several hearings in early August in which the MDC and the city of Quincy participated, no agreements were reached regarding improvements to the Calf Pasture pumping station and the southern metropolitan area's combined sewer overflow infrastructure. In response to the slow progress, Quincy made a request for preliminary injunctive relief. This particular skirmish would be crucial to the future of the harbor, for it pressed Judge Garrity to decide, after hearing arguments from both sides, whether he should officially accept and adopt the special master's findings of fact and proposed remedies, or reject them.

If Garrity were to adopt the special master's report, the MDC faced the specter of a judicial decree that would compel it and the other state agencies to take action within imposed deadlines, enforceable by contempt of court citations. Both personally and as a matter of principle, this represented an appalling prospect to those officials, managers, and bureaucrats who believed—along with the attorney general—that such decrees would eat away at their powers and prerogatives. They chafed at the idea of being bound so closely by the order of one lone judge who could disrupt normal operations if the decree were not followed to the letter. To the executive branch, the courts seemed to be everywhere—schools, correctional institutions, mental health facilities, and now the harbor—and they protested that the result was to substitute judicial fiat for the decisions of elected leaders. (From the other point of view, of course, the courts were so busy precisely because the elected leaders had failed to carry out their duties.)

THE PROCEDURAL ORDER: JUDICIAL INVENTIVENESS AND MORAL COMMITMENT

The political situation became quite volatile. In an hour-long session on August 25, the judge challenged the state's lead attorney to explain his opposition to court intervention when his client, the MDC itself, seemed to have no substantial objections to the report's recommendations. "Quite candidly," Garrity told Michael Sloman, "what you have done is quite different from the agency's public statements."[10]

Throughout August, meetings were taking place at high levels within the state administration. The attorney general found himself under strong pressure from the governor and agency chiefs, Hoyte and MDC head William Geary particularly, to respond more positively to the possibilities contained in the special master's report. While these officials did not necessarily wish to be under legal compulsion to take prompt action, they saw the political advantage—and, to be fair, the real necessity—of adopting the proposals.

The court opened its hearings in September to consider objections to the special master's report, listening to arguments from both sides. Judge Garrity pondered the alternatives before him. If reform was to be achieved, it was necessary to get on board the state defendants who would be charged with carrying out the recommendations submitted to the court. Then, in a sudden development, Judge Garrity abruptly ended the hearing on September 9, 1983, with an announcement that the state defendants and the city of Quincy had come to an agreement. The court declared that "a massive and expeditious effort to clean up Boston Harbor pollution and remove its causes is desired by all parties and . . . further adversarial litigation may be counterproductive to the effort necessary to reach that result."[11]

What was truly remarkable and innovative was the creation of a new legal vessel to accommodate this agreement. Normally, when parties agree to the settlement of an institutional breakdown lawsuit, the terms are incorporated into a legal instrument known as a consent decree that is subject to approval by the judge.[12] Judge Garrity opted to issue a novel judicial construction—a special remedy specifically created for the changed circumstances. "This agreement," he expounded, "is called X—I haven't figured out a name for it yet. But I'm keeping the pressure on." As Garrity envisioned it, this newfangled "procedural order," as he finally would name it, bound the relevant agencies to action not by the threat of judicial sanctions, as is the case with consent decrees, but only by a sense of moral obligation and, perhaps as well, public pressure to reach a common goal.

This unorthodox strategy worked. Garrity's judicial experiment served to bring the parties together: both sides were willing to submit to a "procedural order" as opposed to a consent decree. The state defendants waived their right to challenge the accuracy of the special master's report, the litigation was to be suspended, and the initial remedies set forth in the report were adopted according to the specific timetables it suggested. Paradoxically, because the order's terms were not legally binding on the parties, its scope could be extended beyond the narrow issues presented by the plaintiff in its complaint. With this one stroke the issues in the *Quincy* litigation were broadened by the judge to include the problem of the pollution of the harbor as a whole.

The implementation of the procedural order was less onerous than would have been the case under a consent decree. Under the judge's definition of his order, the parties could withdraw from the proceedings whenever they chose, in which case the *Quincy* trial would resume on an adversarial basis. Furthermore, the parties would be allowed to modify jointly the milestones set forth in the procedural order at any time without the approval of the court. (The court could also modify the order without approval of the parties, since it had no binding effect beyond that of a voluntary commitment.) The one stick retained by Judge Garrity—still a big stick—was the ability to restart adversarial proceedings.

In effect, this timely twist on legal devices placed the future of Boston Harbor and the health and safety of the people of the commonwealth in the hands of well-intentioned parties pledging a commitment to comply with the order's mandate—twenty-three remedies outlined in an attached "Schedule of Tasks."[13] Under its auspices, those responsible for the pollution of the harbor voluntarily agreed to work together with the plaintiff and the court in an historic effort to put an end to the massive fouling of a precious natural resource. The schedule included significant matters not addressed in detail by the special master's report, among them sludge management, combined sewer overflows, and long-term plans to provide for secondary treatment.

The parties agreed to develop, in conjunction with the EPA, schedules for cleanup, which eventually became a ten-year plan that set deadlines for each phase. The court appointed me to monitor adherence to the schedule, and to report from time to time to the court.[14] When a scheduled milestone was reached or missed, or another significant development occurred, the responsible parties were to "give written certification to Professor Haar and the other parties."[15]

From the date of the order, meetings were held regularly with all parties involved, and their attempts to satisfy the schedules and provisions outlined in the order were reviewed publicly. Steven Horowitz, the deputy master, and I reported to Judge Garrity on these developments, kept him notified of evolving issues, and received advice and suggestions from him as to how to proceed.

Eighteenth-century map of Boston Harbor, from *A New Map of New England According to the Latest Observation*, 1720.

Top: Candidate George H. W. Bush at Boston Harbor, September 1, 1988 (AP Wide World photo). *Bottom:* Beach in East Boston (MWRA photo).

Top: William B. Golden with his dog, Hope, around the time the *Quincy* lawsuit commenced. *Bottom:* Peter L. Koff, circa 1984.

Boston Harbor pollution. *Top:* Typical section of polluted water. *Bottom:* Outfall effluent plume. (MWRA photos)

Motors in the pump room of the old Deer Island treatment plant (MWRA photo).

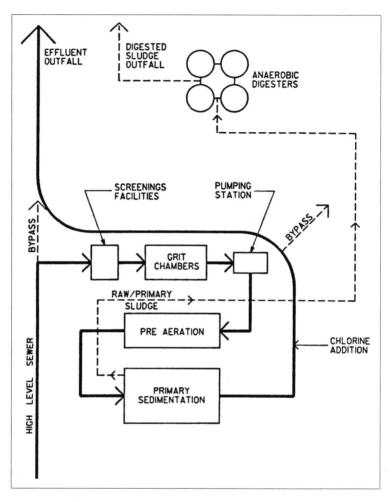

Schematic of Nut Island wastewater treatment plant, early 1980s
(courtesy MWRA).

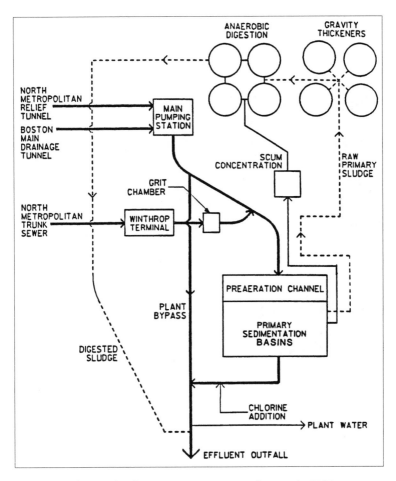

Schematic of Deer Island wastewater treatment plant, early 1980s (courtesy MWRA).

Judge Paul Garrity and the author at work (*Boston Globe,* September 11, 1983; republished with permission of the Globe Newspaper Company, Inc.).

The new Deer Island primary treatment plant, 1996 (MWRA photo).

Top: Governor Michael Dukakis signs the MWRA bill, December 1984. Standing, left to right: Representative John Cusack; Secretary of Environmental Affairs Jamie Hoyte; Representative Royall Bolling, Jr.; Representative William Robinson (Republican Minority Leader); the author; and Senator Paul White (AP Wide World photo). *Bottom:* left, Francis X. Bellotti; middle, Steven G. Horowitz; right, Francis X. Meaney.

Judge Garrity in a widely distributed photo, taken on the day that the MWRA law was signed (photo by Gary A. Cameron, © 1984 the *Washington Post*; reprinted with permission).

Revitalized Boston Harbor and East Boston beach in 1996 (MWRA photos).

By these various measures, including his own prerogative to resume the litigation, Judge Garrity put the power of the court behind a detailed timetable for beginning the harbor cleanup without coercing the parties every step of the way. Even without official sanctions for infringements, the procedural order gave me as special master an unusual measure of authority to shape the negotiations between the parties and to oversee their deployment of resources, even their timing, as they sought to implement its provisions.

In short, this unique adaptation of an existing legal mechanism proved to be a brilliant stroke. Politically astute, Paul Garrity had recognized that the scope and complexity of the task at hand made orthodox strategies and traditional forms of decrees inappropriate. The advantages of this cooperative process became obvious right away. It avoided forcing the parties into polarized, inflexible positions, as adversarial litigation is too likely to do. It allowed for the participation of those who were not parties to the suit, groups and individuals who were players in the political process that would inevitably be a part of the massive effort to regenerate Boston Harbor. It also promoted an informality and a sense of give-and-take missing from a more traditional approach. Even Michael Sloman, the state's assistant attorney general, acquiesced, saying, "This gets to the concerns but without a judicial order. This is essentially the same position we have had all along."

FROM THE COURTROOM TO BEACON HILL

Floating on the wave of good feeling created by the court's action, the various branches of the Massachusetts government began to gear up for the next phase of the effort. The court stepped back and allowed the legislature to take the reins. The Sargent Commission (as the Boston Harbor Cleanup Committee had become known), appointed by Governor Dukakis, pledged anew to "reclaim [Boston Harbor], to make of it the great benefit it can be to all New England."[16] Moreover, just days after Judge Garrity signed the procedural order, Senate President William Bulger announced that he would create a new commission on Boston Harbor development to investigate ways in which the MDC could be improved;[17] among the options to be considered was transforming the MDC's water and sewer divisions into an independent authority that would free the sewage treatment system from politicized and burdensome legislative oversight.

Over the next eighteen months, Steven Horowitz and I were regularly invited to various forums to explain the findings and recommendations of the special master's report and to answer questions raised from the floor. These exchanges were fruitful, in different ways at different times. In many of our earliest speeches and public presentations, we emphasized how crucial it was that adequate funding be provided to truly change the existing sewage system, and that a system that was fair and equitable was the ultimate goal. "To the making of reports there is no end," I also warned whenever the process seemed to be bogging down, for a primary concern was maintaining the impetus for change.

Perhaps predictably, after an initial burst of energy, many months lapsed before any further move was made by the state's officials to support the court's efforts to reform or replace the MDC. During that time, former governor Frank Sargent resigned as head of the Boston Harbor Cleanup Committee, due to reasons of health, and was replaced by Environmental Affairs Secretary James Hoyte, which gave the BHCC, in the words of the *Boston Globe,* the air of "just another administration task force."[18] Meanwhile, friends of the harbor became concerned that the final outcome of the *Quincy* suit, whose resolution had been proceeding with such promise, might be dimmed through a series of legislative initiatives directed at robbing the procedural order of substantive meaning.

Senate leader Bulger's Commission on Boston Harbor Development helped in some measure to put these fears to rest. During the first days of 1984, this commission submitted a legislative bill proposing a multimillion dollar cleanup of the harbor, coupled with a plan to establish a new "Metropolitan Water Resources Authority" independent of the MDC (its proposed title was something of a misnomer since under the bill the new authority would be restricted to sewage disposal). The commission's proposals were approved by Bulger, and what became known as the Bulger bill was also worked on by the various parties, myself included. The Dukakis administration chose to formulate its own initiative, however, adding delay and contention to the emergence of significant legislation.

Cleanup of the harbor continued to defy a tidy or swift solution. Toxic-substance discharge through the sewers, for example, was a new issue being vigorously pursued by environmental groups. "People don't want to—and possibly wouldn't be able to—comprehend the complexity of it all," Commissioner Geary complained. "They just want action and can't understand why something more substantial doesn't seem to be happening. I sometimes look at all these meetings and all these issues and say to myself, My God, this is like Vietnam!"[19]

Judge Garrity endorsed legislative efforts, no matter the source. He included an evaluation of the financial aspects of the Bulger proposal as part of the charge to an independent consultant appointed by the court. In a 154-page study, the Bank of Boston gave its seal of approval to the Bulger bill and supported the notion of an independent sewer authority. Most important, the bank's report confirmed the conclusion that the MDC, as then constituted, simply lacked the financial resources and managerial capacity to carry out the multiple tasks necessary to restore the harbor's health. Therefore the bank backed the recommendation for a new authority with the power to issue revenue bonds in order to pay for a highly expensive series of undertakings.[20]

In the month following the introduction of the Bulger bill, Judge A. David Mazzone of the U.S. District Court in Boston suspended the pending federal lawsuit concerning the harbor, brought by the Conservation Law Foundation, in order to permit the state suit filed by the city of Quincy to be brought to a final resolution. The several variables involved in the development of legislation to establish a new regime were dovetailing.

In the meantime, all the parties closely followed the methodology laid down in the procedural order. Monthly compliance conferences were held with the participants in the *Quincy* case. The MDC, through its various divisions and contracts with the private sector, worked on improving the delivery of sewer services. At first the state agencies mostly managed to keep to the dates in the original procedural order with only minor revisions to the timetable. As one defendant recognized, the schedule was far more aggressive and ambitious than would have been the case without the court's intervention. Having the court monitoring him, James Hoyte told me later, tended to hold his feet to the fire and made sure he moved quickly on things.[21] This "feet to the fire" trope must have captured how the *Quincy* defendants felt about the process; certainly they used it often when speaking of the case and its aftermath.

By spring of 1984, however, little else had occurred in conjunction with the Bulger harbor commission's proposal for establishing a sewer authority. A citizens' seminar, held in mid-April, ostensibly for a public report on how well the harbor cleanup and legislation were proceeding, became instead the platform for calling the public's attention to the slow pace of the executive branch's competing proposal and the resultant drag on process. "Despite the goodwill," I told those in attendance, "the best efforts, the attempt to get out of the usual routine . . . there is no real sense of urgency."[22]

"Haar spoke," the *Boston Globe* reported,

after James S. Hoyte, Massachusetts secretary of environmental affairs, and Michael R. Deland, regional administrator of the U.S. EPA, had assured a crowd of 200 at the Franklin Street offices of the State Street Bank that their agencies were working together closely, cooperating and moving forward. Both also complimented Haar's work.

Their smiles faded and their brows furrowed as Haar's jocular opening gave way to a blunt commentary on their efforts.

"I feel a lack of progress," Haar declared.

Secretary Hoyte responded, "I'm surprised he doesn't see a sense of urgency on the part of the defendants. I think Prof. Haar and Judge Garrity feel very passionately about the harbor. I think Haar's comments characterize that passion. He's holding our feet to the fire."[23]

The *Globe* followed up with a scathing editorial claiming that "Gov. Dukakis and the legislative leadership have only themselves to blame if Judge Paul Garrity places the Metropolitan District Commission's sewer operations under court receivership." "As the weeks have dragged into months," it went on, "the assurances that the harbor clean-up is a top priority for both Gov. Dukakis and the Legislature have become increasingly hollow."[24]

Almost as if in direct response, the Dukakis administration gave its blessing to a proposal severing the sewer division from the MDC, but it augmented the already existing Senate recommendation, the Bulger bill, by expanding the notion of a separate sewer agency to incorporate a water agency as well. In speeches designed to build support for his proposed bill, Dukakis dramatically illustrated the direness of the situation by displaying jars containing a murky brown fluid—water that had been pulled straight out of the harbor.

Despite Governor Dukakis's efforts, the administration bill, although fairly well received, was not quickly processed. Both bills were subsequently waylaid in the legislature for months; it would be October of 1984 before either of them saw significant movement in either the House or the Senate.

On June 18, 1984, nearly a year along in the process of designing a new authority, I appeared before a joint committee of the House and Senate holding hearings on the various bills under consideration. "It is not every day," I said at the outset, "that a court appointee appears to testify in support of pending legislation." But several legislators had urged me to come, I explained, since the creation of a water resources authority presented an unusual opportunity for collaboration among the several branches of state government. I pointed out that Judge Garrity was seeking prompt action, although he felt strongly that the harbor revitalization was a political issue that had to be left in the first instance to the political branches of government, not the court. But if the political system could not act, even given the considerable time it had already had to cope with the pollution problem, he would not shirk his own responsibility: to see to it that the illegal pollution of Boston Harbor was brought to an end.

SNAGS AND SNARLS: THE STATUS OF *QUINCY* AT THE ONE-YEAR MARK

Meanwhile, as the court persisted in applying pressure on the legislature and the administration, it was time to reevaluate the progress that had been made on the more immediate aspects of the *Quincy* case. The court held a brief hearing on August 10, 1984, to review the *Quincy* defendants' report detailing their efforts in complying with the original procedural order issued eleven months earlier. A more thorough status conference was held in early October to determine whether the various parties were fulfilling the obligations to which they had agreed the previous year. Special attention was paid to five basic areas of immediate concern: upgrading existing MDC treatment plants, improvements in sludge management, combined sewer overflow (CSO) remediation, rehabilitation of sewage collection systems, and advancement of human resource programs.

After reviewing the defendants' compliance reports and other documents, including updates on the monitored meetings, we had no choice but to report a somber general conclusion to the court: despite the commitments and efforts of the defendants to implement remedial measures, the harbor was still grossly polluted, perhaps even more so than it had been one year previously, and it continued to constitute a clear and present danger to the health, safety, and welfare of the citizens of the commonwealth.

There were many explanations for the delays that had slowed down even the first and seemingly simplest phase of the harbor cleanup. For one thing, a basic dispute had arisen as to who bore the legal responsibility for carrying out the CSO improvements mandated by the procedural order, and there was little agreement as to how many of these projects were justified in cost-benefit terms. Infighting, rampant among various departments of government, slowed progress further. The agencies had been most responsive to the calls for procedural steps, studies, and sifting of alternatives. They were hindered, we reported, by a continuing lack of requisite legal authority, funding capacity, managerial expertise, and staffing levels—all of which diminished the necessary sense of urgency.

Once again I emphasized for the record the emerging consensus among industry insiders that the only effective way to address the pollution hazards of Boston Harbor was through the creation of a new authority with greater resources and powers than the MDC. Taking note of the bills that had been proposed in the Massachusetts legislature and emphasizing the need for respecting the constitutional doctrine of separation of powers, I recommended to Judge Garrity that he continue to keep a close eye on the process evolving under the procedural order. Furthermore, should the legislature fail to take action, the court would be compelled to take more drastic steps. These might include resuming proceedings to consider the imposition of a moratorium on any development in the metropolitan area that generated additional sewage, or placing the MDC in judicial receivership. My oral presentation to the court ended with an outright statement that the key to the entire harbor revitalization effort was the creation of a new authority that would possess capacities that the MDC currently lacked. Accordingly, the final recommendation was for Judge Garrity to convene another hearing in late November to reevaluate certain critical components of the initial procedural order that pertained to the relationship between the city of Quincy's original suit and the larger issue of the health and future of the whole harbor.

That November hearing was to be the crucial catalyst in the harbor cleanup. The drama that it set in motion, which will be described in Chapter 13 (following a discussion of policy and financial issues in Chapters 11 and 12), caught the public's attention in a way that demanded action from the political branches. Public opinion, that great intangible often invoked in the world of politics, difficult to measure, packed with surprises and contradictions, was to play a decisive role in the resolution of the case.

The role of the media in all of this cannot be overemphasized; their investigations, reports, and evaluations helped clarify issues and were major factors in inducing action. The media coverage laid the groundwork for the passage of the ultimate water resources legislation. The impressions conveyed to the public, generalized and vague as they may have been, eventually added up to an understanding of the need and requirements for action. Key legislators, ever sensitive to changes in public mood, caught the slow stirring of popular sentiment. Public opinion would not punish, indeed might even reward, those representatives who would act. The renewal of Boston Harbor was no longer a losing cause. The public's cry for relief from harbor pollution stimulated by and recorded in the media necessitated the creation of an independent authority that could get the job done.

AWASH WITH IDEAS

A New Authority for Governing the Harbor

11

What is possible would never have been achieved if, in this
world, people had not repeatedly reached for the impossible.

—Max Weber

The single most important recommendation of the special
master's report was the creation of a new independently
financed state authority to take over the roles of planning, constructing, and administering a system capable of cleaning up
Boston Harbor. This was not a remedy sought by the city of
Quincy in its suit over the pollution of Wollaston Beach. But evidence presented at the trial in the summer of 1983 had made it
obvious that the MDC and the other state defendants did not
have the combination of staffing, institutional mandates, fiscal
resources, and political backing necessary to solve the problems
that ended in the release of raw sewage into the harbor's waters,
the poisoning of its marine life, and the degradation of the harbor environment.

During the summer of 1983, Judge Garrity's rulings and dec-
larations from the bench, assiduously reported by the press,
pushed the people of the commonwealth beyond the uneasy
sense that something was wrong and toward a collective demand for change. The findings of the special master's report,
based on a great deal of specific information about the main
sources of the pollution of the harbor, outlined particular steps
that could be taken to begin solving the problem. The direct relationship between environmental degradation and the inadequacies of the metropolitan sewage treatment system was documented and clarified, and the need to restore the harbor as a

positive asset for the Greater Boston area was set forth in a way that most of the interest groups involved—even those parties formally named as defendants in the *Quincy* litigation—could agree upon. Politicians exhibited a growing sense that the long-recognized deficiencies, both in infrastructure and in coordination of efforts, could no longer be shoved into a corner to be forgotten until the next board of distinguished citizens was appointed to "study" the issue. At long last the stage was set for concerted action.

The work promised by the state defendants under the procedural order of September 1983 was watched carefully by the court, ever hopeful that with the increased attention and a sense of urgency, the regeneration of Boston Harbor could be initiated through existing institutions. Beyond that, in the fourteen months after the procedural order was issued, a prospective Massachusetts Water Resources Authority (MWRA) slowly took shape as a new state agency charged with the responsibility of bringing water to and taking wastewater from the metropolitan Boston region in an environmentally sensitive and financially responsible manner. It would be authorized to issue tax-exempt revenue bonds to investors, its operations paid for by user charges for the sewer and water services it provided. Given these powers and responsibilities, the authority would be able to devise a comprehensive strategy for handling the problem of water pollution by fostering efficient systems of water provision and waste disposal, moving toward modern comprehensive planning for the improvement of services, raising money at reasonable rates of interest, and carrying out the revival of the harbor.[1] It would have to attract and retain able staff and consultants. Effectively set up and operated, the MWRA could be a catalyst for raising environmental standards and protecting other natural resources of the commonwealth, thereby establishing environmental considerations as an integral item in the general calculus of public expenditure.[2]

The financial report by the Bank of Boston, commissioned by the judge's procedural order and submitted on February 8, 1984, fleshed out the skeletal outline in the special master's report of what a new authority might look like and what it could do.[3] As the idea lost its jolting novelty the state legislature began to respond. In this instance judicial prodding, whether real or perceived, was the immediate force to which legislators reacted, albeit at times reluctantly—"What does the court want?" was the constant query—but there it was and it did get results.

The procedural order came to be treated as the call to action it was. Engineering solutions were available, but attention, discipline, and the will to confront the pollution of the harbor had been lacking. Three major bills to establish a new agency to oversee sewage treatment in the Greater Boston area were eventually introduced in the legislature: the Dukakis bill, the Bulger bill, and then a third, late entry from Representative John Cusack, the chairman of the House Committee on Urban Affairs, in December 1984. Many of the differences among them were minor, having to do with trifling particulars designed to appeal to different constituencies, but a few key issues distinguished them. This chapter focuses on the policy issues involved in the MWRA bills, while Chapter 12 discusses the financial issues at more length and Chapter 13 concentrates on the political dynamics of negotiating and enacting the MWRA legislation.

ONE AUTHORITY OR TWO?

An immediate and layered question was whether the area's water delivery and sewer systems should be combined under a single entity. An important aspect of a state authority, indeed historically the driving reason for its existence, is that its jurisdiction can be fashioned to fit a particular need without regard to city or county boundaries. When numerous local governments have a part in maintaining infrastructures that work for them, an umbrella organization to coordinate and regulate their efforts to meet common needs can serve them all well. The 1921 compact between New York, New Jersey, and a number of cities to create the Port of New York Authority, which has managed transportation in that region, is a prime example.[4]

The first MWRA bill to reach the floor of the legislature, introduced by the Dukakis administration on April 19, 1984, aimed to combine sewer and water functions. Earlier in the year, Senate President William Bulger, a dominant voice in that body and a veteran of many legislative battles, had fashioned a proposal that transferred only the sewer district to the new authority, reflecting his stated concern that the complicated process of integrating water delivery and sewer services within a single authority might undo any legislative response at all. Introduced for legislative action in the autumn, his proposal would gain Senate passage on October 4, 1984.

Why was Bulger's bill more limited? "I know we jumped the gun and went ahead with sewage alone," he said in an interview on October 10, 1984,

> [b]ut I did it because I foresaw political difficulty if we included water. Legislators in the western part of the state weren't happy about a new authority taxing open lands in and around Quabbin and Greater Boston legislators are nervous about water rate increases. . . . I desperately want to get the thing started. Polluted water is denying millions of people's full use of the harbor, my constituents among them. We have to get going before the Feds reduce their contribution to zero.[5]

In fact, his concerns were borne out, as conflicts about major issues stymied the movement of all the bills: management rights of the new authority, police powers, funding, the composition of the board of directors, protection of open lands around the Quabbin Reservoir, and the availability of the Connecticut River for additional water supplies (which was patently unacceptable to the western Massachusetts constituency).

Discussions ensued at different forums. When several legislators asked my opinion about the choice between a single or a combined authority, I deferred to their legislative competence. But when pressed by the chairman of the House Ways and Means Committee at a private meeting at the Parker House, as to what kind of authority would "satisfy the judge," my response was that it did seem that combining the water and sewer functions could avoid a duplication of administrative structures and create useful synergies.[6]

Debt management was a pivotal consideration that favored a single authority. An uncoordinated competition between two entities, each charged with providing the infrastructure for a major public service, each seeking funding, could increase the cost of borrowing. Moreover, in my experience as a member of the Massachusetts Finance Advisory Board, appointed by the governor and charged with overseeing the scheduling and methods of issuing debt instruments for state projects, I had observed that timing is a crucial element in effective debt management.[7] Coordinated planning by a single authority would reduce the debt burden passed on to ratepayers.

A more parochial interest in a combined system should also be noted here—the belief of local practitioners specializing in municipal bonds (especially Francis X. Meaney, then managing partner of Mintz, Levin, Cohn, Ferris, Glovsky, and Popeo, and a veteran of tax-exempt bond financing) that the introduction of water would "purify" the sewage in the eyes of the investment community, resulting in lower interest rates for what might be charitably characterized as less rational reasons.[8] Traditionally—and apparently not as a result of functional or analytical considerations—water authorities fare better in the debt market than do sewer authorities.[9] So there was considerable behind-the-scenes pressure, exerted by myself, by the law firms, and also by the Bank of Boston,[10] to place the words "Massachusetts" and "water" in the title of the new authority instead of calling it a "metropolitan" and "sewer" authority, as it had been variously named in different legislative proposals.[11] "Water," I was told more than once, "is perceived more favorably in the market."

Yet another issue concerned the possibility that water revenues might be utilized to cross-subsidize sewerage projects. It was clear that the magnitude of the capital program required for the sewerage division might make its consolidation with the existing water delivery system a case of spurious equivalence, along the lines of the classic recipe for horse-and-rabbit-stew made on a strictly "fifty-fifty" basis—one horse to one rabbit; no matter how carefully the rabbit is chosen, the taste is sure to be swamped by that of horseflesh. In particular, the court's emphasis on capital spending for the metropolitan sewerage system, and its limited interest in water projects, raised concern that essentially all of the funding a combined authority could raise would be consumed by the first operating function that entered the market—in this case its sewerage division.

Ultimately the legislature established the MWRA as a combined water and sewer authority, granting it jurisdiction over the areas served by the existing MDC water and sewerage systems, with minor modifications to take care of instances in which local communities received water services alone.

The legislature sought to avoid cross-subsidization through distinct provisions in the authorizing statute to separate water and sewage operations, including:

- a separation of the operating divisions within the authority for water and sewerage
- segregated accounts for each operating division with respect to revenues, expenses, assets, and funds
- separate user charges, based on the cost of service, for each operating division

- an allocation of shared costs (utilities, general administrative and professional services) on a cost-accounting basis
- a stipulation that each division meet its minimum debt service coverage requirements and any financial contract resolution with its own revenues.[12]

The legislature considered these arrangements adequate protection against the danger that the new authority might use its debt capacity for one operating division at the expense of the other. And, above all, by requiring each division to generate sufficient revenues to meet its own financial obligations, each would be required to maintain sufficient rates for the purpose. This seemed sound internal financial management. Just as important, it was required in order to satisfy potential bondholders.

Consideration was also given to extending the operations of the proposed MWRA to the entire state. Ultimately, this was rejected, as there were no pressing problems for services in the western part of the state. However, the legislation gave the MWRA the power to expand its service area if in the future it was financially and technically capable of doing so.

THE BALANCE OF POWER

The Board of Directors

Perhaps the most intricate governance issue in the creation of the Massachusetts Water Resources Authority—one that reflected inherent tensions between the executive and legislative branches of the state government and the interests of the various constituencies—was determining the role and composition of its board of directors. This included the criteria for the selection of board members as well as the nature of the powers and responsibilities conferred upon them.

The Dukakis, Bulger, and Cusack bills represented the most popular elements of many alternative governance proposals. A plethora of bills were proposed, discussed, revised, and reexamined over the fourteen months between the procedural order in September 1983 and the ultimate passage of legislation in December 1984. At times the sheer number of competing proposals so complicated the matter that even the best-willed legislator could not readily determine what provisions made the most sense.

The Dukakis administration's bill called for a board of seven directors, with the secretary of the Executive Office of Environmental Affairs (EOEA) serving ex officio as chairman of the board. Of the remaining six members, one was to be appointed by the governor and serve coterminously with the EOEA chair; one was to be selected by the mayor of Boston, also serving coterminously; a third member was to be appointed by the governor from a list of three submitted by the mayor of Boston and would serve a term of four years; and three were to be appointed by an advisory board, designed to foster community and citizen input, for six-year terms staggered at two-year intervals.[13]

The Bulger bill, submitted by a politician who was intimately familiar with the workings of power on Beacon Hill, also kept the board down to seven members, but set up a selection process that gave the governor even greater potential control over the new authority: in addition to the secretary of EOEA, the governor would appoint two members serving coterminously, one of whom must not be a resident of Boston. Two members were to be appointed for four-year terms from Quincy and Winthrop, selected by the governor upon the recommendation of the two local governments; the mayor of Boston would appoint one member for a four-year term; and, finally, one member would be appointed by the advisory board for a six-year term.[14] Thus, under the Bulger bill, upon assuming office the governor would immediately control at least three members of the MWRA's board of directors.[15] Both bills allowed the governor to remove any member of the board for cause, which was broadly defined; in essence, they provided for what amounted to gubernatorial control of the MWRA's board of directors.[16]

The third bill, called the Cusack bill after State Representative John Cusack, differed significantly from the other two in its recommendations for the board of directors.[17] To begin with, it increased the size to nine members. The two additional seats were assigned to the Connecticut and Merrimack river basin communities, although the actual appointments of individuals would remain in the hands of the governor (these members would serve coterminously with the governor). Second, and showing the strength of local pressures, the two Quincy and Winthrop appointments were to be made by the proposed advisory board—which was also to be responsible for nominating two board members without regard to city of residence—giving the advisory body control over four of the nine seats. All four would serve for six-year terms staggered at two-year intervals, which was meant to insulate them to some degree from political influence. As under the Dukakis and Bulger schemes, the secretary of EOEA was designated chairperson, but the treasurer of the Boston Water and Sewer Commission was also given an ex officio seat. Finally, the ninth director would be appointed by the mayor of Boston. The Cusack bill, then, was designed to shift power toward local communities,[18] as was emphasized by the provision granting the ability to remove directors for cause to the respective appointing bodies rather than to the governor alone.[19]

The final Massachusetts Water Resources Authority Act, coming out of the joint conference committee to which the various bills were referred, took portions from all three of the major contenders—the Dukakis, Bulger, and Cusack bills—and added further elements and compromises. It increased the size of the board of directors to eleven members. Following the Cusack bill, it provided that the governor appoint two members, one each

from the Connecticut and Merrimack river basins, to serve coterminously.[20] It also returned the final say in the appointment of
the Quincy and Winthrop members to the governor, who chose
them from a list of three qualified persons submitted by the relevant city officials.[21] The number of advisory board selections decreased to three; these members were to serve six-year terms
staggered two years apart.[22] Three directors would be named by
the mayor of Boston for coterminous periods. The last seat belonged to the secretary of EOEA as the ex officio chairperson of
the board. The act provided for both a quorum and an acting
majority of six. A new provision that emerged from the final
conference was a requirement that one of the five seats over
which the governor had power be filled by a member of a minority group as defined by law.[23]

Of all the debated proposals, the final act's provisions with regard to the board represented the most politically balanced arrangement, with control lodged in no single official or group. At
first glance the modifications that were adopted represented a
move toward a four-way politics of consensus, a resting point
amid the pushes and pulls of the governor, inland user communities, harborside user communities, and watershed communities.
But when these sections of the empowering act are looked at together with those relating to the advisory board, a second and
more significant goal appears: achieving a balance of power between representatives of the governor and representatives of the
mayor of Boston. This was an expression of the historic power
struggle between the city and the rest of the state; some have referred to the commonwealth's often-acrimonious dealings with
Boston as "political guerrilla warfare."[24] Perennially crucial for
city politicos was the fear that state officials would usurp the
city's control over its own destiny.

More important still, these political maneuvers did not crip-
ple the bill. Despite the lobbying of relevant interest groups who

did achieve modifications on their behalf, final management control of the MWRA's fate stayed with the authority in all drafts of the bill.[25] The MWRA would be powerful.

Directors' Terms, Duties, and Powers
Throughout the drafting of the MWRA legislation, its framers wrestled with a perennial yet largely undiscussed problem with regard to the composition of public boards, even when they are constituted as "broadly representative": the troubling issue of who best represents the general will. Too often, members of old "leading" families, politically connected businessmen, and high-ranking officers of influential financial and corporate institutions are the pool from which directors are chosen. Their willingness to serve often stems from a notion of noblesse oblige; also, it should be noted, this group has less need for compensation. But self-interest is never absent.

Following this tradition of elite dominance, the authors of the financial report of the Bank of Boston, commissioned by the court, recommended independent business leaders as bearing the proper credentials for membership on the MWRA's governing board. Drafters of the MWRA act, however, appreciated how ephemeral this type of political independence is once it collides with the realities of everyday operations. Hence all the bills rejected the recommendation for an insulated board composed of leading citizens, set apart from the formalized parts of government and immunized from politics. Rather than a board selected for managerial, financial, or technical expertise, or on grounds of virtue rather than sordid politics, the legislators chose a more politically representative structure, including directors appointed by the governor, the mayor of Boston, and the advisory board.

The relationship of the board of directors to the authority's management became another slippery issue, one that raised questions similar to those that arise in private corporations concerning the role of boards of directors vis-à-vis CEOs. Indeed, prominent corporate attorneys—not to overlook public-minded investment bankers—seek ways to bolster the position of directors against dictation by management. One common recommendation is the appointment of a lead director in order to discharge fiduciary obligations more effectively. Another proposal is that professional staff, independent of management, be made available to the board so that members are enabled to fully explore, analyze, and cope with financial statements, accounting practices, and alternative policies for acquisitions and investments—all with the idea of equipping directors with tools to assert control over the formulation of policy. But the opposite trend prevailed in the MWRA act, rendering the board less informed and less powerful in relation to the executive director—and perhaps less useful in representing the public interest.

Other issues proved less controversial. The act creating the MWRA contains standard clauses about the terms of its directors. Each serves until a successor is appointed and qualified, and each is eligible for reappointment at the end of the term. Any member may be removed by the appointing authority for demonstrated and documented misconduct or willful neglect of duty. Terms were staggered in order to avoid sudden shifts in the policies of the authority because of appointments by newly elected statewide or local officials.

The major sections of the act conferring power upon the MWRA's board of directors—most notably those regarding the extent of control over finances and general managerial discretion—were fairly standard, similar to those customarily provided to boards of corporations, private or public. And they were changed little in the sequence of drafts.[26]

Finally, all three draft bills showed one common tendency, a reluctance to pay salaries, and in this the final act demonstrated the consensus: directors serve without compensation; only reasonable expenses incurred in the performance of duties are reimbursed.[27] This was representative of a widespread feeling that public service itself is the reward, a privilege that is somehow diminished or tarnished by the payment of compensation.

The Secretary's Preserve

One section that remained constant in all three bills was the designation of the commonwealth's secretary of environmental affairs, a gubernatorial appointee, as the chairperson of the MWRA's board of directors. Yet despite the apparent consensus, this was a provision that troubled many groups—and one that I opposed, albeit without success.

The members of the board of directors of a public agency are expected to use independent judgment and cultivate a nonpartisan outlook in carrying out public policies. The act established a board that is representative, hence one capable of bringing to the table alternative aspects of issues and settling them through debate and negotiation. I felt that the use of the head of a major department of state government as chairperson interfered with the autonomy of the board. It introduced the possibility of a conflict of interest in situations where the authority's actions might run afoul of policies that the secretary of environmental affairs was expected to enforce. And it blurred the lines of responsibility. After all, I argued at the time, the act specifically provided that the authority "shall be an independent public authority not subject to the supervision or control of the executive office of environmental affairs or of any other executive office."[28] Was this to be interpreted as a mere piety, not to be taken seriously in the world of action?

Apparently so. Certainly this section of the act was contradicted by the chair appointment. When it came to designating the secretary of EOEA as chairperson, the choice did seem a painless way for the governor to have a direct say in the policies and management of the agency. The presence of James Hoyte, a capable administrator and well-liked individual, may also have influenced the legislators in coming to this decision.

That the secretary's presence on the board would serve as a beneficial link between the new entity and the executive branch of the state government was argued by the proponents of this provision of the bill. And, it might be said, environmental matters are primarily the concern of large units of government, since pollution recognizes no politically drawn boundaries; environmental issues, whether involving garbage disposal, landfills, smokestack clouds, or the pollution of a river, leap over any political walls that may be set up by local systems of governance. The state government had to be involved.

I maintained, however, that this very factor was troublesome. The secretary's chairmanship of a governmental unit whose operations might violate the policies that are the province of the EOEA would mean that one official would have to play two potentially conflicting roles. Which hat would the secretary don or doff and in which situations?[29]

The Advisory Board

As public corporations, and particularly regional authorities, grow in importance in providing public services in the United States, lawmakers are faced with a vexing question: How to form an authority that from a financial perspective and with regard to its ability to raise capital must be independent, yet keep it responsive and accountable as American democratic philosophy requires? The Commonwealth of Massachusetts, in the legislation creating the advisory boards of the MWRA and the Massachusetts Bay Transportation Authority, has contributed an important component to the governance of such entities. Uninhibited by the review, scrutiny, or restrictions typically imposed upon other areas of state and local government, the

MWRA is—in theory, at least—held accountable to the public by the presence of its advisory board.

The proposals concerning the MWRA advisory board were quite similar in all three of the major bills. In offering citizens a chance to factor local knowledge and desires into the MWRA's decision-making process, the advisory board exemplified the tenet that a way to attain consensus is through a sense of ownership of the process by those affected by it.[30] The final legislation, not in so many words but by its general tenor, established the advisory board as a watchdog over the MWRA's budget and operations and as a liaison between the authority and its customer communities. It served the purpose of giving them representation with regard to actions of the authority that affected them directly, in essence offering a check-and-balance, or even a veto, on the choice of agency policies.[31] Conceivably the advisory board could also exert pressures on the decisions made by the authority's executive director.

The three bills considered by the joint committee and the legislation finally adopted all provided for representation on the advisory board by the chief executive officer of each of the local communities served, or by that official's permanent designee. In the Dukakis and Cusack bills, the number of communities was sixty; in the Bulger bill, which dealt only with sewer services, it was forty-three.[32]

All the proposals specified a weighted voting arrangement for advisory board actions other than the appointment of directors, based on each community's proportion of the total assessed user service charges.[33] Thus the larger municipalities—in particular Boston, the biggest of all—commanded a louder voice when it came to policy and specific projects.

The advisory board provisions of the Cusack bill were adopted in the final act, with the six members appointed by the governor to serve coterminously with the governor, and with the addition of a Metropolitan Area Planning Council representative and two other members representing other interests. In addition, it stipulated that an officer or employee of the state or of a city or town was not thereby precluded from advocating or voting for any particular matter involving the authority.[34] And, as with the board of directors, advisory board members were allowed reasonable expenses but were not compensated.[35]

The powers conferred upon the advisory board changed little over the course of drafting and debates. Special powers were enumerated: the board must approve sewer service contracts lasting more than six months, and it shared with the governor and the legislature oversight of the extensions of the sewerage system. Similarly, it had to agree to any extension of water services.[36]

It is in the financial arena that the advisory board has potential genuine power—should it choose to exert it. It makes recommendations to the authority on current expense and capital budgets, capital facilities programs, and other financial charges. The authority is required to submit its expense budget to the advisory board at least sixty days prior to its adoption, and any expense budget amendments at least thirty days before adoption.[37] Correspondingly, the act added a proviso that the directors of the authority must submit detailed responses and explanations to the advisory board in the event of a substantial divergence between the authority's actions and the advisory board's reports and recommendations regarding finances.[38] Moreover, the authority is required to consult with the advisory board in the preparation of its capital facility programs.

Importantly for both individual and business consumers—and addressing the frequently uttered concern about the sprint upward in rates that would be occasioned by the expensive Boston Harbor cleanup and a new environmental regime—the legislation charged the advisory board with holding public hearings prior to any change in rates. The authority was also obligated to open its books to public scrutiny at such times. Rate hearings could be held jointly with management at the discretion of the advisory board.[39] And this, it should be noted, is the only true restraint on the MWRA with respect to fiscal policy, since otherwise it operates as a monopoly, unfettered by regulatory agency reviews or antitrust liability.

Another relevant provision of the act—paralleling the advisory board's mandate to review and comment on the annual report and to hold hearings—was a residuary clause empowering the board to make overall recommendations to the governor and the legislature regarding the authority and its operations.[40]

Representative Democracy versus Efficiency

In a number of its provisions the MWRA act tried to strike a balance between the pragmatic demands for an efficient system for raising and allocating capital and the messier principles of representative democracy. Quite naturally, fears were expressed during legislative negotiations that the size and composition of the seventy-member advisory board could well suffer from "town meeting" syndrome, which would impede balanced discussion and be inconsistent with the rational weighing and swift resolution of complex and competing issues.

On the whole, the structure and powers of the MWRA's two boards—the board of directors and the advisory board—indicate a deep and abiding ambivalence in the legislature toward the mechanism it was parenting. Although it recognized the demands of localities for representation as well as the need for some check on the powers of the authority, it was determined to keep the advisory board purely advisory. In this instance the democracy-versus-efficiency conundrum found its Massachusetts solution in the decision to create a powerful board of directors with clearly demarcated functions and a representative membership, rather than to divide powers between a board of directors and an advisory board. Illustrative of the difficulties and subtleties of the situation is the contrast with earlier legislation establishing another major independent authority, the Massachusetts Bay Transportation Authority, whose advisory board was given power over the budget, whereas the MWRA's advisory board has only the right to be informed and to comment—a substantially weaker prerogative.

The requirement that the members of the MWRA's advisory board be either chief executive officers of cities and towns or their permanent designees raised another set of concerns. Surprisingly, experience has run contrary to commonsense expectations: with rare exceptions the influence of local governments has tended to decrease, rather than increase, when elected local officials are named to the governing board of a regional public authority. Such officials are already busy people. Time devoted to their local duties is time not spent learning the authority's business or reviewing frameworks for bond covenants and prospectuses, feasibility reports, program targets, planning methodologies, research reports, project proposals, and performance analyses. Busy officials may retain ex officio seats to the detriment of advisory board functions of supervision, and, in practice, this may diminish the quality and character of decisions.

THE EXECUTIVE DIRECTOR

Perhaps the most important power conferred on the board of directors of the new MWRA was the appointment of the executive director. It is the exercise of this individual's remarkable powers as the day-to-day head of the organization that determines the fate of the authority's operations and how it will be judged by those affected by its actions. On the larger scale, the performance of the executive director has turned out to be pivotal in the success or failure of public authorities nationwide.

By the terms of the act, the chief executive officer of the authority must be a person professionally skilled and experienced in law, finance, public works, or public utility programs, or in public administration with significant experience in wastewater pollution abatement.[41] Most significantly, in practice no major limitations were ever placed on the appointment of this officer. The executive director is hired for a term not to exceed five years, is eligible for reappointment for another five years, and is subject to removal for cause.[42]

"Administering the affairs" of the authority is entrusted to the executive director, who is authorized to make all decisions on matters relating to contracting, procurement, personnel, and administration.[43] The director's performance is placed under the general supervision of the board of directors, with any additional terms of authorization as the board "may from time to time reasonably adopt and continue in force."[44]

In many public bodies the personality and outlook of the executive director become the key to the authority's performance, for with knowledge, time, skill, and patronage come dominance. In theory, the executive director provides informational and managerial support to the board of directors and enables it to discharge its policy-setting role. But as is the case with many large private corporations, the day-to-day reality of the operations of the authority reverses that order: decision-making on policy and management issues is predominantly the province of the executive director, with the board playing the supporting role. Responsibility for implementing the board's decisions is also lodged in the executive director, of course, and here too that officer's discretion is quite wide.

The entire MWRA staff reports to the executive director, with the exceptions of the Affirmative Action Office and the Special Audit Unit, which report to both the executive director and the board. The executive director's dominance is reinforced over time because the legislation fixes a longer term for that office than for other employees whose initial contract of employment cannot exceed three years.

A SPECIAL AUDIT UNIT

Another novel contribution by Massachusetts to the theory and practice of public agencies is the Special Audit Unit, for which provision was initially made only in the Cusack bill. After some legislative debate the final legislation settled this internal unit "under the direct supervision" of the executive director. Concerns regarding the needs of the board of directors for direct staff input were answered by giving the audit unit a mandate to report to both the executive director and the board on the "quality, efficiency, and integrity" of the agency's operating and capital programs. It is also authorized to make periodic recommendations to the same officeholders. If knowledge is power, as Francis Bacon reminds us, such a group can be a significant force within an organization, and one, not coincidentally, whose actions carry a potential for splitting the executive director and the board over crucial decisions at difficult times. With these considerations in mind, the act requires MWRA employees serving in this unit to devote their efforts to it full-time. It further mandates that they shall not be assigned direct operating responsibilities within the authority.[45]

CONTROL OF LEGAL AFFAIRS

In crafting the act, legal matters received special consideration. Although many provisions were fairly routine and changed little throughout the eight months of negotiations, several sections did add significant curlicues.

To begin with, the MWRA would be required to notify the state attorney general in writing of any legal proceedings in which environmental damage is the issue.[46] This and related recommendations introduced by the conference committee dismayed environmentalists and conservation groups, who felt that the attorney general's failure to act was partly to blame for the past failures to achieve administrative and legislative commitments for a cleanup of the harbor. Attorney General Francis Bellotti's position on the *Quincy* litigation, as exemplified in the actions in court of his deputy, Michael Sloman, meant that the state defendants had continued to fight that suit well beyond the point where doing so served a useful purpose.[47] And, since the attorney general is an independently elected official, for political reasons the governor's office was unwilling to suggest outside counsel for the MDC; thus Bellotti retained control over the defendants' presentations in *Quincy.*

For these and more abstract reasons, environmentalists were hoping for an authority responsible for its own legal affairs, and hence independent of the attorney general's office. They seemed to be succeeding at first, as this was the approach initially taken in the various draft bills. But in conference strange things popped up.

First, the act prevented the authority from entering into any consent decree without the prior approval of the governor and the legislature. Second—and again directed against the proposals of environmentalists and in some way reacting sharply against what Paul Garrity's court had been advocating throughout the *Quincy* litigation—the act required the attorney general to represent the MWRA in any case in which water pollution is an issue.[48] Hence, even though the new authority was given managerial autonomy and its own sources of revenue free from the legislative appropriation process, the legislation provided that the political officials of the commonwealth, especially the attorney general, would retain control when it came to actions in any federal or state litigation. The legislature announced through the litigant's backdoor that political forces would remain in play.

A parting surprise measure: the conference committee, apparently smarting under the treatment of the legislature in the *Quincy* litigation, removed all cases in which water pollution is an issue, and all MWRA suits, from the state superior court jurisdiction. In a truly nose-thumbing mode, the act gives the state's highest court, the Supreme Judicial Court, original and exclusive jurisdiction over all state actions in which the MWRA is a defendant and water pollution is an issue.[49]

A final result of this jurisdictional coup was to force future water pollution cases into the federal courts, but the more immediate purpose of the last-minute amendments was to serve as an assertion of state legislative supremacy.

STATE CONTROLS

The Commonwealth of Massachusetts features a highly decentralized structure of government. Aside from the bully pulpit, even the governor has limited powers. Many top officials are elected independently and so are inclined to pursue their own agendas, as was brought home vividly in *Quincy* by the attorney general's insistence on litigating the defendants' case and barring any settlement. Also, the state has a history of relying on boards, commissions, and multilayered administrative bodies; this too tends to weaken the power of the governor. The upshot has been legislative dominance over state policies, although this institution itself has been badly divided on major issues over the years.

Because of this history, the struggle of reformers in several realms has taken the form of an ongoing campaign to increase the governor's power and so to impose changes from above. Naturally, this was keenly advocated by Governor Dukakis. He called for the replacement of autonomous boards and authorities with officials appointed by and directly answerable to the governor. But this campaign did not prove successful.[50] That much care was taken to make the MWRA's advisory board and the board of directors broadly representative and carefully balanced among potentially competing interests—indeed, the resort to a two-tier system—bespoke a political culture averse to centralization.[51] The balancing of forces in the commonwealth produced a politics of negotiation, in which every interest affected must be heard and often may hold a veto. Of course, one drawback of the system is that it encourages incremental solutions. Another is that, contrary to hopes, it may lead to a politics of retribution. In any event, the highly intricate structure found in the traditional workings of the state government helps explain some of the complexities and contradictions of the MWRA.

Establishing an autonomous authority represented a desire to decentralize harbor-related decision-making outside of the regular structure of the state government but to concentrate within that authority the power to attain results. A driving purpose was to keep the future management of the greater Boston area's water and sewer services out of or, if you prefer, above politics: the new agency would run operations based on the specialized expertise of its own management, according to policies formulated by its board of directors, for the greater public good. A major goal was to achieve autonomy and insulation from pressure groups. However, in the last days of drafting in December 1984, the legislators seemed to ask themselves, Are we creating a Frankenstein monster? They rushed to impose fresh requirements, albeit of limited consequence, that reflected their concern that the authority would be entirely too independent.

One restriction was increased transparency, which was also a response to the financial bulldozer. The act subjected the board of directors to the requirements and provisions of Massachusetts administrative procedure regarding open meetings and public disclosure of records, and the conference committee also added bidding and contracting regulations and investigative procedures. Extension of sewer service to additional communities required the approval of both the Department of Environmental Quality Engineering and the advisory board; similarly, various regulatory bodies, such as the Executive Office of Environmental Affairs, must give their permission before a new community could receive water services.[52] Along the same lines was another requirement that approval of service area expansions be given by both the governor and the legislature.

Still other restraints upon the power of the authority center upon freedom of information. Annual reports are due to the governor, the president of the State Senate, the speaker of the House of Representatives, and the chairs of the House and Senate committees on ways and means,[53] and progress reports must be prepared every five years with the assistance of a citizen and advisory panel selected by the authority and approved by the advisory board.[54]

Inevitably, the location of new sewage treatment sites was expected to be a source of intense controversy—such facilities are rarely welcomed as neighbors. The legislators took account of the particularly sensitive rub of an MWRA override of the will of local governments or, for that matter, holders of private property. The act incorporated the Bulger bill's conditions that both the governor and the legislature approve any takings by MWRA of public-use lands.[55]

Finally, it should be noted, the MWRA was explicitly made subject to the general laws of the commonwealth. The relevant laws enforced, for example, design standards, environmental grant procedures, air pollution reductions, dredge and fill requirements, and environmental impact statements. As an authority created by the legislature, the MWRA was also subject to state audits, to be conducted both at the discretion of the state auditor and regularly at least every two years.

INTEREST GROUPS AND THE MWRA

When the MWRA proposal came out in its initial form as a bill put forth by the Dukakis administration, considerable discussion ensued in the newspapers. Such a major undertaking as revamping the vital sewer and water services of a large metropolitan area cannot avoid a flurry of comment by countless groups that have a legitimate interest in the outcome. Yet just as predictably, the general public may remain relatively indifferent to the particulars of the complex legislative effort required, even apathetic to the details of a chosen financial route (as were, in fact, most individual legislators). The idea that *someone* would be put in charge of coordinating the planning, financing, and management of the harbor cleanup represented a commitment that sufficed for many. Residual public attention focused on general efforts to protect the property tax base. Obviously there were exceptions, people who devoted considerable attention to how an enabling act would function, but these efforts came primarily from the ranks of lobbyists, some motivated by dedication to a cause and others who were employed by groups that had a financial or administrative interest in the legislation. Perhaps the three most influential lobbies exerting pressure upon the drafting of the act were public interest groups on behalf of municipalities, environmentalists, and consumer organizations.

Among the groups most directly affected by the legislation were the local governments, each in charge of its own local sewer collection system. By and large they were successful in achieving their quite limited goals—the creation of a new state Division of Watershed Management,[56] an expansion of the Quabbin Advisory Committee, limitations on system enlargement,[57] and the addition of a management rights clause.[58] A 10 percent limitation on the capital cost contribution required of local entities was also included in the final MWRA act,[59] and along with it the outlines of a classified rate structure that assigned different rates to different types of users of a given service, based on criteria such as volume of water and time of use. An ongoing fiscal battle between state government and local governments was mitigated by the act's provision for in-lieu-of-tax payments to localities for nontaxable authority property situated within their jurisdictions. Local communities were also successful in gaining greater autonomy with respect to operations, billing, and collection for their own water and sewer systems. Local governments, however, were not well enough organized to be able to speak with one voice in a lobbying effort. Communities abutting the harbor waters had different agendas from those located further inland, and the water supply interests of the western localities added yet another set of perspectives. Even where the towns had common interests in making the act more responsive to their needs, the Massachusetts Municipal Association, the lobbying group for all towns, was unable to reach a consensus on various MWRA proposals. A "User Group Steering Committee," composed of representatives of local governments, was formed to deal with the eventualities of legislation, but it did not come to terms with the broader issue of whether the legislation should strip away some of the MWRA's political insulation so that the public, through its locally elected officials, could have more of a say over what projects the authority would undertake, how they would be carried out, and how costs were to be shared and allocated. In the end the advisory board remained the one means of input for local governments, and even in this realm only limited powers were conferred.

As the legislation was being developed, consumer groups raised sporadic claims that did not command rapt attention from legislators. Their concerns were based on the financial impact of the new authority's activities on the individual pocketbook. For instance, they argued for state assumption of the MWRA's operation and maintenance costs, for a classified rate structure that placed a greater share of costs on business and industrial users as opposed to residential users, and, rather less frequently, for measures to encourage conservation. They also applied continuous pressure—to no avail—to reserve seats on the authority's governing board for directors who would be elected rather than appointed.[60]

By dint of effective public relations, various environmental groups ranging from those concerned with boating and recreation to those representing the people who worked the clam flats also managed to be heard. But the major organizations representing environmental concerns focused on the water supply portions of the various bills, calling for representation for water donor communities on the MWRA's board of directors, water quality improvement and conservation, and the creation of a state Division of Watershed Management. The environmental movement had not reached its full power. The Conservation Law Foundation action against the MDC and EPA was still in abeyance in the federal court, and the harbor imbroglio had not yet drawn the attention of the public nationwide.

AUTONOMY AND ACCOUNTABILITY

To adequately realize its numerous and varied goals, the act afforded the MWRA a level of autonomy deemed necessary to enable the authority to make decisions from an objective, scientific perspective, protected from overintensive pressure by interest groups or the threat of cooption by the state executive or legislative branches or by local authorities. It was expected to stay free of vulgar politics. But this came at a price, since at the same time the authority was also supposed to be responsive to the overall fiscal policies of the commonwealth, to its environmental enhancement goals, and, always, to public opinion, especially on the matter of rates. Informed and intelligent balancing was required between business-like efficiency, the avoidance of political influence, and the exercise of political skill in a highly political commonwealth.

Some important questions went unanswered in the negotiations that produced the final act. To what extent were the benefits of efficiency in providing sewer and water services to be emphasized over the general principle of citizen involvement in and ultimate control of public services? And how did the state legislature and governor, acting through appointments and review powers, figure in the accounting?

As one shakes the MWRA statute book for closer inspection, it becomes clear that members of its board of directors are directly accountable neither to state government nor to local governments nor to the general public. Only slight public constraints on the directors' powers were forged. And the private oversight by the bond market was confined to limited areas. Is this wise? Surely the argument can be advanced that while the legislators satisfied part of their responsibility to the people of the commonwealth by setting up an authority that was powerful enough to rehabilitate Boston Harbor, they slighted the corollary obligation for a system furnishing enough prudent oversight of MWRA actions to ensure a continuing embodiment of the people's will. The enabling act concentrated responsibility primarily in the executive director and the director's staff, and secondarily in the appointed board of directors. Unless carefully modulated, such empowerment of a cohort of experts in science and technology—even granting that the long-lasting pollution crisis demanded drastic steps—compromises principles of representative democracy.[61] The old democratic political regime had nearly killed Boston Harbor; now the pendulum had swung toward technocracy.

A QUESTION OF BALANCE

The legislators and their advisers had carefully examined the history and theory of public authorities. Consequently, a powerful reality emerged with the birth of the MWRA. It highlighted the role of the independent state authority, with its combination of public and private powers, almost a secret government, as a solver of complex large-scale societal dilemmas. The full significance and power of these independent agencies are still not yet generally recognized. Public enterprises, with their monopoly over public services, are increasingly coming to dominate state and local credit markets. They frequently set the framework for all other borrowings.[62] Whether styled as authorities, metropolitan agencies, or special districts, independent agencies such as the MWRA draw their essential character from their reliance on financing from the private capital markets, which insulates them from the legislative appropriation process—and also from the democratic process. As a direct result they enjoy independence from their governmental parents in the way they formulate and execute policy.

They are given full and free access to the capital markets, and the standards of those markets matter more than governmental rules. Legislative restraints of the past have not persisted; even judicial checks and balances have tended to wither away. In addition to specific, exonerating statutory language, long lines of cases in Massachusetts and many other states hold public authorities exempt from the constitutional doctrines historically applied to curb financial abuses by municipal governments. The major restraint had been the public purpose doctrine: that actions and spending, for both local governments and public authorities, be for the public welfare, as determined by the judiciary, in order to pass muster under the public use requirement of the Fifth Amendment and analogous provisions in state constitutions. This standard has been whittled down, not least by the sweeping U.S. Supreme Court opinions of *Berman v. Parker*[63] and *Midkiff*.[64] As a result, it is hard to find or even think of a "use"—be it football teams, or coliseums, or sales of frankfurters at sports events—that will not be found to be "public," and hence enfolded within the constitutional powers of a public authority. Debt limitations on state governments, often articulated in exhaustive detail in state constitutions, are not applicable to authorities, since they are considered to have an existence apart from the government. Again, the common prohibitions on state lending or on state credit guarantees are not brought into play; in many cases the prohibitions have been so narrowed, either by express language, by the creation of subsidiary and intermediary corporations, or by other legal loopholes, that they have no bite. And, as a final course to straight sailing, public enterprises are generally free from judicial review in the exercise of their specific functions, including, most importantly, the setting of rates.[65]

Throughout, the MWRA act struggles to reconcile the conflicting goals of agency effectiveness and public accountability, perhaps putting its thumb on the scale slightly in favor of effectiveness. Ideally, the fusion set up by an enabling statute for a public authority requires a careful delineation of powers, activities, and limitations, lining them up one by one—and also leaving room for flexibility and the lessons of experience. At various points the legislature tried to reconcile the tensions between vigorous action and democratic accountability through the requirement of annual reports, access to records, notice requirements, and hearings, all facilitating public awareness of the MWRA's actions and plans. Yet authorities have earned a reputation for running their operations as far removed from public scrutiny as possible.

The basic form of the MWRA act was determined according to a financial structure aimed at securing the judgment of the financial market that the MWRA was truly an independent authority with its own source of funding, free from external tampering. This separation from accountability to the government and the general public was further emphasized by the reliance of the board of directors on the analyses and expertise of the staff of professionals reporting to the executive director. The financial and managerial structure succeeded in producing an extraordinarily centralized and self-contained (and not very public) authority carrying out vital public functions.

Still, it is unclear how the results might differ if the enabling legislation had emphasized public accountability. Neither the

Massachusetts legislature nor the governor has much of a basis for questioning recommendations made by a highly competent staff whose depth of experience increases with the passing of the years. It is hard, moreover, to penetrate the armor of technological complexities (and verbiage) in which alternative choices in the area of sewerage operations are dressed by the scientists. And how public "values" might shape specific decisions remains murky—with no obvious channels for articulation or criticism.

METROPOLITANISM

The legal blueprint set up in the 1984 legislation had another significant, although little discussed, impact on local government powers. The MWRA exemplifies a new species of public agency in yet another major way: it is an experiment in rational regionalism, for it is on a regional basis that the authority exercises its powers and provides its essential services. This was a point emphasized in my reports as special master—the weakness of the MDC's wastewater system operations pointed up the inadequacy of a small multipurpose agency besieged and outgrown by its problems. Important legislators believed that a regional (and powerful) public agency would be better suited for dealing with the maze of governments and regulations that had paralyzed the MDC, and that a geographically extended body would provide a mechanism whereby parochial local interests could be traded off and balanced. Ideally, with testing and experience, the MWRA could establish sound sewer and water services for metropolitan Boston and contribute to the better governance of the region.

The whole notion of combining or coordinating local governments in a joint or concerted action, such as metropolitan planning and zoning, or furnishing affordable housing on a regional basis, was still relatively untried. The concept had not yet been studied in depth by academics or verified by experience. The MDC itself, formed in 1919 by a merger of special-purpose public entities dealing with water, sewers, and parks in order to provide services spanning multiple jurisdictions, was a significant advance in metropolitan governance for its day.

In later decades this outlook dimmed. There was slight interest in regional solutions to what were regarded as essentially local problems, and less desire to cede local power to regional bodies. But recently a move has been growing toward a more favorable appraisal of metropolitanism in response to the pressures of population density, transportation congestion, pollution, lack of affordable housing, urban sprawl, and environmental crises. The MWRA is part of this trend.

SAFE HARBOR
Paying for the Vision

12

The state of a civilization may be inferred from the state of its plumbing.

—Adolf Loos

If the new Massachusetts Water Resources Authority was to avoid the pitfalls that caused the breakdown of the Metropolitan District Commission (MDC) system, it needed, above all, financial independence. Testimony from witnesses in the *Quincy* litigation left no doubt that a lack of adequate funds had led to the deterioration of the MDC's plants, the lowering of staff morale, and ultimately the routine dumping of raw sewage into Boston Harbor. Under the old regime the MDC had no direct access to the funds raised from the cities and towns it served. MDC revenues were not earmarked in the state's coffers; instead, water and sewage charges went into the general fund. As a result, money to run the agency came by way of appropriations gingerly made annually by the legislature—in which a majority of members represented non-MDC communities—from the general pool of state funds. The MWRA enabling act would remedy that by granting the agency control over its own revenue and financing.

But decreeing the financial independence of the MWRA would also mean that substantial sums of money and a considerable number of business contracts would pass through its hands—and dollars plus patronage make for an irresistible combination. Conferring upon the relatively few individuals who would manage the MWRA the power to employ thousands of people and to raise, borrow, and spend hundreds of millions of dollars carried the potential of generating a huge economic and political power center. Thus the financing of authorities like the MWRA raises issues of adherence to democratic values in a compelling way. Should large aggregations of wealth and patronage of a monopolistic nature—accumulated through the performance of community services and bedecked with the legitimizing labels of "public" and "government agency"—be allowed to exist beyond the control of publicly elected officials and legislators?[1] The MWRA was likely to become the proverbial 800-pound gorilla that can pick its own feeding time and place, make its own rules, and follow its own will and whim.

Therefore, granting the MWRA full power over its own finances raised sharp questions of discretion and its abuses. The necessary trade-offs and line-drawings between power, efficiency, and insulation from politics as the main objectives of the authority, and accountability to the public as a countervailing component of the vision, determined how the funding provisions of the MWRA enabling act were drafted.

ACCESS TO PRIVATE CAPITAL

Long-term financing provisions in each of the three draft bills would enable the MWRA to set water and sewerage rates and to ensure sufficient revenue to meet operating and debt service requirements, no matter how conditions fluctuated in the outside world. This meant that guarantees were required that the agency would be immunized from loss due to future political pressures.

From the perspective of analysts and financial experts, the public authority would have to be able to satisfy the lending market that it was sufficiently insulated from the political process to secure repayment of its debt through its own system of revenues, monies that would remain under its control for the foreseeable future, certainly at least for the term of the debt. As the enabling act put it straightforwardly, in the very first paragraph of its statement of purpose, "[the authority's] financing re-

quirements . . . are substantial and require independent financial resources, including the ability to rely on user charges to
recover costs of providing such services and the ability to fund
capital programs without undue reliance on the general obligation credit of the commonwealth."[2] And it went on to give the
MWRA the right to set rates independent of any other state or
local governing body.[3]

Unlike the normal public utility, the authority would not be
subject to regulation in its operations, most sensitively that of
the fixing of rates. The advisory board and the ombudsman,
placed in the position of liaison between the users and the authority in the setting of rates, would have no power other than
issuing recommendations, which the MWRA could accept or reject. The state showed a further commitment to the MWRA's
financial capacity, at least in the eyes of potential investors and
underwriters, by inserting a statutory rate covenant (one that
would probably have appeared in bond indentures, anyway) to
the effect that rate charges must be set to meet operating expenses, debt service, funds, and reserves.[4]

What form and covenants of a bond would satisfy the competing requirements? Drafters of the enabling law had a choice
of arrangements to make, since tax-exempt bonds may be issued
either as general obligations of the agency or, in the alternative,
may take the form of special revenue bonds.[5] Historically, the
capital needs of state and municipal sewerage systems were met
by the issuance of general obligation bonds pledging unlimited
ad valorem taxing powers to guarantee long-term indebtedness.
Such a total assurance was, in the early eras, the sort of security
ordinarily sought by bondholders, for full faith and credit of the
issuing entity guaranteed coverage of debt service (the interest
charges and amortization of the principal) through the levying
of taxes, and, if necessary, through tapping general resources.
Bondholders slept peacefully on such an assurance.

By the early 1980s, however, local authorities began to view wastewater facilities as enterprise operations that are self-supporting rather than dependent on subsidies from state and federal grants or from real estate taxes. The MWRA legislation took its cue from this model—authorities as entities that construct and operate revenue-producing facilities and pay their bondholders with self-generated user charges.[6] Consequently, revenue bond funding became the borrowing method of choice for the MWRA. Indeed, in the following years, the special revenue bond continually increased as a percentage of all municipal and regional financing in the United States.

In two sweeping provisions, the enabling legislation granted the MWRA broad authorization to issue bonds for any of its corporate purposes by resolution of its board of directors, and to receive and apply revenues toward "the purposes of the Act" without approval or authorization by the commonwealth or any political subdivision thereof.[7]

Special factors over and above a general reluctance to resort to state-guaranteed bonds that might overextend the full faith and credit of the state also played a part in the legislative choice. Legislators feared that borrowing the large sums of money that the special master's report indicated would be required for the improvement of Boston Harbor would lead to a rise in interest rates for all debt issuances by the state. This put at risk the capital-raising ability of the commonwealth as a whole, as well as that of its individual municipalities. To protect and insulate the state, the MWRA legislation provided that the authority's bonds, except for a guarantee of initial issues, would not be deemed a debt or pledge of the faith and credit of the commonwealth or any of its political subdivisions.[8]

The provisions that finally emerged in the enabling act therefore reflected a determination to stamp out any lingering doubts or wishful hopes about state backing for MWRA bonds.[9] The MWRA would be financially autonomous, but it would also be on its own.

But to what extent? On paper, the state could simply wash its hands after passing the legislation, since MWRA capital obligations and operating expenses would be payable solely from the funds of the authority—although the state might face financial as well as moral penalties when it next turned to the bond market. But the voice of the private market is not stilled. Despite the declared absence of state legal backing there was a ubiquitous winking of the eye, emblematic of the belief—denials and the best-drafted covenants notwithstanding—that if need be the state would step up to the plate and rescue a beleaguered agency.[10] Reckless spending or inadequate internal financial controls would bring about a call for the state to come to the rescue, a call that could not be denied.

Anyway, it was (and still is) highly unlikely that user charges would fail to meet the authority's revenue requirements: the MWRA enjoys a monopoly position over a vital asset that no individual or organization in the commonwealth can do without. If worse came to worst and bondholders were obliged to foreclose, they would end up with a revenue-producing asset that generates income adequate to pay the obligation—and no recourse to the state treasury would be necessary. Contrary to Governor Al Smith's argument, offered in jest in 1933, that "a sewer never can be made a self-liquidating project," the plain fact that a water and sewer system is indispensable for the life of a modern metropolis makes it a creditworthy asset even to the most cautious investor.

One public restraint did remain: a simple, yet significant, limitation on the grant of bond-issuing powers to the MWRA survived the wholesale legislative delegation of financial authority. The enabling act placed a ceiling of $600 million on the aggregate amount of bonds that could be issued.[11] This cap reversed the scheme as it stood in earlier drafts, which had imposed no such limit. In this realm caution prevailed, though subsequent events demonstrated the elasticity of the limit. In 1989 an "emergency act" substituted $1.2 billion for the $600 million, and even this whopping addition was followed by a 1990 statute raising the ceiling to $2 billion, and still later it rose to $4 billion. In sum, the legislature, recognizing the breadth of its delegation to the MWRA, was careful to retain a modicum of control over the amount of bonded indebtedness—although the cap was lifted almost automatically as crunch time arrived. Still, the possibility of contrary action served as a brake on MWRA debt and spending.

The MWRA statute assumes that the private sector calls the financial tune. The act is quite clear on this point; it provides a measure of bondholder protection that is as wide as possible without in so many direct words turning the authority over to Wall Street. For instance, the bondholder may bring suit, either at law or in equity, for relief, including proceedings for the appointment of a receiver to take possession and control of the authority and its properties, and to fix, revise, and collect charges.[12] Moreover, the MWRA's corporate existence cannot be terminated so long as there are bonds outstanding.[13]

Consistent with typical revenue bond financing, the law subjects the refunding of bonds to private market controls, none of them requiring approval by any state agency.[14] The enabling act allows the board of directors to agree to any trust agreement or bond covenant that might be insisted upon by the underwriters. As if to make still clearer what was already clear, it reinforces the point by allowing the directors to pledge limits on the purposes and activities to which bond receipts will be put and provides further extensive remedies for bondholders, including legal and equitable remedies, extraordinary writs, and specific performance or pledges and trust agreements.[15]

Informal restraints on bond-financed agencies abound in practice and should also be taken into account. An organization raising funds has subsidiary and corollary goals in mind: to obtain the lowest interest rates and financing costs, to secure prepayment privileges, to create a marketable issue, to accomplish its objectives with a minimum of restrictions on its future ability to borrow or to make plans for new construction and rehabilitation activities. In order to meet such goals, which at times may be internally contradictory, the borrower needs to maneuver through the minefield of custom, regulations, and practices in the highly conservative and standardized arena of banking and municipal finance. So what becomes most pressing for a public authority, overriding other considerations, is keeping up good relations with its investors.

Hence, looking at the picture as a whole, the authority's board of directors is basically free to issue debt instruments on whatever terms and with any timing the market requires. While it is obliged to advise the state's secretary of administration and finance, the authority's advisory board, and the Massachusetts Finance Advisory Board prior to the initial issue of any bond series, the requirements of conformance to public standards are perfunctory. In the end, the role of private financing trumped governmental oversight.

To enable the agency to meet the financial market's demands, the legislature conferred upon the MWRA a high degree of internal control of revenues, budgets, and debt issuance and service, all immunized from external governmental checks. This money power was to be its spear and shield: the authority did not suffer from the subsequent difficulties of the commonwealth's bonding capacity, nor was it ever called upon to compete against other state priorities or, more importantly, other bond issuances. In fact, in a final irony, its credit rating by both Standard & Poor's and Moody's rose higher than that of the commonwealth itself. And throughout it is the private market that has the final say; in fact, it has its say all the time: the market decides the terms of capital availability whenever there is a transaction, favorable or not.

HOW TO START A NEW AUTHORITY?

Special consideration was given by the legislature as to how the authority, an untested and unknown entity, would be able to issue debt at the outset. As a freshly launched enterprise, with massive icebergs of expenditure looming in its future, shadowed by an undistinguished past record (based upon MDC mismanagement in financing), and facing uncertainties, at best, in federal aid, the MWRA was bound to encounter difficulties in the issuance and sale of its first revenue bonds.

Interim aid from the legislature filled the vacuum, taking the form of a five-year grace period during which the state would use its full faith and credit to guarantee the authority's bonds. The interim state guarantee would provide the MWRA with the opportunity to develop a financial plan at the same time that it was getting its administrative structure moving. That the start-up funding guarantee was short-term meant limited exposure for the state and, it followed accordingly, little risk that the state would use its temporary financial power to take control of the agency. Benefiting from this transitional aid, the authority would soon be able to enter the credit market under its own steam; indeed, the legislators estimated that by the end of 1989 MWRA operations would be self-sustaining, and even conservative bankers would be ready to buy bonds secured solely by the authority's own revenues.

The MWRA would make the most of the opportunity. Once it was in operation, the agency wasted no time in assembling a financial team to prepare for entry into the financial markets. Studies were undertaken to determine the need for (and costs of) expanding facilities and building new ones, the availability of state and federal aid, the amount to be financed, and the timeframe within which the financing would be completed.[16]

The overall creditworthiness of the new agency, as it related to the issuance of bonds, was a constant worry. Belts were added to suspenders. Each local community in the service area was evaluated for financial soundness by the rating agencies; all were called on to supply three years of audited financial statements, current and proposed budgets, and demographic information. Going still further to overcome lenders' initial reluctance, a self-insurance fund was established to reinforce the authority's creditworthiness; the Community Obligation and Revenue Enhancing Fund was sized to provide one-tenth of the annual debt service amount. Like the lender's ability to intercept local aid grants from the state, this served as an additional line of security against defaults. This reserve fund was advocated by myself, included in a version of the draft bill, and developed in the course of legislative negotiation about the terms of the enabling act. The extra support helped; the MWRA would receive an A rating from Moody's, and A- from Standard & Poor's.

The MWRA would assume responsibility for all its predecessor's property and debts. Ownership rights to both the waterworks and the sewer system were vested in it. In return, the MWRA took over all general obligation debt previously issued by the commonwealth on behalf of the waterworks and sewer portions of the MDC operation. Each employee of the metropolitan sewerage district automatically went onto the payroll of the MWRA without impairment of civil service status or seniority and, most pressing, without reduction in compensation or benefits.

As a result of the transfers, the MWRA was born as one of the largest start-ups in the nation at the time, with $2.3 billion in assets, 800 employees, a current expense budget of $95 million, and a capital program of $1.1 billion. The authority also assumed immediate water and sewer debt of $207 million, of which $88 million comprised the sewer debt.[17]

Since the MWRA would have to commence immediate borrowing in order to implement long-range capital improvement plans, the enabling act cleared the way in other respects. One hazard was Proposition 2½, which had raced through Massachusetts, a product of the taxpayer revolt that began with Proposition 13 in California; it prevented any increase in local property assessments of more than 2.5 percent per year without the approval of local voters. A minor problem it turned out, though it was worrisome and loomed large in the drafting phase of the MWRA act. Circumvention occurred quickly at the final stage of the legislation, primarily through a sleight of hand by Senate President Bulger: Proposition 2½ was bypassed in the enabling act through the delegation of fiscal power to the agency.

USER CHARGES: HOW SHALL THE PEOPLE PAY?

The financial history of the MDC proved to be the Banquo's ghost of the *Quincy* litigation, and it was an object lesson for the MWRA legislation. The commission's inability to raise funds had led to the harbor crisis. A further burden was the combination of functions piled onto the MDC, which had charge of diverse and scattered programs other than water and sewerage: police, parks, roadways, and recreational facilities—even a zoo in Franklin Park. And finally, one other factor, somewhat hidden, needs to be considered: psychoanalysts of the appropriation process conclude that sewer infrastructure, being for the most part underground and therefore invisible, carries less weight in inducing appropriations or, for that matter, other forms of attention than do visible structures, such as schools, ice skating rinks, or roads.[18] Clearly the MDC system could not achieve funding catch-up.

Also paralyzing executive branch officials and legislative representatives was the fear that raising sewer and water rates would infuriate voters. Taking into account the improvements recommended in the special master's report, it was estimated that annual water and sewer bills for the average household would amount to $180 in 1986, would rise to $545 in 1993, and keep rising. Politically it was risky for any legislator to take a step that would increase the rates, however necessary for the protection of the metropolitan environment. Although improved services would enhance the economic development of the Boston metropolitan area, such a generalized future benefit did little to appease ratepayers.

Certainly, the costs of the revitalization of Boston Harbor could have been distributed through various taxation mechanisms, including property, income, or sales taxes. But the legislature preferred to rely on a user charge system to fund the MWRA. For this, there is a cogent fairness argument: those who use a service should pay for it. As a majority of economists argue as well, a fundamental notion behind user charges is that of efficiency through the pricing mechanism: user charges place a price on each unit of the publicly provided services, and if the price is set to reflect true cost, then users' consumption will reflect their informed preferences. Such a test also enables a society to improve its resource allocations, spending only those amounts needed to achieve the goals—health, convenience, or aesthetics—that the society wishes to attain.

A pragmatic reason for the choice was that unlike some other public services, water and sewer systems have identifiable users. There are, at least in the abstract, no free riders, and all those who ought to pay can be charged. Furthermore, in a recent extension of the efficiency argument, user charges can create a motivation for conservation; by setting the price high enough to meet the cost of the additional capacity needed, user charges provide reasons to eliminate waste and less beneficial uses. Also, not to be minimized, a fee system is feasible administratively, in that the costs of measuring usage, billing, and collecting charges can be kept within tolerable limits. Finally, there was no denying another fact of life that conveniently outweighed theory: since user charges are not deemed a tax, they could be assessed on institutions that are otherwise tax-exempt; for the Boston area, dominated by schools and hospitals, this promised to be a most important advantage.

In addition to its internal cohesion, a user charge system has to surmount a major hurdle perennially facing all public funding schemes: acceptability to the bond community.[19] The law had to be straightforward and clear, not challengeable, so that the system could be seen to comply with all legal requirements.

Achieving the desired financial self-support system required an effective billing and collection system. As the various MWRA bills went through the legislative mills, alternatives were proposed and the experiences of other metropolitan areas were compared and analyzed. A heated debate erupted over whether the MWRA should bill users directly. With all of this in mind, the final legislation adopted a billing system under which municipalities, rather than end users, would be responsible for payments to the MWRA. The result is a modified wholesale billing system by which the authority, the wholesale supplier of sewer and water services, charges each of the municipalities for its proportional use of the services on a cost-of-service basis.[20] Since municipalities are made wholly responsible for payment of charges set by the MWRA, it becomes their obligation to assess the homeowners and businesses. Thus the local governments act as conduits passing their costs on to retail customers through a user charge system incorporating state agency and local rate charges as separate items of one bill.

The system was rendered complete by excluding other decision makers. The MWRA's board of directors sets the authority's wholesale rates independently, although the rates are derived from a budget subject to review by the advisory board.[21] The enabling act states only the most general factors in setting charges: actual costs of providing services; incentives "to promote conservation of resources and protection of the environment"; contributions made by local authorities to I/I reduction projects, leak detection, system reduction projects, and the separation of combined sewers; reasonable provisions to reflect historically disproportionate investment in the sewer and waterworks systems; and reasonable interest charges and penalties for delinquency in payment.[22]

Two strong collection techniques were made available, the right of settlement against local aid from the state, and court actions against delinquent municipalities. The enabling act required the state treasurer to pay to the authority on demand any amounts otherwise certified for payment to the local body. This was effectively a lien on the local aid grants made by the state. With respect to unpaid municipal bills, the authority had the right to impose penalty charges for delinquent bills, and it could sue in Superior Court to recover any unpaid principal plus interest or other damages. Two other remedies considered but rejected were the placing of liens on property and curtailing provision of services to delinquent end users, as those incentives were deemed more appropriate to a retail billing system in which the provider had direct interactions with users.[23]

Beyond the benefit of simplicity in charging end users via the municipalities, this hybrid system had a further advantage in that it allowed for individual flexibility: provided that municipalities met the overall charges imposed by the authority, they could reduce charges to those unable to pay due to "age, infirmity, or poverty." This was a surprise welfare provision that emerged in the enabling act after the conference.[24]

During the final discussions on the MWRA's billing system, the legislature's choice was reinforced by a countrywide survey conducted by the Bank of Boston. It revealed that wholesale billing was the national trend; survey results showed that major providers of similar services were choosing to bill as wholesalers.[25] As a new agency the authority needed to adopt practices consistent with the industry standard accepted in the financial marketplace. And, to clinch matters, there was an overwhelming commonsense advantage: billing the system's fifty municipal customers, as opposed to, say, a half-million end users, required little organizational and institutional change and minimal administrative support and expense.[26]

ANOMALOUS FREEDOM

The primary impetus behind the creation of the MWRA was financial need—some means had to be found to pay for the Boston Harbor cleanup. The goal was to raise money as cheaply as possible without indefinitely burdening the state's credit; it would be realized through the issuance of tax-exempt bonds supported by a stream of income generated through user charges. This concept guided the financing recommendation of the special master's report, and the need for a reformulation of institutional structure and outlook became increasingly apparent after Judge Garrity issued the procedural order.

The end result—the MWRA as an autonomous and self-financing agency—is not without its critics. To some commentators, "authorities are created only for anti-democratic purposes," that is, for the evasion of rules—including rules embodied in state constitutions—that apply to the running of government itself.[27] Some truth lurks in this extreme statement. Authorities do constitute a type of separate government, often wealthier and more politically influential than the government of a state.

Authorities, it seems, want to eat their cake and keep it, too. They claim attributes of government, such as tax exemption, eminent domain power, and immunity from suit. Then, turning around, they deny other governmental attributes they consider obnoxious, such as civil service provisions, local debt limits, bidding requirements, disclosure of books and records, and judicial review. And they are not directly responsible to the people or to those who created them in the first instance—the people's representatives. How to fix acceptable limits on their freewheeling functions?

Establishing the MWRA as a financially independent public corporation required a recognition by all sides of the significant impact of a powerful authority on the governance structures of the state. But the issue of controls was not faced straight on or adequately fleshed out.

The essential point is that with access to private capital, public authorities become relatively immune from legislative dictation, but contrary to theory, they are also relatively independent from the other potential brake of close oversight by the private sources of funding; investors judge an authority's financial soundness, but do not closely monitor its policies and operations. Authorities are thus largely unfettered by traditional checks on the exercise of public power. Moreover, unlike the ordinary corporation, authorities are not subject to restraints either by way of the performance of their stock in a market, or the registration requirements of the federal Securities and Exchange Commission. And in reality, investment bankers, insurance companies, bondholders, trustees, underwriters, and fiduciary investors are surprisingly indifferent, once they have made an investment in an established authority, as to how individual projects under the cover of the bond are faring. Once they find that the agency has sufficient backing for debt repayment, their supervision, in practice, is tepid.

Typically unconcerned with the day-to-day operations of the enterprise—let alone how successful it is in achieving the social objectives set forth in its enabling act—lenders buy bonds on the strength of the agency's revenue sources and its connection to government. And they do so with little regard to the absence of a commitment by the general government to stand behind the agency debt, assuming, as private market investors tend to do, that an authority's debt remains a governmental obligation; even if this is not literally true, the assumption is that the government will step in if one of its agencies is in danger of defaulting. This is the setting that gives the agency's management remarkable freedom of action, and poses such a conundrum for those trying to frame accountability for the authority.

Ultimately, the reasoning behind granting the MWRA extraordinary financial powers was not the result of economic determinism but was instead a commonsense recognition that the Boston Harbor cleanup was not in fact a "cleanup" in the traditional sense—it was not a maintenance operation—but rather a capital construction program that would eventually result in cleaner waters. Rehabilitating old plants and pipes, as well as building new plants, pumping stations, tunnels, and secondary treatment facilities, required vast infusions of money. At the time the projections in the special master's report indicated that the necessary capital investments would make the Boston Harbor effort the largest single public works project in New England's history.

In order for the project to succeed, a somewhat uneven balance was struck between democratic theory and the necessities of the situation—the harbor would eventually regain its health, with the intervention of a powerful and independent public authority backed by private providers of capital. The two values of efficiency and accountability formed an uneasy alliance, with efficiency carrying the heavier weight. This was the outcome of the research, the probing of the experts, the articulation of contending opinions, and, based upon that foundation, the recommendation of the special master and the judgment of the court. By the end of 1984 the legislature would adopt the same reasoning and grant the MWRA in the enabling legislation the unrestricted powers required for successful action.

PARTING OF THE WATERS   13
The Showdown between Court and Legislature

Laws are like sausages. It is better not to see them being made.

—Otto von Bismarck

The legislation that created the Massachusetts Water Resources Authority barely escaped a political train-wreck between the legislative and judicial branches.

By mid-October of 1984, two competing bills (by Governor Michael Dukakis and Senate President William Bulger) for creating a new sewer and water authority were being tinkered with in the Senate but were stalled in the House—not to overlook a third bill submitted by Representative John Cusack, which called for extensive local control over the new entity. Then troubling signs appeared of a serious split within the Dukakis administration.

At the eleventh annual Boston Harbor Issues Forum, held October 11, 1984, the state director of economic development insisted that the power to accomplish all necessary harbor rehabilitation projects was "already well entrenched" in existing state and municipal institutions. He rejected the idea of a new super-agency, asserting that the present commitment of public officials was sufficient to "make these things happen." He further told the audience that the governor's own development cabinet could provide any coordination that might be needed.[1] Rumors persisted that the legislative proposal closest to the governor's heart was a piece of pending legislation for state financing of infrastructure known as the Massbank bill. The governor, it was believed, would marshal all his political forces to create that agency, and this "state bank" would eliminate the need for a specialized authority to fund the Boston-area sewer system.

In response to the prospect of further delays, Judge Garrity had warned on October 9 that he would put the sewerage system into court receivership and ban new sewer tie-ins unless the legislators acted promptly to resolve their differences and come up with a compromise law. With the House and Senate wrangling over three proposals and numerous amendments regarding a new authority, the judge suggested that the legislature should reach an agreement before the next court hearing, which was scheduled for mid-November.

"It's a shame that the court has to get involved in situations that are the functions of government," Garrity said in open court. "But I probably made a terrible mistake in waiting four years with the Boston Housing Authority before I took it over. We have to make a fresh start. . . . This case is my highest priority, and I won't leave it."[2] Governor Dukakis's press secretary responded that the administration was not surprised by Garrity's stand: "The judge has been very patient but firm and clear about what he expects from the state." Another spokesperson added, "Everyone understands Garrity's frustration. The harbor has been polluted far too long."

The judge wrapped up the hearing of October 9 with his own ruminations on the harbor problem:

Let me tell you what my reaction is. . . . When I was a little kid about nine or ten years old I can recall being brought to the City Point Beach in South Boston by my parents on the T. My mother and father would say don't go near the water and I would ask why. Just don't go near the water. Can I go down and take a look? No, you can't go down and take a look. And like every obnoxious nine- or ten-year-old I would go down to take a look at the water and there was human excrement. . . .

A year ago when this case first came before me there was human excrement floating around the harbor. And a couple of weeks ago when I was out there, there was human excrement floating around the harbor. And if I'm somewhat impatient it's not because this was a fairly long hearing this afternoon, and it's not because it's been a year since this case came before me; it's been thirty-five years of my life, just from a very personal perspective, that this darn harbor, which is the greatest resource the city of Boston probably has, has been polluted. And it's been polluted for long before then. . . .

I guess my stance is that my own patience is rapidly coming to an end. It's clear to me and the political branches of government have to realize that . . . a fresh start has to be made. And my sense is that it has to be made this year; it has to be made within the next month or so. And very, very specifically for that reason that's why I'm going to continue this case, at the suggestion of Professor Haar, to the second week of November.

The parties left the hearing with a feeling that the urgency of the situation would impel legislation forward. Once again realities overrode dreams and good intentions, however, and the next month passed with no substantial advances toward passage of the Dukakis or the Bulger bill, or the Cusack variation. November 15, 1984, found the parties back before the court.

Serving as spokesperson for the bench, I was quoted in the press as saying,

Eighteen months after taking jurisdiction over the complex issue of who bears responsibility for the harbor, Judge Garrity cannot afford to wait any longer. The long promised deadline for action has arrived. . . . The administration and the Legislature have had ample time to study the . . . legislation, to air their differences and to negotiate an acceptable compromise. I can assure you that Judge Garrity, however reluctant, is prepared to act.[3]

On November 16, the judge announced in open court that unless significant legislative progress occurred by the next scheduled hearing on November 30, he would take steps to place the sewer division of the Metropolitan District Commission into judicial receivership. He set the cutoff date for action as the Monday after Thanksgiving, November 26.

The specter of judicial receivership pushed the legislature to resolve the issues. Two separate major initiatives—Bulger's bill for a sewer authority and Dukakis's bill calling for a combined sewer and water authority—were pending in the House Ways and Means Committee. (Representative Cusack's alternative, and several other provisions, were seen as variations on these two major proposals.) Legislators feared the probability that a court-created entity would raise funds by imposing stiff sewer taxes on the forty-three cities and towns in the MDC's sewerage district. A legislatively created authority, on the other hand, could fund harbor cleanup efforts by floating bonds, which would spread the cost over generations. Judge Garrity, in detailing the consequences of legislative inaction, also made it clear that receivership would entail an immediate moratorium on new connections to MDC sewer pipes—bringing development in the metropolitan area to a virtual standstill.

Nonetheless, on November 28, the joint House and Senate conference committee postponed action on all legislation concerning the proposed authority after lawmakers from central and western Massachusetts expressed concern over the harbor project's impact on water resources. On November 29, House Ways and Means Committee chairman Michael C. Creedon stated that swift action on any compromise legislation was unlikely. He added—most ominously—that if any bill came to the House floor it would carry an adverse committee report. "This is not going to be solved between now and December 13, that's for sure," he declared, referring to the date already set for the adjournment of his committee for the remainder of the current legislative session.

At a news conference that afternoon, Governor Dukakis was dismayed by Creedon's stance. "I can't believe that this legislature is going to go home and let Judge Garrity bring the economy to a halt," he warned. "The judge has indicated clearly what he will do if we don't act." Nevertheless, the committee voted to adjourn for a week.[4]

This postponement prompted House Republican leader William Robinson (who, in the Democrat-dominated legislature, was often silent on major political struggles) to chime in with an offer of a motion to discharge the legislation from the committee: "By discharging the bills we will send a good faith message to the court that we intend to deal with this issue now." The legislative session was scheduled to end on January 1, and the House committee had spent days debating a major education bill. Robinson called for a vote to suspend work on that bill and move the sewer-water measure ahead. Committee chairman Creedon, however, had a different reaction to the pressure being exerted by the court: "I have a belief about court orders," he fulminated. "I ignore them."

As this cliff-hanger scenario developed, Judge Garrity and I almost welcomed Creedon's short-tempered outburst as carrying the seeds of its own undoing. As it turned out, this was a correct appraisal. A sharply drawn cartoon by Paul Szep on the editorial page of the *Boston Globe* depicted Creedon tripping over his own sewage, reflecting the damage he had done to his credibility. Public reaction to the chairman's comment focused on legislative fumbling and inaction.

Queried by the press, Judge Garrity declined to comment for the moment. Instead he chose to act.

GETTING THE JOB DONE

In the days leading up to November 29, Steven Horowitz, the deputy master, and I prepared a memorandum of law to the judge on the court's authority and capacity to put the MDC into receivership, as well as the advantages and drawbacks of such a stratagem. In the *Perez* ruling,[5] the appellate court that had upheld Judge Garrity's earlier move to place the Boston Housing Authority into receivership set out a three-part test for such action: repeated or continuous failure of the institution's officials to comply with a previously issued decree; a reasonable forecast that continued insistence by the court that the officials conform to the decree would lead only to confrontation and delay; and a lack of leadership within the institution that could be expected to turn the situation around within a reasonable time.[6] The appellate court in *Morgan* had enunciated the reasoning we followed: where the usual remedies are inadequate, a court of equity is justified in turning to less common ones, such as a receivership, "to get the job done."[7]

Funding was a potential sticking point, we reported to the judge, since it was unclear from the precedents whether the court had the power to compel the legislature to appropriate funds for an entity in receivership;[8] furthermore, it would be difficult for the agency to borrow, sell bonds, or issue commercial paper. But these were questions that could be faced later on.

On November 30, 1984, Judge Garrity stunned the state's political and economic establishment by imposing an immediate ban on all new tie-ins to the MDC sewer system and halting work on current MDC sewer construction projects.[9] Furthermore, he stated that he had scheduled a trial for Tuesday, December 4, to consider putting the sewerage division of the MDC into receivership, a remedy the city of Quincy had requested in the summer of 1983, with a judicial appointee named to run the sewer system and oversee the harbor cleanup.

The government's failure to take action to build an adequate sewerage system threatened to keep Boston Harbor "a cesspool in the region's front yard," Garrity announced. Formally accepting the report I had recently made on the lack of progress, he signed a moratorium order and held it up before the courtroom. "It is effective right now, retroactive to June 13, 1983," he told the state defendants and other parties. "And you can appeal."[10]

In chambers with the parties, the judge made it clear that he would "back off with pleasure" if the legislature created a sewer authority in the next few days, even after a trial was under way.[11] Once he appointed a receiver, however, he would not relinquish the court's hold on the cleanup for several years. "I have been biting my tongue for a year," Garrity said, "deferring to the political branches of government. . . . But what, sir"—here he turned to Assistant Attorney General Michael Sloman—"is a judge to do after a year?"

A summation of the day's events that appeared in *Time* magazine provided a fair evaluation: "After more than a year of pleas, threats, deadlines and back-room bargaining with the Massachusetts state legislature, Superior Court Judge Paul Garrity had decided enough was enough."[12]

Now willing to talk to reporters, the judge emphasized that his injunction was inspired by the House committee's decision to postpone action on legislation. "A political solution is not in sight—that is the problem here." The necessity for the action had become clear to him, he told the *New York Times*, after watching interviews with state legislators on the local television news the preceding evening; several legislators had indicated that "it would be a great idea if the court took the matter over, and let them off the hook."[13]

Two weeks earlier, in an interview with the *Boston Globe*, Judge Garrity had taken care to warn the public that his patience was wearing thin, pointing out that "it is not manipulation of the Legislature [for the court] to defer for almost 20 months to the political branches" to solve the harbor's pollution problems. He abhorred interfering in legislative affairs, he went on, but the situation was dire: "This is the 11th hour, the 11th minute, of the crisis in the harbor."[14] On this occasion and many others he had made it clear that as long as there appeared to be something approaching a good-faith effort to solve the metropolitan area's sewerage problems, he would not step in and take matters out of the hands of state officials. This time, however, the legislature's decision to recess in spite of the deadline he had set was a challenge and a flouting of the court that he could not overlook.

To emphasize its impact, the ban on new tie-ins was made retroactive to June 13, 1983. This could imperil an estimated $12.3 billion worth of new construction; it might end a $500-million-a-year building boom. Since the order affected the entire Boston metropolitan area, the judge's action also halted work on at least twenty-four additions to the MDC system then under way. Single- and two-family housing was exempt from the ban, however, and permits to link with the MDC system were authorized if the unit under construction would produce less than 2,000 gallons of sewage per day.

Public reaction to the moratorium and the promise of further judicial action was varied but loud. The business community labeled Garrity's order and pronouncements a ploy, designed to transfer to them the burden of putting pressure on the legislature. Some called the ban unrealistic and extreme. Others assessed it more evenly. Frank Basius, the general manager of the Turner Construction Company, commented, "This is simply a question of a judge saying to the legislature, 'If you guys think it's so unimportant that you think you can take a holiday, then I'm telling you it isn't.'" All in all, spokespersons for the construction industry estimated that in the short run alone the judge's ban could stop $100 million worth of construction, most notably the completion of nearly finished downtown buildings that could be denied sewage hookups indefinitely.

Reaction at the governmental level was tumultuous. Some officials were outraged at Judge Garrity's audacity in usurping legislative functions, labeling the action "Draconian." The Municipal Association warned that any lengthy moratorium would put cities and towns "in a tremendous bind." Many state representatives fretted that the intervention would hit their constituents with astronomically high water bills.[15]

But other public officials were supportive, either directly or obliquely. Some legislators were glad to hear of the court's ruling. One commented, "Frankly, I'm delighted that the judge has said enough is enough."[16] The EPA's regional administrator, Michael Deland, was quoted as saying, "I have already instructed EPA employees to cooperate with the state court order, so there will be no federal funds diverted to any of the named [sewer expansion] projects under way."[17] Boston mayor Raymond Flynn reminded the public that his plans for two thousand acres of parks and facilities along the waterfront depended on the health of the harbor's waters. "I am confident," he said, "[that] the state government will enact swift and appropriate legislation to clean up Boston Harbor."[18]

John DeVillars, the governor's chief of operations, put an administration spin on the matter. "With jobs and economic growth threatened, the need for legislative action on the governor's proposal is clear and compelling. As the governor said . . . , there must be action, and action now." Broad-based support for the governor's draft legislation had come from environmentalists, local officials, and business and labor, he stated, and if the bill could be moved to the floor of the House he was confident of success.[19]

Nevertheless, Attorney General Francis Bellotti announced that he would take an appeal to the Massachusetts Supreme Judicial Court in order to revoke Garrity's moratorium. "We intend to seek immediate relief from the effectiveness of the order prohibiting the sewer hookups," Assistant Attorney General Sloman told the *Boston Globe*.[20] To the *New York Times* Sloman complained that the judiciary should not be permitted to interfere with the executive branch's efforts (the MDC's sewer expansion project, for example), especially in light of the fact that the delays in the cleanup had been caused by the legislature.[21]

A hearing date was set by the Supreme Judicial Court, but in legal circles it was generally considered doubtful that an appeal would succeed.

HIGH WATER AND STRONG WINDS

December 3 was a fateful day as two events crossed paths: a legislative panel approved and sent to the full House a measure to create a new authority with a mandate to clean up the harbor, and the attorney general appealed to the Supreme Judicial Court to lift the trial court's recent order on the ground that it would severely harm the region's economy.

Judge Garrity's willingness to take a stand galvanized Beacon Hill and produced a flurry of action. House committee staff members worked over the weekend of December 1 and 2 and into the early hours on Monday to produce a compromise measure that largely mirrored the Dukakis bill that had been introduced way back in April. After endorsement of the committee was secured, the proposal was sent to the full House for final approval. Meanwhile, the Bulger bill, similar in its creation of a new authority but differing in that it placed only sewer services under its jurisdiction, was reported out favorably from the Senate.[22] But it was the judicial proceeding that riveted the parties' attention. Supreme Judicial Court Justice Joseph Nolan was scheduled to hear arguments on the state's appeal at a hearing on December 5 at 9:30 A.M.

Tensions mounted. In separate news conferences held on December 3, representatives of conservation groups and the construction industry called for immediate passage of the legislation. The Homebuilder's Association warned that if the House and Senate failed to act, the hookup ban would result in the loss of thousands of construction jobs.

In the middle of what he termed a media circus, House Ways and Means Committee chairman Michael Creedon had been targeted for intense criticism by the press and by public interest groups. And his credibility as a legislative leader was not enhanced by an investigative reporter's recent revelation that Creedon had gone off deer hunting in Maine with his budget director, missing more than fifty roll-call votes, while the House was left behind wrestling over which bills and which amendments it should enact. "I don't set the hunting season," Creedon protested, "and the hunting of bucks and deer is allowed for only one week."

The compromise legislation, the latest version of which was drafted as a public service without charge by the Boston law firm of Palmer & Dodge, pleased nearly everyone but Creedon. "The governor's bill is the most Mickey Mouse bill I've ever seen," he lashed out. "It's not even written as a statute. What did you people pay for this?" When told the work had been done pro bono, he declared, "Well, you get what you pay for."[23]

On December 4, the EPA weighed in to announce that it might impose its own ban on new tie-ins to the sewer system if Judge Garrity's order was overturned. The agency was taking this step, its spokesperson stated, to forestall any attempt to persuade the upper court to overturn the ban. "We have the authority to do this," he announced, "and we want everybody to know we are backstopping the judge on this."

Seemingly indifferent to the slings and arrows aimed in his direction, Judge Garrity convened the separate state trial to reconsider the issue of receivership for the MDC. On December 4, as the hearings began, Assistant Attorney General Sloman went on record as suggesting that because of the judge's previous public statements about the *Quincy* litigation and all its unresolved consequences, his "impartiality might be questioned." Garrity flatly refused to disqualify himself—"I'll decide the case on the evidence presented to me in the courtroom"[24]—and his steadfast drive toward a solution dominated the news.

As special master, I outlined four options at the hearing on December 4:

- continuation, modification, or rescission of the current moratorium on all new sewer connections, extensions to the system, and construction as outlined in the order issued by the court on November 29, 1984
- receivership of the MDC sewer division
- a two-for-one system-wide reduction requirement under which two gallons of untreated sewage would have to be removed from the system before one new gallon of sewage would be allowed into the system
- an infiltration/inflow removal requirement under which peak flows of sewage within the system would be reduced to rates at or below the actual maximum treatment capacity of the plants serving the system

Both Peter Koff, the attorney representing the city of Quincy, and Assistant Attorney General Sloman were scheduled to submit briefs on these questions by 10:00 A.M., December 7.

Then came a shock on December 5th. The cause of the Boston Harbor cleanup received a major blow from an appellate judge who apparently failed to understand the environmental and, above all, the political implications of his decision. Without writing an opinion or giving any written or oral reason for his reversal, Justice Nolan overturned the six-day-old ban on tie-ins to the sewer system. This stunned virtually all participants and observers, including the trial court's staff. We had no clue as to what was going on in the judge's mind or what had so disturbed him about the moratorium Judge Garrity had ordered.

Nevertheless, we struggled to discern the reasoning behind the ruling. Was it the retroactivity of the trial court's decree that bothered him? The speed of the proceedings? Something about the environmental formulas? Did he feel the remedy was too extensive? That it put construction projects in jeopardy? Was he influenced by a fear of a court-legislature showdown? By a dislike for Garrity's strong personality? Was it laziness on his part that accounted for failure to write a reasoned elaboration of the judgment? Justice Nolan chose to remain silent, cloaked behind his robe. One statement he made was suggestive. During Peter Koff's argument Justice Nolan had raised a question, "Should the court be in this business?"[25]

We had thought that, with the help of experts, we had identified the main causes of the gross pollution of Boston Harbor. And that by the exercise of logic, and by mobilizing the ideas of engineering, economic, and financial specialists, we had settled on the most prudent course of action: to set up an authority that would be independent, would be able to raise its own funds, and would develop a staff with the ability to plan and carry out a strategy for the improvement of the harbor. Our reasoning and the basic framework for an authority had been set out in studies, in various newspapers and editorials, and in published statements of interest groups. The proposal had received the endorsement not only of conservationists and dedicated environmentalists but also of businesspeople, public health officials, and experts in the formulation of public policy.

Confronted by a case whose only true remedy carried vast implications, Judge Garrity had walked a careful path between restraint and risk-taking. His approach during the trial in the summer of 1983—laying out the logic of the situation, examining problems and looking at causes, seeking a wide range of possible solutions, weighing the costs and benefits of each before reaching any conclusions—had been judicious in the best sense of that word. Since then he had taken pains to respect the prerogatives of the legislative and executive branches of government, patiently waiting for public opinion and the body of evidence that had been submitted in court to persuade the administration and the state's lawmakers that drastic steps were necessary, but leaving it to the political process to decide how and when, and in what form, those steps should be taken. He had done nothing further until that process had once again failed to work.

The case had gone this far only to be entrapped by a higher court decision that seemed to stem from an outmoded idea of the role of the judiciary. Along with Judge Garrity, we understood that affected interests might oppose formation of an independent authority. The existing MDC, for instance, would be greatly reduced in size, scope, and influence, and perhaps the state's politicians would not appreciate the attendant loss of patronage and political control over this piece of administrative machinery. But we thought that these and other parochial concerns would be seen by the public for what they were and would ultimately fade in light of the advantages to be gained by establishing an independent agency with the power and resources to take effective action for the greater good. That the law, which we regarded as an instrument for helping society advance in terms of economic growth as well as in its aspirations for fairness, justice, and environmental health, should function as a brake on reform was disappointing. All our efforts would end up suffering the same fate as previous attempts to undo the degradation of Boston Harbor, becoming just another link in the long chain of failed reforms.

Depressed but not conceding defeat, we went back to work. The sphinx-like silence of Justice Nolan was especially troubling for those of us who had recommended the idea of a moratorium on sewer connections as both a remedy for pollution and an Archimedean lever for inducing legislative action. Which case or precedent had we overlooked, or which argument that should have been rebutted? We studied analogous cases: moratoria had been imposed by courts, but they had been upheld on appeal only as a portion of general remedies imposed by an administrative agency. Was it possible to issue a moratorium with minimal retroactive impact and hope that it would pass muster on an appeal to the full Supreme Judicial Court?

Hurriedly, Steven Horowitz and I drafted a new memorandum of law justifying a revised, more limited moratorium. We spent time with EPA administrator Michael Deland to ascertain what was on his agenda and discuss other pressures the federal agency might bring to bear on the situation. We considered whether the time had arrived for the Conservation Law Foundation to take action in its sidelined federal lawsuit. Meanwhile, the print journalists and TV people were milling about in the corridors outside the courtroom, trying to find out what the next stage in the drama might be. Over the next few weeks, their probing and investigative efforts kept the harbor on the front pages of the newspapers while nightly TV news updates and interviews maintained the excitement.

The undeniable facts were widely reported: the city of Quincy had brought a case to the court involving the gross pollution of its beaches, the court had found that both federal and state laws had been breached, liability was determined, court-ordered remedies issued, and the requirements of the remedies had not been met by the state defendants. *Ubi jus, ibi remedium*—where there is a right, there is a remedy. By this fundamental legal principle, our system of justice is supposed to provide full redress for violations of legal rights. How could the judicial branch withdraw from the case? Had Justice Nolan decided differently or even simply delayed his ruling for a day or two, the situation might have been resolved successfully while all the parties were under urgent pressure to act. For the present though, it seemed that all the efforts of the *Quincy* litigation might be going down the political drain.

Following the course he had set earlier, Judge Garrity continued the hearings on Quincy's plea to put the MDC sewer division in receivership, and he pledged to keep going "every day, night and day" until the matter was resolved.[26] The judge was irritated by the state's decision to appeal his ban, and publicly stated that he held the executive branch accountable for the ongoing pollution of Boston Harbor. When Assistant Attorney General Sloman countered that the Dukakis administration was eager to win passage of pending legislation to speed the harbor cleanup, Judge Garrity responded, "I don't believe it. . . . We would have had legislation today but for what took place in the last couple of days." At this point, the governor's legal counsel took cover with the statement that, by statute, it was the attorney general, not the governor, who made all decisions concerning litigation.

As Garrity phrased it, the *Quincy* litigation had become a matter of "people over polluters." Putting a related thought in the plainest of words, he commented, "It is regrettable in terms of the vitality of democratic institutions that a judge has to kick ass to get the political branch to do what is in the public interest."[27]

Two hours after Justice Nolan's ruling on December 5, Michael Deland announced that he had received approval from Washington in a telephone conversation with the head of the EPA, William Ruckelshaus, to proceed with a federal suit against the MDC in the U.S. District Court that would seek to impose federal supervision on the harbor cleanup. Deland also stated that he would request a federal ban on new sewer tie-ins to the MDC system as "an entirely appropriate remedy" if the legislature did not vote for a new sewer authority.[28] The Conservation Law Foundation joined the band. "Boston has the worst sewage system in the country," said Douglas Foy, CLF's president, in the course of announcing that his private organization would reactivate its own dormant lawsuit against the MDC and EPA over the pollution of the harbor.[29]

Meanwhile, as could have been predicted, only hours after Justice Nolan announced his decision the Massachusetts House once again voted, this time by 92 to 52, against continuing debate on the two pending bills authorizing an independent sewer authority. Its legislative session was scheduled to end January 1, 1985. According to Representative John Cusack, who had contributed so much to the debate, the effect of the Nolan decision was "to take the pressure off" the lawmakers.

PLAYING AGAINST TIME

In view of the looming expiration of the legislative session, our first concern now was beating the clock. After nearly six months of intense debate on top of years of discussions and proposals, the prospect of having to wait for the next session and then start all over again on drafting a statute was daunting, to say the least. Opponents of a proposal have many opportunities for ambush near the close of a legislative session, and it is always easier to delay a bill into oblivion than to kill it outright. In the guise of avoiding a spate of last-minute special interest legislation, the Democratic caucus that dominated the legislature, including the House Ways and Means Committee, voted to take up no substantive matters after December 13. In addition, although flexible in his timing, Judge Garrity had already set the end of the *Quincy* case as the point for his retirement from the bench and reentry into private practice.

With the passing days, Garrity maintained his course. He offered no reaction to Justice Nolan's reversal of his ban on new sewer connections other than to say that he was still entertaining the possibility of issuing a new moratorium order, perhaps one that would not be retroactive, if the evidence in the ongoing trial justified such action. The court had become convinced—perhaps committed by the many months of work we all had put in—of the rightness of the cause, not only for itself but for the national environmental movement as a whole, and of the necessity for a new government institution if the harbor was to be saved. The city of Quincy had alleged and had proved violations of law, and now, nearly two years later, these infringements still continued. A failure of the court to use its powers to rectify the wrongs that it had found through the trial process would not only render nugatory the adjudicated rights of the plaintiff, we felt, but it would also undermine the rule of law in our society. On December 10, Judge Garrity stated that he had prepared another moratorium order, this one banning metropolitan-area sewer hookups for proposed buildings and those currently under construction. He would refrain from imposing it, however, while the legislature was considering whether to create a new authority to deal with harbor pollution.[30]

Under the renewed threat of a court-ordered ban on commercial sewer connections, on December 11 the Massachusetts legislature resumed debate on the measures for a new sewer and water authority. Informed of this action in the midst of the trial by a telephone call from the state house, Judge Garrity delayed his threatened ban for "at least twenty-four to forty-eight hours" to give the lawmakers time to act. He would, he announced, defer the ban on an "hour-by-hour . . . day-by-day" basis. But he also noted that the order imposing the ban was "prepared and ready" and that he had asked the special master to "determine the progress of the legislation" and to remain at the state house to answer any questions the legislators might have about the proposed new authority.[31] He then continued the trial on the receivership issue.

During its first six hours of debate, the House considered some fifty amendments to the Dukakis administration's bill, adopting several technical changes such as a definition of per-

sonnel policies but rejecting the substantive ones. One amendment, offered by the House majority leader and adopted without
debate, would guarantee that no community pay more than 10
percent of the sewerage construction costs required in its area,
with the state and federal governments asked to pay the remainder. An amendment that would have capped the executive director's salary at $50,000 a year was defeated. House minor-
ity leader William Robinson stated publicly that a number of
amendments had been withdrawn in order to demonstrate to the
court the House's willingness to act. Its members wanted "to
show the courts we are willing to give this bill a strong reading."
He added, "We are trying to develop a bipartisan consensus."

The clock ticked on while the House and Senate met in joint
session, where the Dukakis bill faced a slew of additional
amendments. Representative Cusack, now a floor leader for the
bill, remarked, "I'd be happy if I see only forty more amendments in the hopper." But as the legislature pushed to a holiday
recess, one last impediment threatened to derail the whole process: only a bill that restricted the new authority to sewer services alone, as in the Bulger bill, was given a chance of passage
by the Senate.

On December 12, by the overwhelming vote of 133 to 12, the
House passed and sent to the Senate legislation creating a combined sewer and water authority. After an evening recess, the
Senate, on a voice vote taken at 11:00 P.M., authorized the creation of a joint conference committee to work out differences
between the House and Senate.

The conference committee worked all the next day and into
the night of December 13. In a rare move, Senate President Bulger appointed himself to the committee, and he told the other
conferees that he still favored the creation of a sewer authority
alone. "I agree reluctantly that an authority is necessary but it
should be limited to what has to be done right now. There is no

question that water is a serious concern but the question is do we have to do it now?"[32]

At midday on Friday, December 14, House Speaker Thomas McGee announced that the House would recess at the day's end until after Christmas. All seemed over. Nevertheless, at 1:00 P.M. the conference committee convened once more to see if it could iron out the differences between the House and Senate on the structure and scope of a new authority. Then yet another glitch: at 1:05 P.M. the committee recessed at Bulger's request. At 2:00 P.M., Judge Garrity announced that receivership hearings would reopen at the beginning of the next week and that he would place the MDC's sewer division into court-appointed receivership if the governor did not have a bill on his desk by Thursday, December 20. At 2:15 P.M., the conference committee reconvened in the Senate Reading Room, and Bulger listed his conditions for the passage of a law establishing the new authority, then requested a fifteen-minute recess to discuss changes with his staff. This request drew a testy reaction. Long-term resentments flared up as Representative Creedon pushed his chair back from the table and stood up to leave. "Take all the time you want," he told Bulger. "Every time I look at that portrait of silent Cal Coolidge I think, 'Jeez, there's the Senate.'"[33]

Disagreements continued, with Bulger contending that the court's announcement amounted to an ultimatum "to finish this afternoon and that is already impossible for us." But Speaker McGee announced that if the conference committee came up with a workable bill he would call the House back into emergency session to deal with it. At 3:15 P.M., the committee recessed, supposedly to reconvene at 4:30 P.M. and work through the evening and into the weekend, but scheduling conflicts, miscommunications, and ill feelings made this impossible. At 4:30 P.M., the committee failed to reconvene. At 7:30 P.M., committee chairman Cusack announced that the committee would not meet again until 9:00 A.M. on Monday, and, when the full House adjourned, its committee members left for the weekend. Illustrative of the confusion that reigned, a previously scheduled committee meeting for 9:30 P.M. did convene, but only the Senate members appeared.

A new meeting of the conference committee was hastily called for early afternoon on Saturday, but this too fell through. A plan emerged to meet at 2:00 P.M. on Sunday, December 16. But House minority leader Robinson let it be known that he would not attend, later blaming miscommunication for his absence on Friday evening and Saturday, and adding that he had talked a half-dozen times over the weekend with Bulger by telephone. "I had family commitments that had to be honored," he told the press. "I was willing to work all night Friday—I'm not angry with anyone." "Tempers are flaring a bit," Cusack explained. "People are tired and I think we need a day off."[34]

Despite rancor between House and Senate members of the committee, a pared-down group (which included only Cusack of the three House members) worked for an hour and a half on Sunday in open session to resolve their differences. Returning to his preferred option of separating out the water facilities, Bulger pointed out that there was no provision in the bill for water meters or meter reading, noting "these are the sort of things you've got to be careful about in a bill that runs more than 100 pages and which Senate members have not had a chance to study."

By Monday, December 17, Cusack could report to the press, "We're very close on this now. I see no reason why we can't have a bill ready to be taken up by the Legislature Wednesday." Bulger agreed, if a bit ungraciously. "I think our differences can be resolved," he said. "We have been working at the task of performing our constitutional function here. The court must do what it must do." Continuing its work, the full conference committee agreed with the Senate's proposal for a billing scheme that would charge communities for services on a wholesale basis, as against the House version that chose payment collection from users.[35] Another divisive issue related to control of the board of directors, with Bulger favoring gubernatorial appointment of enough members to ensure control over that body, while others advocated a more independent, diffuse board (the ultimate outcome).

At long last the conference committee agreed on a compromise bill—one that would create a combined water and sewer authority. The House was formally in recess until after Christmas, but Speaker McGee immediately called it back for an emergency session set for Wednesday, December 19, at 1:00 P.M. The Senate was to convene at 11:00 A.M. on the same day. "A great deal of hard work has been done by the members of the conference committee," McGee declared. "Hopefully their recommendations will be acceptable to both the House and Senate members and this most important issue can be resolved."[36]

Representative Cusack praised the role Judge Garrity had played: "He gave us the push that was needed. It proves government can work, but perhaps it works best in a crisis situation." Governor Dukakis struck a similar note of comity: "I'm very pleased with the progress that has been made by the conference committee. This is, of course, their work, and I cannot become involved, but I am pleased." On a slightly different note, as leader of the Senate, Bulger declared, "I want it clear that I want all Senate members to stay, through the night if necessary, until this is completed," adding, as an apparent afterthought, "I cannot speak for the House." Asked for his view of the situation, Judge Garrity responded carefully: "It would be improper for me to comment on an event that has not yet taken place. I have said all along, though, that if a legislative and political solution is reached by the Legislature, then these [receivership] proceedings would stop in their traces."[37]

THE FINAL PUSH

Altogether, the six-member joint conference committee had met
for five days in the shadow of the judicial receivership hearing
now scheduled for the coming Thursday, December 20. "Both
branches worked hard under pressure," John Cusack said on
Tuesday, December 18. "I feel very, very sure that both the
House and Senate will have no problems with [the bill]."[38]
Bulger predicted the Senate would pass the measure Tuesday,
December 18, or early Wednesday, December 19. "The Boston
Harbor question has been with us a long time," he said. "It's regrettable we didn't have the initiative or self-confidence to do it
without being nudged by the courts."[39]

Judge Garrity delayed hearings on the receivership to give
the legislature more time to work out a political solution. Recognizing that the deal was not yet done, he reminded the legislators
and the administration of the new ban on future sewer hookups in the metropolitan area that the court still held ready, and
he repeated once again that the time might soon come when he
would be forced to exercise his responsibilities in the case. Those
of us who had watched the proceedings and spoken with individual legislators advised the judge that he had no other choice.
On the key issue of separation of powers and the appropriate role of courts in institutional litigation proceedings, Garrity
simply observed, "I'm not in confrontation with them. They
have to do their legislature thing and I have to do my judicial
thing."[40]

Meanwhile, the economic impact of a new ban became
clearer. At least two major buildings would be in serious trouble:
the sixteen-story Marketplace Center at 200 State Street and the
twenty-three-story building at 260 Franklin Street were not yet
hooked up to the MDC system, although both were well along
in the construction phase. Forty-three other properties in the
Boston-metro area were identified as targeted by the injunction.

Construction industry spokespeople feared even more for developers who had yet to begin projects that had already been approved, citing difficulties in securing financing as a potential threat to the industry as a whole. Others warned that the ban would cause the loss of thousands of construction jobs in the commonwealth. Those users already hooked up to the system feared less for their properties, since, as I had stated, "as a practical matter, those with permits dated after June 13, 1983 probably would be unhampered by the order."[41]

Experts agreed that the ban, if imposed and allowed to extend for a long period, would devastate economic development. For example, the South Middlesex Area Chamber of Commerce warned that development in Framingham "has for all intents and purposes ceased," stopping $100 million worth of construction. According to Environmental Affairs Secretary James Hoyte, a moratorium on sewer tie-ins would have an immediate impact on many projects in various stages of development throughout the area, including office buildings, the Bentley College Development Project, a science and engineering project at Boston University, and housing developments in Charlestown and other communities. The president of Beacon Construction Company likened the consequences of the proposed decree to "setting off a nuclear bomb on the corner of State and Congress streets." Executives at Wang Laboratories were said to be scrambling to determine whether they would be allowed to flush the toilets at the company's building near Chinatown when it opened the following spring. Judge Garrity's new moratorium plan assured that the business community would continue to push the legislature to act. Pressure intensified.

Another snag in negotiations occurred at about 6:30 P.M. on Tuesday, December 18. Representative Cusack attributed the problem to fatigue. "People had been working around the clock. They were exhausted and trying to define language. After a while, nobody knew what anybody was talking about, but we've finally gotten it worked out as far as I'm concerned."[42] The legislators toiled on. Yet another last-minute hurdle loomed but was avoided: working out refinements of the wording delayed printing of the final draft compromise bill past the 11:00 P.M. deadline normally imposed to allow for a bill's reading and consideration, but the legislators agreed to suspend the rule in order to take up the bill the next day.

On Wednesday, December 19, after three days of frantic lawmaking following fourteen months of lawsuits and nine months of legislative arguments, divisions, and compromises, the Massachusetts Water Resources Authority Act became law.

Final passage came with wide majorities in both houses. After one and a half hours of debate, the House enacted the bill at 7:35 P.M., on a roll-call vote of 120 to 11. The Senate passed the measure at 8:05 P.M., on a roll-call vote of 29 to 1. That very evening, Governor Dukakis signed into law the legislation creating the Massachusetts Water Resources Authority, narrowly averting a court-ordered takeover of the MDC's sewer division and, possibly, a moratorium on construction in the metropolitan area.

"This is one of the most far-reaching and important pieces of environmental legislation in this state in the last century," Dukakis affirmed, putting into words the general feeling.[43] But, he cautioned, "there is an extraordinary amount of work to be done. . . . [This is] just a beginning in a larger effort to clean up the harbor."[44] Barely concealing a sigh of relief, House Speaker McGee told a press conference that he "wished to hell someone out there in the press area" would give the House its due for putting partisanship and self-interest aside and resolving a critical policy struggle.[45]

"Whoopee!" Paul Garrity was reported to exclaim upon hearing the news. "I know it would seem injudicious, but—*whoopee!*"[46]

CALM AFTER THE STORM

As the tumult subsided, Judge Garrity restated that he had always thought receivership of the MDC would be inappropriate. "Judges," he said, "should not take over and run the functions of the executive branch of government."[47] Satisfied by the actions of the legislature and the governor, he canceled the scheduled hearing on a possible court takeover of the MDC sewer division.

MDC Commissioner William Geary declared that he was delighted with the creation of the new authority, even though it took two divisions and 800 employees away from the agency he headed. "Now those good people will have the money . . . they lacked to do their jobs properly," he predicted, adding that he was not overly concerned about potential federal court orders "as long as they are as reasonable as were the Superior Court orders."[48]

In response to a reporter's question, I pointed to July 1, 1985, the starting date for the new authority, and indicated that the court intended to keep the pressure on the MDC for the interim period. "This is no time to coast. Passage of the legislation is a wonderful step, but we should keep in mind that while we speak, the harbor continues to be polluted." In this connection, Judge Garrity promised to issue a series of secondary orders "to keep the pressure on the MDC to work toward controlling pollution." "Professor Haar," he went on to say, "also will be directed to monitor the progress of the MDC. . . . Haar will be doing nuts and bolts stuff if necessary, that is, actually taking a look [to see] if there is a pump not working at the Deer Island sewage treatment plant and reporting on why that condition exists." As his last action involving the harbor, the judge appointed me as the court's monitor to assist in the transition from the MDC to the MWRA and to ensure that the MWRA's operations would remain under court supervision, according to a stringent schedule of corrective actions, for the next three years.[49] And thus Judge Garrity issued the order that, except for the ongoing monitoring proceedings, laid to rest the suit brought by the city of Quincy back in 1982.

A few final details remained. Representatives of the MDC's successor, the MWRA, stated in court that the new agency planned no new pleadings or motions; they intended to carry on with the meetings that had been set up by the court's procedural order and to work in good faith to accomplish its provisions. The EPA and the attorney general's office expressed their desire to remain involved in the process, and the attorneys for the city of Quincy kept up their support for the cooperative effort as the most economical and satisfactory course. The Conservation Law Foundation, however, had some thoughts about reviving its case in federal court, and recommended that the special master work for both courts. I believed that coordinating proceedings in two venues would be difficult, but I was willing to have the technical meetings continue while the federal case went on and to monitor progress under the procedural order.

Judge Garrity turned the remnants of the Quincy case over to the Superior Court for reassignment; its chief judge, Thomas R. Morse, Jr., took it on, and I worked with him until the end of December 1985. Monitoring of the MDC and of the fledgling MWRA as it was being assembled thus continued under the supervision of the state court.

All this was accompanied by a procedural square dance in the federal court in which the EPA—wanting to escape its status as a defendant in the suit that had been brought against the MDC by the CLF and suspended by Judge A. David Mazzone—filed an action against the MWRA. The two federal suits brought by the EPA and the CLF were then consolidated. The EPA, switching to the role of plaintiff, was dropped as a defendant in the CLF's suit, and the towns of Quincy and Winthrop were allowed to enter as intervenors. Somewhat later, on September 5, 1985, Judge Mazzone granted the motions of the EPA and the CLF for partial summary judgment against the MWRA, finding it liable, as successor to the MDC, for violations of the discharge permit and also of the Clean Water Act.[50] Thus the provision of the MWRA legislation that attempted to insulate the new authority from any liability for past violations by the MDC was dealt with sharply and summarily by the judge in order to ensure the MWRA's compliance with the remedial process set in motion by *Quincy*.

The eleven members of the MWRA's board of directors were sworn in by Governor Dukakis on February 27, 1985, to prepare for the transfer from the MDC. On July 1, 1985, the long-troubling issue of Boston Harbor came under the purview of the MWRA and its executive director, endowed with the power to design a comprehensive harbor rehabilitation plan, raise funds through tax-exempt bonds to pay for it, and marshal the human resources to carry it out. The Boston metropolitan water and waste treatment system was "under new management" for the first time since the 1890s, and the cleanup began in earnest.

There were real gains here. The general public was now aware of the threats to its health and general welfare. Benefits of a restoration of Boston Harbor, as well as the costs, were clarified. A new, powerful, and financially independent institution would henceforth be able to monitor and guide the future of the harbor and keep its well-being in sight. The "flush and forget" mentality went out with the tides.

In establishing the MWRA, the Massachusetts legislature created the first state agency in the nation with a mandate and the resources to develop, finance, and carry out a large-scale program to correct wastewater pollution. The environmental movement found a stronger voice and became a force in judicial, legislative, and executive branch decisions. In the process it gained a more hardheaded and determined vision of its aspirations. Above all, the public was now alerted to the beauties and economic potential of the interplay of nature and culture when the harbor and the city come together, as well as the historical and spiritual significance of natural resources such as Boston Harbor—and to its own power to force all three branches of government to restore and protect them.

And the Superior Court had converted a tragedy of the commons—the spoiling of a great natural resource "owned" by everybody and hence by nobody—into a situation of promise for everyone, and for the future.

THE COMMONS RESTORED
Courts and Social Change

14

There is nothing more difficult to arrange, more doubtful of
Success and more dangerous to carry through than to institute a new order of things.

—Niccolo Machiavelli

The use of judicial remedies to save Boston Harbor raises legitimate questions as to whether this is the proper business
of courts under our system of governance. Indeed, the related issue of judicial competence to navigate such complicated scientific, technological, economic, and political considerations was
identified at the outset by Judge Garrity in his first ruling on June
27, 1983. Is resort to the courts to solve complex social and environmental conflicts—even to the extent of formulating policies
for the future—becoming a necessary part of modern society, or
does it raise the specter of an imperial judiciary undermining the
authority of the democratically elected executive and legislative
branches of government, upsetting the system of checks and balances set forth in the Constitution?

For my part, I remain convinced—as I was from the start as
special master in *Quincy*—that it was both "appropriate and
necessary" (living up to the standard set by David Hume) for the
court to fashion judicial remedies to ensure the regeneration of
Quincy Bay and Boston Harbor. By "appropriate," I mean that
the court was neither overstepping its authority nor improperly
impinging on the prerogatives of other branches of government.
By "necessary," I mean that without judicial intervention the
environmental pollution that posed an imminent threat to the
health and well-being of the citizens of the Boston metropolitan

area would have persisted for the foreseeable future. This latter conclusion is supported by the testimony of expert witnesses during the trial, by official and consultants' reports and documents, by the statements of the participants themselves, and, most significantly, by the outcome of the *Quincy* litigation.

APPROPRIATE AND NECESSARY

Judicial fashioning of remedies in this case was *appropriate*, I reasoned then and would argue now, for five major reasons.

First, a legal wrong had been asserted. The Massachusetts state court did not enter into the controversy on its own initiative; the problems of Quincy Bay and Boston Harbor were thrust upon it by the city of Quincy as plaintiff when it initiated the lawsuit. The Metropolitan District Commission, charged by state law with the responsibility for building, operating, and maintaining a sewerage facility for the metropolitan area, had failed to honor its obligation: its Deer Island and Nut Island plants routinely released sewage that was only partially treated. The Boston Water and Sewer Commission's Moon Island outfall was routinely used to discharge raw sewage whenever the MDC plants were overwhelmed by high volumes of inflow, and the Division of Water Pollution Control's infiltration/inflow reduction program had proven ineffective in reducing excessive flows to the system. In sum, all of the evidence revealed that these and other state defendants were directly or indirectly responsible for violating existing law by systematically discharging huge quantities of highly polluted effluent into the waters of Quincy Bay and Boston Harbor.

Once liability is established, it is the court's responsibility to rectify past wrongs and to seek an end to present and future violations of the law. It is worth repeating that under our system of governance, courts are not roving law enforcers seeking to right wrongs wherever and whenever they may be found. Quite the contrary: courts are reactive, which means that someone outside the judicial system has to bring a suit in order "to transform," as Justice Robert Jackson put it, "judicial power from a potential to a kinetic state."[1] Once the city of Quincy's claims were substantiated, in turn, failure to provide appropriate relief from the defendants' ongoing wrongful practices would render nugatory the original judgment and ultimately serve to undermine the role of the judiciary in guaranteeing the rule of law in society. Acting to stop infringements of the law, or to redress the failure of other branches of government to enforce it, is central to the mandate of the judicial branch under the Constitution.

Second, disputes that revolve around environmental matters are peculiarly susceptible to judicial enforcement. By its nature and composition, a court can serve as a relatively disinterested and objective referee in cases that involve environmental decision-making, since it is not answerable to any special interests and is held to be subservient only to the fair and equitable application of legal norms and societal goals as they are formulated by duly elected legislators and construed by prior courts. This is not to say that the court may not ultimately become an advocate for a particular position or side. Indeed, once a finding of liability is established, the court may, in ascertaining the most appropriate remedy, drift to the plaintiff's side, as it did in the *Quincy* litigation, and in seeking an end to the illegal practices of the defendants thereby promote the vindication of public rights. In doing so, of course, it must continue to recognize the prerogatives and appropriate roles of the executive and legislative branches of government.

Third, as a practical matter, especially in cases involving the environment and the health and safety of the populace, the court acts as a trustee for future as well as present generations. This was Judge Garrity's emphasis in *Quincy.* As political institutions, the legislative and executive branches of government were buffeted not only by changes in their understanding of the scientific issues concerning Boston Harbor, but also by political and economic currents exerting daily and even hourly pulls and tugs of influence. Paying attention to this swirl of pressures is by no means improper; undoubtedly it is an essential component of the democratic process. Nevertheless, such day-to-day concerns sometimes lead decision makers to respond only to the crises and assembled forces of the moment, to the detriment of generations yet unborn and unrepresented in public debate. For instance, as the *Quincy* litigation unfolded, Governor Dukakis was worried about being outflanked on the right by politicians like former governor Ed King, who stressed economic development, and on the left by those who advocated more aggressive action in attacking the problems of water and air pollution. In matters concerning the environment and health—where present-day activities may result in long-term, potentially irreversible, and frequently incalculable harms—the court, as the most politically insulated branch of our government, can act more forcefully than the other branches as guardian for the future. This generational fiduciary role—reinforced by the immunity of a judge's life tenure—played a major part in Judge Garrity's thinking.

Fourth, there are many unknowns in environmental health sciences, especially in areas that are on the frontiers of scientific study. While explorations and empirical studies go on, courts are experienced and proficient in dealing with delicate balancing issues such as those involved in the interaction of economic development and increasing scientific knowledge of the health and safety effects of pollution. Over the centuries our courts, familiar with picking out the bounds of the regulatory police power, have developed interpretive guides for dealing with environmental, public health, and safety considerations, and the reasonable relation of means to the ends of health, safety, and welfare. Assessing and balancing the various factors involved in determining equitable relief is a province of the trial court.

Fifth, judicial intervention in a matter of common interest can stimulate public awareness and debate, thus enhancing rather than obstructing the democratic process. Judge Garrity's rulings and memoranda, his interviews with the press, and his outspoken comments from the bench helped galvanize public opinion. Talks by Steven Horowitz and me, as officers of the court, amplified Garrity's impact by explaining the actions of the court, discussing the legal contours of the case, and responding to questions. As a result public participation overcame legislative inertia. On the one hand, the use of this alternative point of entry into the political process inspired citizens' awareness of the need for a new agency with powers sufficient to undertake the rehabilitation of Boston Harbor; on the other, the court's recommendations and decrees as to how the monumental task of cleaning up the harbor could be conducted led administrative agencies, interest group leaders, and legislators to approach old issues with a fresh perspective and a new sense of hope. When provided with clear and compelling information, the media could and did arouse public interest and reaction—and this brought political pressures to bear on the legislature and the state's executive officials.

But the mere fact that it is appropriate for the court to fashion judicial remedies may not be enough to support such intervention—the question must also be posed as to whether intervention is *necessary*. Previous experience and my participation as special master lead me to the conclusion that in *Quincy* it unmistakably was, for three interrelated reasons.[2]

First, the findings of fact in the trial demonstrated a long-term pattern of mounting contamination of Boston Harbor and a continuous failure on the part of the agencies responsible for oversight of the metropolitan sewage system to devise a strategy and course of action to overcome this clear and present danger to the environment. Clearly this failure was not the product of a lack of knowledge. The many reports, studies, and investigations that had already accumulated spoke eloquently of official concern; in fact, the appointment of the Sargent Commission by Governor Dukakis during the *Quincy* litigation was but its latest manifestation. Nevertheless, the beaches, bays, and outer reaches of the harbor remained unacceptably polluted and environmentally degraded. A seemingly interminable series of plans, proposals, and schedules marked the decade preceding *Quincy,* but the necessary administrative approvals—let alone actual dollars of funding—were either lacking altogether or agonizingly slow in coming. It was eminently reasonable, therefore, to view with skepticism the state's vociferous contention that it had a definite "plan" to clean up the harbor. (In fact, in their response to the draft report of the special master, the defendants, seemingly indifferent to the public need, baldly stated that "pollution, while unfortunate, is not necessarily a legal wrong.") In *Quincy* the immediate necessity was that, without direct and bold judicial action, the situation of Boston Harbor threatened to fall beyond repair in a classic case of a tragedy of the commons.

Second, the question of political will aside, no one agency involved in the case had the governmental authority or ability to clean up the harbor. A problem as complicated and intricate as the pollution of Boston Harbor can rarely be solved by a patchwork of decentralized local governments, each with limited powers and its own agenda to consider. The state court, however, is an institution charged with looking out for the welfare of the commonwealth as a whole. Exerting its comprehensive equity jurisdiction, the court can overcome the administrative overlapping and fragmentation that impede solutions and perpetuate ongoing and systemic wrongdoing. By providing an overview for the government (as well as the public), the court could spur the appropriate bodies into fashioning a comprehensive and realistic program of action; it could help them coordinate their efforts within the framework of the welfare of the region as a whole.

Third, environmentalism was still a relatively new social movement in the mid-1980s, one that had not yet captured the imagination or the full political backing of the governor of Massachusetts or of key legislators. The comprehensive statement in the *Quincy* trial documentation of the facts regarding the deterioration of the harbor and the resulting danger to the health and safety of the area's residents, released to the media and backed by the authority of the court, opened discussions and debates in a way that had never before occurred in the commonwealth. It became a prime example of what Justice Felix Frankfurter underscored in 1962 in the *Baker v. Carr* decision: "In a democratic society like ours, relief must come through an aroused popular conscience that sears the conscience of the people's representatives."[3] Democratic discourse and a free exchange of ideas could then push the condition of the harbor—and environmental issues in general—high on the political agenda as worthy of public attention and the allocation of adequate state resources, both human and financial.

As Judge Garrity pointed out repeatedly, although at times it seemed to fall on deaf ears, the court had no desire to usurp the administrative functions of the commonwealth's operating and regulatory agencies, nor to interfere with day-to-day governmental decision-making processes, nor to replace or ignore the assembled expertise and experience of public officials and consultants who had been struggling with the harbor's problems for so many years. Instead, the court strove to fashion remedies that would rectify past, present, and potential future wrongs in a way that was least intrusive on the prerogatives of the other branches of government, leaving it up to the executive and legislative branches themselves to determine how compliance with the decreed framework could best be accomplished. This judicial task of delicately balancing competing values is not an enviable burden. But when administrative inaction or misconduct leads to substantial harm, the courts cannot dodge their obligation to take it on.

As in *Quincy*, the courts, when faced with a situation of exceptional scale and urgency, can develop, organize, and sharpen the tools they possess in order to produce significant social restructuring. There is no iron law of limited societal energies that poses an insurmountable barrier to judicial action. Courts operate within limits but also wield great powers. The legal process that led to the creation of the MWRA and the cleanup of Boston Harbor is a tribute—no less fervent a word will do—to judicial persistence and courage in a tinderbox atmosphere under adverse circumstances. And its success inspires lessons for future environmental litigations.

A SEPARATION OR BLENDING OF POWERS?
PRINCIPLE AND PRECEDENT

The actions of Judge Garrity in the *Quincy* litigation hark back to a debate of profound historical significance in the United States about the proper scope of the authority of the judiciary. Today, the theory of separation of powers, often invoked in support of a rigid demarcation of the powers of the three branches of government, is once again being reexamined. This is certainly not surprising in an era of the formation of new constitutions around the globe seeking to express a post–Cold War political vision of how nations conceived in democracy should structure political power. In the industrial sphere similar questions concern how economic decisions are to be delegated to the private sector and the operations of the market.

The dispersion of power among the various branches of government takes many forms in different states. There are considerable variations concerning the precise governmental functions to be divided and the degrees of separation, as well as distinctions in terms of the relationship of the courts with the other branches of government.[4] A major agreement in the history of the doctrine is that functional dispersion is essential for a constitutional, democratic society, but wide differences of opinion abound. It is clear that resort to the shorthand phrase "separation of powers" as the guide for the appropriate conduct of judges is too facile and often stands as a rhetorical weapon for blocking change and reform.[5]

Montesquieu, the French sociologist and theoretician credited with formulating the doctrine and whose writings influenced the framers of the U.S. Constitution, maintained that the three functions of the government, which he identified as the legislative, executive, and judicial, should be kept separate. The partition was to ensure that no one of the three could assemble powers that would be tyrannical (in the parlance of the eighteenth century) or dictatorial (as we would put it in the twenty-first). Since his time, separation of powers has been increasingly identified as a central axiom of democratic government.

The limitations imposed on the authority of the court by the doctrine of separation were obviously central to the decision-making process of Judge Garrity as he came to the formulation of remedies in the *Quincy* case. This judicial dilemma was further heightened by the fact that the principle is more explicitly incorporated into the Massachusetts constitution than in the federal constitution or, for that matter, in most other state constitutions.[6] Article 30 of the Massachusetts Declaration of Rights, written by none other than John Adams, is a ringing declaration of the doctrine:

In the government of this Commonwealth, the legislative department shall never exercise the executive and judicial powers, or either of them. The executive shall never exercise the legislative and judicial powers, or either of them; the judicial shall never exercise the legislative and executive powers, or either of them: to the end it may be a government of laws and not of men.[7]

On its face this text is as clear a proscription against the intrusion of one branch of government into the affairs of the other two as could be put into writing, a supreme try at creating sealed compartments of governmental power.[8]

Historically, however, right from the outset it was deemed to be a precatory warning, not a realistic description of how government should or does in fact operate. Opposition to such an extreme interpretation of the principle is especially prominent in the writings of James Madison, the singular mind behind the formation of our national constitution and one of Adams's intellectual opponents. The separation of powers doctrine, Madison argued, was not intended to impose upon the branches a rigid specialization of function:

> If we look into the constitutions of the several States, we find that, notwithstanding the emphatical and, in some instances, the unqualified terms in which this axiom has been laid down, there is not a single instance in which the several departments of power have been kept absolutely separate and distinct.[9]

For Madison, the doctrine could be only a limited restraint on government: "It goes no farther than to prohibit any one of the entire departments from exercising the powers of another department." In no state constitution, he pointed out, "has a competent provision been made for maintaining in practice the separation [that is] delineated on paper."[10]

Over time, Madison's construction of the doctrine won out. A series of twists and turns aside, the U.S. Supreme Court has come to rule most often in favor of a "pragmatic, flexible view of differentiated governmental power . . . not to a hermetic division among the Branches."[11] As Justice John Paul Stevens put it in 1986,

> One reason that the exercise of legislative, executive, and judicial powers cannot be categorically distributed among three mutually exclusive branches of Government is that governmental power cannot always be readily characterized with only one of those three labels. . . . [A] particular function, like a chameleon, will often take on the aspect of the office to which it is assigned.[12]

State courts are even freer in this regard than their federal counterparts. They are not required to adopt separation of powers, nor are they beholden to federal interpretations of distinct roles.[13] The more conservative Massachusetts state courts, however, continued Adams's traditions as late as 1911. In *Rice v. Draper*, decided that year, the petitioner sought a writ of mandamus to compel the governor to perform his official duty, in this case to pay money to veterans who had served in the war with Spain. In its decision the court cited a split in legal doctrine among the states, with some holding that in carrying out political functions a governor is not subject to direction by the court, while others maintained that in the performance of ministerial (that is, administrative) duties a governor could be compelled by the court to act. Coming down on the side of strict construction, the court ruled that the governor of Massachusetts was not accountable to the court for the performance of any part of his official duties.[14]

The argument that dominated the court's thinking was that no clear distinction could be drawn between duties deemed political and those considered ministerial, and that to attempt to draw one would open the door to "an endless train" of litigation. For this reason, and for ease of administration as well, the court ruled that the duties of the executive were not subject to judicial process. Otherwise, in the court's opinion, it would be asserting "a right to make the governor the passive instrument of the judiciary in executing its mandates within the sphere of his own duties."[15]

Subsequently the Massachusetts courts, creeping like a snail, gradually changed course. This resulted in a broader understanding of the separation of powers doctrine not as an abstract maxim of political philosophy but in terms of practical experience.[16] Steven Horowitz and I prepared a memorandum of law for Judge Garrity that emphasized the relaxation of the separation rule over time as the Massachusetts state courts yielded to new circumstances and demonstrated a willingness to share their powers with the legislature—with the expectation, we noted, of reciprocity from the other branches of state government.

A turning point had been reached in 1975. In dealing with an appeal involving a serious injury to a minor in an accident at the University of Massachusetts, the commonwealth's Supreme Judicial Court acknowledged the existence of major issues, notably the state university's claim of sovereign immunity, that could be addressed by either the court or the legislature. In finding against sovereign immunity in the case—*Hannigan v. New Gamma-Delta Chapter of Kappa Sigma Fraternity*—the court chose initially to defer to the legislature, since it believed that that body was better suited to complete the task of changing the law and that it should have a reasonable opportunity to accomplish this by statute. But the court also made clear that if the legislature failed to act, it would: "[I]t is preferable that the Legislature should act to accomplish this necessary change. We shall continue to refrain until the legislature acts, or until events demonstrate that it does not intend to act."[17] Judge Garrity adopted a similar forbearance during the *Quincy* litigation, but he too stressed a willingness to step in and exercise judicial powers in the event of a default by the legislature.

Three years after *Hannigan*, the Supreme Judicial Court hammered the final nail into the coffin regarding the extreme interpretation of the doctrine of separation of powers. In *Blaney v. Commissioner of Correction,* it upheld a lower court's orders to a state official, this time in a sphere that clearly involved official discretion. In mandating changes in the way that prison officials treated protective custody inmates, the court stated outright, "We see no merit in the claim [by the commissioner] that the scope of the judgment intrudes into the executive branch in violation of art[icle] 30 of the Declaration of Rights of the Constitution of the Commonwealth concerning separation of powers." If officials failed to carry out their lawful obligations, the decree made clear, they would risk contempt of court. There are no exclusive provinces, the opinion implied, and the three branches of government are all engaged in tilling the same ground. "Indeed," the court added, in an unconscious invocation of the older language in which this perennial debate has been conducted, "the executive's refusal to obey such judicial orders itself seems to violate art. 30, by abrogating judicial decrees, an exclusively judicial function."[18]

Appropriately enough, the most direct Massachusetts precedent for a more flexible interpretation of the separation of powers was *Perez v. Boston Housing Authority,* an affirmation by the Supreme Judicial Court of an earlier action by Judge Garrity —one that placed the Boston public housing authority into receivership.[19] In that case, public housing tenants brought a class action in district court to vindicate their statutory rights to decent, safe, and sanitary housing. After Garrity, as the trial judge, attempted a number of expedients to guide and compel performance, all of which failed, a comprehensive consent decree was formulated. This also was doomed to failure, owing, as it turned out, to a lack of willing and competent leadership on the part of the authority's board of directors. Finally, as an ultimate recourse after nearly five years of litigation, the judge ordered the appointment of a receiver. This drastic remedial step was the one appealed and upheld. After stating that "it must be confessed with remorse, not unmixed with shame" that the system had failed to find remedies appropriate to restore the housing authority's apartments to the standards of fitness for human habitation prescribed by law, the higher court cited the wisdom of Justice Brandeis: "Courts have (at least in the absence of legislation to the contrary) inherent powers to provide themselves with appropriate instruments required for the performance of their duties."[20]

In its ruling the court rejected directly the housing authority's argument that Judge Garrity's action had violated the separation of powers:

> BHA argues that the judgment herein would offend against the principle of separation of powers which finds expression in Art. 30 of the Declaration of Rights of our Constitution. But if it is a function of the judicial branch to provide remedies for violations of law, including violations committed by the executive branch, then an injunction with that intent does not derogate from the separation principle.

When an executive body "persists in indifference to, or neglect or disobedience" of a court order, the opinion went on—echoing the *Blaney* decision—it is the executive that "could more properly be charged with contemning the separation principle."[21]

In deciding *Perez,* the Supreme Judicial Court had come a long way from John Adams's original pronouncements as well as from its own astringent 1911 decision in *Rice.* Abstract schemes of the powers of government had gradually given way to reality: the court's respect for the responsibilities of the executive and legislative branches was maintained, while at the same time it held in reserve its own power to act in the case of failure by the other branches.[22]

And indeed this development seems inevitable. The so-called separate powers are not fundamentally distinct types—they are three manifestations of one power, that of state sovereignty.[23]

The categories overlap as a factual matter. In practice the doctrine of separation has become an acknowledgment that a government function can usually be carried out more effectively if entrusted to those who devote more or less constant attention to it, rather than an absolute rule stipulating precisely which arm of government alone shall carry out listed functions. Always the realist, Justice Brandeis was right on target: separation of powers "did not make each branch completely autonomous. . . . [I]t left each in some measure dependent upon the others, as it left to each . . . [the] functions in their nature executive, legislative and judicial."[24]

Under this orientation the separation principle assumes a context of mutual reinforcement that makes the work of governing feasible. This interpretation was memorably expressed by Professor Woodrow Wilson before he became president:

> Government is not a machine, but a living thing. It falls not under the theory of the universe, but under the theory of organic life. It is accountable to Darwin, not to Newton. It is modified by its environment, necessitated by its tasks, shaped to its functions by the sheer pressure of life. No living thing can have its organs offset against each other as checks, and live. . . . There can be no successful government without leadership or without the intimate, almost instinctive, coordination of the organs of life and action.[25]

This interdependence, he concluded, requires cooperation and an "amicable community of purposes."[26] As the court eloquently pointed out in *Rice*, the checks and balances of our system of government "were meant to be checks of cooperation, and not of antagonism or mastery."[27] Strong and positive judicial initiative is not excluded, and at crucial points of governmental failure, the coordination of powers calls for judges to intervene.

SEEKING AN "AMICABLE COMMUNITY OF PURPOSES"

Judge Garrity's actions in the Boston Harbor litigation reflect a consistent attitude about the role of the court in entering the political fray to address the complex issues that arise in a world far different from that of John Adams. The realities of a sprawling metropolitan region strained the machinery of the legal system no less than they overwhelmed the broken-down facilities of an antiquated water and sewer system. Rather than retreating to an isolationist posture of making a ruling but offering no guidance, or dictating from on high a set of remedies in *Quincy*, the judge was determined to engage in a constitutional dialogue, to use the court's powers to persuade the political branches of government finally to address the problem of the pollution of Boston's treasured harbor. Since action was required, pointing out the need for performance by putting politicians' feet to the fire was a legitimate judicial function; the specific form and the means adopted to modernize the law and meet this vital interest of the community, however, were for the legislature to decide.

In cases where proceedings to solve formidable problems for the greater good may threaten entrenched and vociferous interest groups, the court can act as an insulating shield, providing cover for the other branches. In the *Quincy* case, blame for the inevitable increases in sewer fees could be placed on the court (and the new agency), rather than the legislature and governor. In this way judges can enforce accountability on elected officials without causing them to lose face or, more importantly, elections. In the *Quincy* litigation, Judge Garrity sought to use the court's powers to leverage the political branches into solving the problem themselves, rather than unilaterally imposing a resolution. And his unique approach, including the use of a special master to facilitate negotiations between the parties, allowed him to do so without pitting one force against another or threatening the independence of legislative and executive officials, although he did, of course, turn to the media to influence public opinion and exert pressure for action.

When one branch of government fails to discharge its responsibilities or to carry out its duties as intended—as was the situation in Boston with the legislature's and the MDC's inability to move against the pollution of the harbor—the need to act falls upon the others. But confrontation alone may lead to further deadlock. This was a central concern of the court. The "Quotation of the Day" in the *Boston Globe* on December 12, 1984, was a comment of mine on the harbor bill: "It's time we stopped fighting each other and started fighting pollution."[28] "What happens in lawsuits," as MDC Commissioner William Geary had noted the week before, "is that parties focus on liability, not on how we work together to clean up the harbor. It degenerates into squabbling rather than the spirit of cooperation that is essential if we are to clean up the harbor."[29]

In *Quincy*, William Golden and Peter Koff, the plaintiff's attorneys, went to court to alter a legislative regime already in place and to recast the existing strategy for treatment of the harbor. Judge Garrity seized the opportunity to capitalize on the newfound spirit of cooperation evoked by the way in which the special master's report was presented and received, for even in Massachusetts positive legislative-court interaction is not the rare event it is sometimes claimed to be. The need to stir the other branches of government in order to break the gridlock over a controversial issue was a logical justification for Judge Garrity's actions in *Quincy,* and the successful outcome vindicated them.

In the end, I would argue, the narrow traditional interpretations of separation of powers does more to obscure than to illuminate how judges make decisions—not to speak of how they *should* make them. The old theory argued for passivity in policy and direction and the worship of rigid procedures over the goals and results that might legitimately be sought. To enable government to discharge its responsibility to the general public in complicated matters, such as overcoming the pollution of a harbor, requires not a segregation of powers but collaboration among various branches of government, each exercising its separate powers but not in blind isolation. The task of governing demands the cooperation of all three branches; to what avail, then, is an excessive concern with the drawing of boundaries, either in theory or in practice? The judge's role is a difficult one that obliges courts to operate as a safety valve when existing pressures on the other branches of government produce political paralysis. In such instances judicial action that recognizes the interpenetration of the powers of government becomes a conscientious duty, even at the risk that the court will become a target of criticism.[30]

But a specific question remains: Just when should a court feel comfortable about breaching the boundaries (assuming they are fixed, if only temporarily) that separate the sovereign powers of government? I believe that courts are obliged to intervene—even to force the reordering of major social institutions or, more frequently and certainly less controversially, to exert their influence to initiate legislative or executive action—when another branch of government is systematically delinquent in discharging constitutional obligations or in carrying out the popular will, as expressed in legislation, and the result is an ongoing wrongful practice. Difficult as it is to imagine a standardized method for dealing with the unanticipated situations that will inevitably emerge in the future, we can look to the past for a few guidelines as to the applicability of the separation of powers doctrine in modern society, and how each of the grand departments should be protected against encroachment.

A workable standard for judicial intervention in an institutional restructuring case would require that the court first find:

- the breaking of the law by the government;
- evidence of illegality that is not isolated but systematic, indicating a persistent pattern of lawbreaking over time;
- that this illegality is entrenched and will continue into the future—and that the executive and legislative branches of the state are unwilling or incapable of correcting the situation; and
- that this illegality has a detrimental impact on the legal interests or constitutional rights of a large number of persons.[31]

Such a framework would enhance the court's ability to serve the public interest in the contemporary world, especially in situations that require change with minimal interference with democratic choice. The new arena of modern society calls for a full deployment of forces by the court to implement remedies when the democratic machinery of the other two branches, like the MDC machinery of pollution control, breaks down.

THE CALL OF THE BUGLER

15

Tools and Tactics of Effective Judicial Intervention

It is the function of our courts to keep the doctrines up to date with the mores by continual restatement and by giving them a continually new content. This is judicial legislation, and the judge legislates at his peril. Nevertheless, it is the necessity and duty of such legislation that gives to judicial office its highest honor; and no brave and honest judge shirks the duty or fears the peril.

—Arthur L. Corbin

When citizens appeal to a court for relief from government's systemic wrongdoing or failure to act, that court has no choice but to intervene. Its constitutionally mandated task takes on added urgency in litigation that targets persistent institutional breakdown, because in such cases the judiciary is, as a general rule, the only branch of government willing and able to lead the effort to right a public wrong. Success in these efforts is usually a function of the court's ability to break stubborn political stalemates, and this chapter will analyze some of the means and mechanisms available to the judge for this purpose. These instruments were battle-tested in the Boston Harbor litigation and earlier cases. Some of them extend the ambit of judicial action into new realms; I believe this is cause for celebration, not apology.

INSTITUTIONAL REFORM LITIGATION AND JUDICIAL STRATEGY

How can the power of the equity court in the *Quincy* litigation to intervene so sharply in political issues be reconciled with Alexander Hamilton's designation of the courts as being "the least dangerous" branch of government? As Hamilton pointed out in terms that have been reemphasized ever since, courts lack the prerogative of the sword or of the purse and may truly be described as having "neither FORCE nor WILL, but merely judgment" and thus are "least in a capacity to annoy or injure."[1] Within the world of constitutional scholarship, Hamilton's statement is taken as both a description and a prescription, a warning to the third branch to be keenly aware of the limited scope of its powers to effect social change. "We, the People" must ultimately rule according to majoritarian values—including a refusal to act where others would have us tread—without interference from elite officials sitting on the bench. Yet if Hamilton's formulation still has resonance, it hardly applies either as an accurate description of the Boston Harbor experience or as an adequate prescription to judges in institutional reform cases beset by complex forces and competing views.

In the *Quincy* dispute the continued inaction of the legislative and executive branches reflected their inability under the existing political structure to cope with the increasing pollution of Boston Harbor, and the plaintiff turned to the judiciary as the only state institution that could break the deadlock. Moreover, in this particular case, while Paul Garrity's life tenure on the bench immunized him from the tugs of war of the political process, he was well versed in the role politics plays in implementing governmental decisions. Nor is this rare, since many if not most state court judges are initially political appointees drawn from the ranks of politically active lawyers. In the face of the legislative stalemate and the executive branch's failure to manage the area's sewage disposal in a way that would safeguard the harbor, Judge Garrity, like many other trial judges, was fully equipped to gauge the political atmosphere and act forcefully to make the state come to grips with the problem.

In situations requiring the fundamental restructuring of public institutions, the main judicial task is to shape a workable remedy that looks to the future rather than to the past. Unlike classic trial procedure, which concentrates on assigning liability and recompense for previous actions, remedies in institutional reform situations bear the more problematic burden of anticipating the future with all its uncertainties. In fashioning equitable relief for an institutional breakdown, a court should operate with awareness of contemporary situations and needs, and devise broad-gauged remedies. It is this wide-ranging remedial approach of the *Quincy* decree that jars the conventional model of adjudication and prompts scowls from traditionalists.

Ordinarily, the term *litigation* evokes a picture of an adversarial process involving two parties locked in combat before an impartial body that has the power to decide between their competing claims. A long history of jurisprudence dictates that established procedures be followed in order to assure society at large (as well as the immediate parties) of the fairness of the proceedings; a collective evolutionary wisdom warns, for instance, that evidence not introduced as part of the record should not be considered in the court's decision-making process and that matters not subjected to testing by cross-examination should be excluded. But the task of correcting a continuous pattern of wrongdoing or a government agency's failure to act properly, as in the Boston Harbor case, shifts the center of gravity. It necessitates a different perspective on how the debate should be conducted and how the judge should conduct the proceedings. In short, the adversarial process model just does not work when extended to the remedial phase of institutional reform litigation.

Thoughtful scholarship abounds about—indeed, is dominated by—the need for judicial restraint.[2] Yet the history of the *Quincy* litigation, including the court's invention of the procedural order as a means for coping with the remarkable scale and intricacies of metropolitan governance, makes a powerful case for the opposite course: judicial action as a positive and indispensable element within the balance wheel of government whenever official actions repeatedly violate the law and fail to meet societal needs. The actions of the *Quincy* court represent the evolution of novel judicial methods, a set of trial tactics adapted to meet the needs of a major metropolitan area. The use of ex parte investigation, trained experts, the broad discretion conferred upon the special master within guidelines laid down by the judge, and other experimental approaches taken to clarify and expedite the issues before the court—all of these adaptations of procedure represent problem-solving devices for a modern regional community.

The harbor case vividly illustrates that in complex public litigation the court's principal burden is not to parse procedural niceties but to absorb and analyze vast bodies of specialized data and to weigh technical necessities against political realities. *Quincy* itself ventured so far from conventional litigation that it concluded without an explicit finding of liability. Only the most doctrinaire proceduralist would judge it a failure for that reason.

The judicial tools discussed here are useful, even indispensable, in the war against institutional inertia. Tactics and timing matter, too. Especially at the outset of litigation, swift and effective judicial action establishes the court's authority and puts the contending parties on notice that they are expected to produce results. Without such action the parties feel free to continue temporizing as political momentum fades and public cynicism spreads.

JUDICIAL TOOLS AND TACTICS FOR OVERCOMING DEADLOCK

Speeding Up the Process

Experience teaches that chronic governmental deadlocks yield only to rapid and decisive action. They are impervious to more gradual measures, and besides, by the time a case of *Quincy*'s magnitude reaches the courts, public patience has, by definition, been sorely tried.

To quicken the normally glacial pace of institutional reform, the court can frame its rulings as challenges to itself and the other branches of government for expeditious action. Such a ruling came right at the outset of *Quincy*, when Judge Garrity set a thirty-day deadline on the submission of the special master's report. Throughout the litigation the judge employed an urgent tone that moved matters along, although it elicited the disapproval of observers accustomed to incremental methods for fashioning judicial remedies, in which sanctions are added, slice by slice, only after earlier and lighter remedies have proved ineffective.

The gradualist approach comports with the findings of eminent scholars in related fields, notably Robert Dahl and Charles Lindblom; they argue that for instituting social change a succession of small steps is preferable to a running leap.[3] Such incrementalism, however, has proven an inadequate response to catastrophes that are themselves the result of incremental societal changes, whether environmental or social. And when an opportunity presents itself to focus public attention on pressing but long-ignored issues, judicial diffidence can look much like dereliction.

It is difficult to overstate how much depends on the signals broadcast by the judge assigned to a case. The epoch-making *Mount Laurel* affordable housing cases demonstrated the need, especially on the local level, for speed and decisiveness. In his precedent-breaking opinion, Justice Frederick Hall of the New Jersey Supreme Court rejected traditional deference to municipal exclusionary zoning. But he chose not to proceed to an immediate remedy, thinking it desirable to leave it to the locality to work itself pure, inch by inch. The result? Six years of inaction in the supply of affordable housing in the New Jersey suburbs. The state supreme court's patience was taken by the localities as a sign that the justices did not really mean business. Not until the second *Mount Laurel* opinion, with its vigorous statement of the court's vision for the metropolitan future—backed by specific procedures designed to hasten the development process—was affordable housing built.[4] As Judge Garrity likewise learned from the *Perez* case in Boston, while due process is requisite before dropping the guillotine, action, once resorted to, must be rapid.

When speed is of the essence, judges must be prepared to trim their tolerance for the customary delays of the judicial process—the endless, endlessly-argued motions, the lobbing of requests for discovery, the posing of interrogatories, and all the rest of the zealous litigator's tactical arsenal. One useful technique for expediting matters is the trial by affidavit. Moreover, direct intervention by the judge, most especially when the exploration is of expert testimony, can quicken the tempo without sacrifice of fairness. By taking this course in *Quincy*, the court was able to gather evidence at an accelerated pace.

The very complexity of a case such as *Quincy* affords a rich store of judicial levers. When the legislature chose to recess rather than take up the Massachusetts Water Resources Authority enabling legislation, the court countered almost instantly with a moratorium on sewer hookups and a hearing on receivership. An advantage of such sanctions is that they are temporary and can be terminated quickly, which helps the court retain public sympathy and makes it easier for the contending parties to accept judicial supervision. But even in the face of criticism and hard feelings, judges need the fortitude to act quickly and decisively, both to project the necessary authority and to give their remedial programs a chance at life.

Absorbing Technical Knowledge

Among the tactics that emerged in the *Quincy* litigation, one in particular is transferable to other institutional breakdown cases—the court's mechanism for the effective interaction of lawyers with scientists, engineers, and other professionals. Its chief tools in this undertaking: the special master and the independent experts. The court's successful cooperation with professionals who had spent decades studying the vagaries of Boston Harbor challenges those critics who argue that the judiciary is incapable of gathering and analyzing technical data or, for that matter, absorbing the contributions of other disciplines.

With liberal resort to the office of the special master and its own appointed experts, the court proved itself capable of dealing with the most recondite material: population and engineering projections, assessments of the benthic and marine environments, the pros and cons of assorted sludge treatments, and even the organizational and financial structures of several intertwined agencies. When the court drafted the procedural order, it took into account the managerial challenge of setting up a new sewer and water agency, and suggested administrative and financial structures with careful attention to the seemingly paradoxical demand that the new authority be both independent and accountable. Advisers from financial service organizations helped anticipate and overcome potential financing obstacles and navigate the often treacherous currents of the credit markets. With the close cooperation of experts, the court proved itself capable of planning and executing extensive institutional restructuring.

Finding Common Purpose

Note a key word, "cooperation." In a complicated situation that calls for sensitivity to local feelings and to fears of perceived outside meddling, peremptory commands from the bench are counterproductive. The *Quincy* court recognized this axiom with its frequent assertions that it was neither willing nor able to indulge in judicial micromanagement, leaving the details of compliance with its decree to the defendants and the executive and legislative branches of government. The court's task, as Judge Garrity formulated it, was to prescribe performance standards, present options, and goad to action those who had previously failed to accomplish the tasks confronting them. He did not fix blame, but he was relentless toward anyone who hindered a resolution.

A general rule of complex public litigations, then, is that judicial autocracy must yield to cooperation under the leadership of the court. Correcting systemic wrongful or ineffectual governmental conduct requires the participation, however recalcitrant and forced it may be, of the government officials being prodded. Self-correction is key: the whole enterprise has a better chance of success if each of the parties can be persuaded—defendants no less than plaintiffs—that they have a stake in the desired result and a voice in reaching it. It is the judge's task to guide the parties to that understanding.

Alertness to Details

Once the court's jurisdiction is invoked and it takes charge of the proceedings, generalities do not suffice. First principles stated alone smack of a hortatory sermon. What is needed are strategies for implementation: extensive, situational programs for correction—details, in short.

Judge Garrity took painstaking care in reviewing the remedies ordered; he conducted what in effect were joint drafting sessions with the parties' lawyers. The phrasing of the procedural order meticulously set forth, one by one, the standards and outcomes for combined sewer overflow remediation, sludge treatment, toxics reduction, and other aspects of the overhaul of the Metropolitan District Commission system. The judge insisted that the commission establish time schedules and milestones for each and every phase of the cleanup, though carefully reserving to the agency administrators the responsibility for determining methods.

The Archimedean Lever

One overarching consideration: if intervention is to prove successful, the court needs to augment its powers, which, as Hamilton pointed out long ago, are otherwise feeble compared to those of the legislative and executive branches. In *Quincy*, the court recognized from the outset that it would need political or economic levers in order to rouse the establishment to action after so many years of paralysis. A moratorium on all office and hotel development in the city designed to prompt developers and lenders into pressuring the legislature to act—as well as the threat of receivership of the MDC—suited this purpose admirably. Judge Garrity's past actions in *Perez* showed that receivership was a tool he was prepared to use. His readiness to issue a revised moratorium, after the unexpected reversal of the first one by Justice Joseph Nolan, revealed a determination and tactical resourcefulness without which the MWRA would not have been brought to life.

The moratorium in *Quincy* inspired the private sector to join in the campaign for creating the MWRA. Similarly, the *Mount Laurel* court in New Jersey found its own strategic lever: in order to break down barriers to low-income families seeking homes in the suburbs, the New Jersey court's Builder's Remedy made certain that the builder who won an exclusionary zoning case would be the one to receive the permit to develop. Engaging the energy of the private sector made possible the implementation of the *Mount Laurel* doctrine of inclusionary housing. Marry the private profit motive with the public interest and the couple becomes irresistible.

The Use of a Special Master

The extensive use of a special master was a striking feature of the *Quincy* litigation. The special master has been an adjunct to the equity courts since the time of Henry VIII. Its role was characterized by Justice Brandeis as an "instrument for the administration of justice." In effect, the special master enables the court to complement adjudication with mediation, the formal with the improvised, standard practice with flexibility. The fact-finding, synthesizing, mediating, and remedy-shaping activities of the special master in the Boston Harbor case illustrate the potential benefits of using this instrument in institutional breakdown cases, although along with those benefits come dangers of wandering too far afield. Before designing a remedy, a court must have before it an adequate factual record. In complex cases involving major institutions and controversial social issues, however, the typical judge has neither the time nor the expertise to carry out a thorough investigation. This is a job better suited to a special master, an individual with relevant experience appointed by the court to work full-time to assemble information and clarify the issues at hand.[5] It may produce unanticipated rewards. For example, in an earlier Boston school finance case in which I served as master, our "discovery" of $9.4 million squirreled away in the footnotes of the city budget allowed the public schools to avoid a shutdown and remain open until the end of the academic year.[6]

In *Quincy*, seeking out the facts about the environmental degradation of Boston Harbor, soliciting the (at times conflicting) opinions of multiple experts, and investigating the actions of the numerous public agencies charged with building and running the sewerage system comprised a series of tasks almost unthinkable for a busy judge with an overcrowded docket. Steven Horowitz and I, unlike the judge, were able to work on the problem full-time. Drawing on the accumulated knowledge of scientists, engineering firms, and government agencies, we were able to present the court with contending approaches and ideas that could be tested and explored at trial.[7]

But Judge Garrity, as we knew well, would not be the only reader of our report. Before the findings were published, the magnitude of the harbor's pollution problem was not fully understood by the public or the legislature. The evidence had been mostly anecdotal—excrement seen floating on the waves, the poisoning of a youngster by contaminated clams. The report's comprehensive overview of the condition of the harbor, bearing the stamp of experts, helped to educate the public and capture the attention of the legislators.

Ex Parte Communications and the Special Master
The public good is best served by a judge who recognizes that an environmental crisis is far from the classic winner-take-all courtroom conflict. To different situations belong different processes. One such unconventional process is the ex parte communication. Productive discussions can go on behind the scenes—attorneys and officials can dispense with public posturing and argue frankly over specific issues; opposing experts can clarify and reconcile their differences. If the court permits and the parties agree, the special master can meet privately with any of them unconstrained by courtroom formality, and the special master's office can serve as a sounding board for various theories and remedies or act as mediator between parties whose lines of communication have broken down. In this spirit, the parties to *Quincy* were able to float proposals for improving Boston Harbor—and in most cases, discard them—without generating the sort of public controversy that leads to wasted time and intransigence.

This was in sharp contrast to the earlier Boston school finance case. As the parties' contending interests deepened, the mayor and the city council traded harsh insults. The council sought to exact the last ounce of political flesh from Boston Mayor Kevin White by loading up the legislation needed to solve the school finance problem with restraints on the chief executive's power. The mayor, for his part, refused to accept increases in the council's budgetary power. As for the third party, the school committee, all sides sought to strip it of many of its elaborate powers, while it insisted on a fiscal autonomy not enjoyed by any other school committee in the commonwealth. Animosities were vented in public, with the mayor designating the council as "a goddamned disgrace." The compliment was returned in kind: if anyone but the mayor had done what he had, one council member opined, "he would be in prison." This was mild compared to other epithets for the mayor emanating from the council: "unsound," a "birdbrain," a "mental case." "This man," shouted one member in a council meeting, "will not finish his term. He'll either quit, be indicted, or somebody'll kill him."

While no such depths were reached in *Quincy,* when discussions grew heated, as often happened, the master could provide an outlet for venting frustrations and anger. This helped cool down the adversarial heat. Everyone involved was able to speak forthrightly—and even discuss possible concessions that could later be withdrawn without penalty. Support for the formation of the MWRA on the part of officials of existing government agencies came out of such interchanges.

What emerged from the ex parte process was a sort of two-level negotiation. The parties postured for the media, then retreated to the special master's office to haggle and horse-trade. This umpiring accommodated the political need for public poses without allowing them to poison the proceedings. It led to agreements on the timing and extent of rehabilitation under the procedural order.

While some participants feel uncomfortable with the directness and freewheeling character of this kind of mediation, the elimination of the judicial filter and the absence of the sometimes awesome figure of the judge are actually conducive to effective problem-solving. In *Quincy,* for example, the consensus among all the parties was that some remedial program ought to be adopted to begin the restoration of the harbor, but the state defendants did not want to be forced to take action, or be subject to contempt powers should they fail to act. Behind the scenes, ex parte discussions with the special master allowed them to use the litigation process to create the MWRA while gaining political credit for being among the "good guys."

The ex parte discussions in *Quincy* led to what I believe was a triumphant outcome, but this approach still leaves open tantalizing questions, such as the proper balance of personal due process rights and judicial efficiency. Did the informality of the arrangement compromise any party's rights to due process of the law? It is hard to know. I assuredly struggled with the issue. As a strategic matter it was important to be up-front with all the defendants and secure their agreement ahead of time, and to put on the record their assent to the procedure.[8] Moreover, for findings of fact, the special master's report relied only on evidence officially submitted for the record; all other conversations were used simply to gather background information and advance an understanding of the issues.

But can we compartmentalize our thinking in this way? Can our minds draw such boundaries between gathering information and reaching conclusions? We combed the record for testimony and evidence submitted formally to the court because we wanted to ensure that the special master's findings of fact were buttressed by the record. But even where on-the-record evidence supported a finding that, for instance, Moon Island effluent could not have flowed from the north and fouled Wollaston Beach, it is conceivable that the original impetus for that finding came from an off-the-record conversation.

Yet our findings of fact were not legally unacceptable simply because we solicited expert opinions before publishing them. Ex parte data may stretch boundaries of procedure, but influences beyond the evidence and testimony formally set before the court are at work in ordinary litigation too. Trial judges look at the expression on the face of a witness, for instance, or a deponent's dress or manner of speech—and these influence the court's findings of fact even though they are not "record evidence." In the end the finder of fact is always asked to make judgments. In cases such as *Quincy* there is an immense body of knowledge to absorb and, as a purely practical matter, ex parte contacts may be the best way to acquire it. Indeed, it is often the only way people will tell you what they really think.

Ambiguity

The special master's admittedly ambiguous position allows him to serve as a liaison to the court while at the same time insulating it to a certain extent from pressures and criticisms.[9] Concerned actors who are not a party to the case, such as legislators and business and community leaders, can initiate contact with the special master without raising the questions of propriety that would follow an approach to the judge.

In this capacity the special master can serve as a channel for views that extend beyond the immediate matter at hand. In *Quincy,* for instance, the differing concerns of the water-rich western part of the state, although not directly involved in the action, could be taken into account. And the city of Winthrop, home to the Deer Island treatment plant, which had not participated in the legal proceedings, was added later on as an official plaintiff. Such new developments need not await the convening of a court session or an opening on the judge's docket. The special master's quick response to the sudden give-and-take moments that occur sporadically in the course of long negotiations can allow the court to maintain its official distance, yet get things done.

Finally, the special master is a useful instrument for monitoring remedies. This was especially relevant with regard to the novel procedural order in which almost nothing was binding and the defendants retained all their options. The use of a monitor to cajole and nudge keeps the interests of the court and the public alive as the private dispute is worked out, while also protecting the judge's position as an impartial arbiter. Ultimately, this left time for solutions to grow and ripen, in this instance the creation of the MWRA.

The Larger Perspective

Thus did *Quincy* differ sharply from ordinary adversarial proceedings. By itself the city of Quincy could not have proposed a sweeping remedy for its complaint: the cleansing of Quincy Bay depended on a rehabilitation of the harbor as a whole and the creation of a new institutional structure for handling the treatment of metropolitan wastewater. Devising the remedy required a knowledge not only of pertinent scientific data but also of the workings of national financial markets, of the methodology of billing and collecting sewer charges, and of the political history and internecine relationships among bureaucracies. So multifarious an undertaking demanded a different judicial apparatus improvised by the court, supported by expert advisers and ex parte communication, and orchestrated through a master.

This returns us to the master's role as the advocate for a larger perspective in cases involving the public interest. A major restructuring of the whole metropolitan water and sewage treatment system went beyond any of the proposals put forward by either the plaintiff or the defendants, although the process revealed the need for a modern, independent authority. Nonetheless, the court's frequently stated belief that a solution to the crisis was within reach, provided that the administration and the legislature would but act, aroused public opinion. The outlines of a possible state authority were made public and came to the attention of the press. The special master's assurances that a sound financial plan could be devised for the new authority helped marshal public support.

And the trial court's willingness to impose sanctions, should there be a failure of action, intensified pressure on the political branches of government. By December of 1984, a shocked public, alerted by the comments of the judge, saw the MDC edging toward judicial receivership, a casualty of political brinkmanship. The resulting outcry finally convinced the governor and the legislature to resolve the crisis underlying *Quincy*.

Professional Expertise

The legal maxim that "general propositions do not solve particular cases" has special relevance for institutional reform litigation. Because of the complexity of the issues these cases present, the trial court must be flexible enough to adapt its methods, including its central task of assessing the facts, to the character of the problem it is confronting. A growing body of experience indicates that in such cases a court should not proceed except with the help of professional experts.[10] This raises questions related to the ex parte problem: How should a special master and court-appointed experts communicate with the judge and the parties involved in the litigation? How can the uncertainty of scientific research and the prejudices of experts be taken into account when evaluating their judgments? What is the countervailing check against the undue influence of the special master? Although legitimate concerns underlie such questions, a judge must have access to the skills, knowledge, and level of analysis regarding technical matters that someone trained only as a lawyer cannot be expected to possess.[11] This is why I argue that resort to special masters and to court-appointed experts should be allowed as a matter of course. The use of a wide range of professionals in *Quincy* is instructive for the effective management of future cases that involve technically and politically complex interdisciplinary issues.

Effective incorporation of technical information into court proceedings requires education on many fronts. The judge and the special master must be able to work together to tap and coordinate the expertise that different professions can bring to a problem. The lawyers from both sides should participate in the process of learning and incorporating the insights from other disciplines. Likewise, scientific experts must learn how to target their analyses to the needs of the court. Such interplay opens possibilities for constructive action by the judiciary—avenues that should no longer be closed off by cries for adherence to "separation of powers" and traditional views of judicial comportment and competence.

Furthermore—and this became clearer as the Boston Harbor case evolved—the extensive use of experts lends credibility to the judge's decisions. It encourages acceptance of the court's recommendations by the parties to the litigation, by other stakeholders, and by the public at large. This was certainly true in another state court experience, the *Mount Laurel* litigation, where the expertise of city planners designated as masters enhanced the legitimacy of the court's work.[12]

Abuse of Discretion

Like the ex parte proceedings upon which the court relied, the use of a special master has drawn its share of critics. Rule 53 of the Federal Rules of Civil Procedure, like its equivalents in state rules, permits the appointment of special masters only rarely. Some commentators call for standards that can clearly (or even fuzzily) set out the extent of the special master's discretion; proposals have been drafted, including a new federal rule of civil procedure, that would circumscribe the powers bestowed. One critic from this camp notes sharply that Judge Garrity's "deferral comes perilously close to an abdication of the judicial process in favor of the special master."[13]

This is a natural reaction by lawyers and law professors, who constantly strive to set clear criteria for governmental actions in order to put limits on the abuse of power. The troublesome factor—to all observers—is that the exercise of discretion brings along with it possible misuse. But, I submit, the movement for rigid standards to govern the relationship between judge and special master is shortsighted. Institutional breakdown cases are complex and nonuniform, and the choice of a special master must be a highly individualized one. The collaboration between judge and special master should not be subject to fiat or decree except at its outer limits. It is a personal association requiring feelings of mutual trust and respect.[14]

In the ordinary course of things, important limits exist. Binding decisions are made only by the court itself. The extensive findings of fact in the Boston Harbor case were subject to Judge Garrity's ongoing critical evaluation and his acceptance or rejection of them on the basis of his judgment. A special master's findings and recommendations are no more than advice to the judge, and as such can be freely disregarded. They can also be contested in public hearings and upon appeal. The subjective realization of the special master is that he is an officer of the court and remains an instrument to assist the court's judgment. As in all civil litigation, in institutional reform cases society relies ultimately on the character of the judge.

The special master occupies a crucial middle ground between the political realm, with its internecine struggles and its self-interested bargains, and the neutral realm of the judge. As fact-finder, the special master may assemble the complex information necessary to establish the baselines from which the parties can negotiate. In addition, the special master is informally available to the parties, helping to articulate their demands and desires and if necessary suggesting reformulations in order to achieve compromise. As a conduit for communication, the special master is available to the media and can provide public explanations for the court's actions. The special master also can ensure that communities and interests not directly represented in the lawsuit are heard.

Paradoxical as it may sound, the use of a special master may mean that the court itself will interfere less, not more, in administration and the political process. In *Quincy,* I could talk to the

MDC staff members themselves, not just the agency's lawyers and official spokespersons, to discover the concerns of high-level executives, supervisors, and the rank and file. And I could consult with the state's legislators and executive officials as to the advisability of forming the new authority, the powers and resources it would require, and how it could best be structured to achieve the ultimate goal of regenerating the harbor. In this way the court was able to gather crucial information and exert its influence, while staying within manageable limits and avoiding unnecessary confrontations.

To be sure, the court's resort to pressure on the governor and legislature provoked complaints of an imperial judiciary. But the court did not directly intervene in the business of the governor and the legislature; it merely pointed toward a remedy and fixed a price for ignoring it. The court's aim was to advance collaboration among the parties—thereby increasing their control over the outcome. And it took much of the political heat off the parties, allowing more room for them to act. In essence, Judge Garrity threatened to strip the parties of authority to devise a solution of their own and then gave them an opportunity to devise one. It worked, and everyone won.

THE COURT, THE MEDIA, AND THE PUBLIC

Intelligent reporting and editorial support were instrumental in thrusting the pollution of Boston Harbor to the forefront of the political debate in Massachusetts and making it impossible for politicians to avoid the issue. The media stirred public outrage and channeled it into pressure for the legislation that brought the MWRA into being. One lesson of *Quincy,* therefore, is that judges, too, need a media strategy.

As historically formulated, the canon of judicial ethics limits the presentation of the judge's views to the written opinion handed down at the end of a case. Up to that point, a judge "should abstain from public comment."[15] I would argue, however, that with regard to cases with such major implications for society at large this view is outdated. Recognizing the special nature of institutional reform litigation, the judge should be willing to engage in what is in effect a community education program.[16] In the *Quincy* case, a public consensus had to be developed on the need to rehabilitate the harbor. This was a task well suited to Judge Garrity's personality and experience. He moved between traditional judicial argument, including the use of precedents and standard techniques of statutory interpretation, and the emerging conception of litigation as judicial power exerted to bring about institutional and societal change. He was ready to engage in dialogue and released the special master to do the same, so that the reasoning behind various motions and special rulings, the lengthy and comprehensive procedural order in particular, could be explained in a way that might reach the average citizen outside the courtroom.

The imperative to educate the public collides with the reluctance of many judges to appear in the public eye. To cite a typical instance, the three trial judges selected by the New Jersey Supreme Court after *Mount Laurel II* to administer litigation relating to affordable housing were disinclined to deal with, even to respond to, the media. Although earlier in their careers, in their incarnation as lawyers, they were involved in politics, as a group they recoiled from the steamy cauldron of the political process. "We cannot be seen as salespeople for our products," was the rebuff of one judge. Another of the three confessed later to a sense of missed opportunity: "Every judge has a responsibility to try to convince the listener, the public, of the rightness of what's going on. . . . Because we are educated in the field, we can't simply say, 'Oh, well, we understand what the judge's role is,' and be complacent about that."[17]

Judge Garrity's use of the media to call attention to the state defendants' inaction during the remedial phase of the *Quincy* litigation certainly discouraged complacency and foot-dragging.

And earlier the special master's hearings generated public pressure by inviting representatives of the press and television to accompany inspection tours of Deer Island and Moon Island. This created visual witness to the repulsive piles of sludge pouring untreated into the harbor, an image that exerted a powerful influence on reporters, viewers, and readers.

This power can be and has been misused. There is a discernible difference, however, between using such an opportunity as part of a larger educational mission and staging a sound-bite event designed to exploit public feeling.

As part of an educational effort, press briefings, formal or spontaneous, that explain legal terms and concepts, unfamiliar motions, or fresh developments can be quite helpful; one-on-one explanations to reporters are well worth the judge's or special master's time. Care must be taken, of course, to avoid inappropriate comments that might jeopardize a ruling on appeal. But newspapers report events to the public, and if a reporter is told enough to understand the legal intricacies of a case, then the ensuing article will present a more accurate picture of the court's actions. A well-informed press functions not only to report but also as a critical watchdog, providing its own evaluation of issues and events, thereby bringing about a higher level of public comprehension. If a belief in the law and faith in our constitutional system are to be sustained, ordinary citizens must understand the working of the court and be able to conclude that it is operating fairly and in the public interest.[18]

Sitting down with the editorial boards of newspapers is yet another way to help ensure a balanced exposition of public issues. This adaptation of tradition may be a questionable action for a judge, but it is less so for a special master. When I met with the editors of the *Boston Globe* on several occasions, I could answer their questions directly, keeping in mind Judge Garrity's admonition to describe and explain while refraining from evaluating, and without leaking confidences or discussing personalities.

Dialogue may not win over hearts and minds, but it can surely lead to an appreciation of the rationale behind the actions of the court. The underlying reality is that in a case involving institutional breakdown, a court order does differ from ordinary adjudication. A court's decision alone is highly effective when imposed on parties to a private litigation, but when the court seeks to propel an entire state to a greater awareness of its obligations, public communication is crucial. Further judicial reasoning and exposition—both within and beyond the written opinion that accompanies a decree—is necessary where the case involves extensive institutional change and large financial investments. In environmental and other civil litigations that draw wide public attention, the newsroom can serve as an auxiliary forum to the courtroom.

This can be tricky. In the Boston Harbor case, explanations of the social purposes behind the actions undertaken by the court were carefully advanced in brief public statements by Judge Garrity himself, and in more detail by myself and Deputy Master Steven Horowitz in many public forums. In addition, although it is rare that a court-appointed official will testify before a state legislative committee, in the summer of 1984—with one bill to authorize the creation of a new authority before the Senate and another under consideration in the House—I did so at the behest of several legislators. In response to a question put by a member of the joint committee, I emphasized that since it was the legislature's task to repair the breaches in administrative dikes that led to the pollution of Boston Harbor, the determination of the form a new authority might take was its prerogative. While the court would not flinch from imposing drastic measures if needed to remedy lawbreaking, it was the primary responsibility of the legislative branch to act, as it thought most desirable, to rehabilitate the harbor. The court was not telling the legislature how to act, but was insisting that the legislature must act—and consistently with its previous commitment under state law to provide a decent sewerage system.

This raises further issues on another side of the question. A court is not supposed to be swayed or deterred by what the political barometer shows to be the prevailing sentiment. "Enforcement of rights cannot await a supporting political consensus," as Chief Justice Robert N. Wilentz of the New Jersey Supreme Court declared in the sensitive *Mount Laurel* affordable housing cases. However, in institutional cases where political action is necessary, the court must try to make its work understandable to the public on whose behalf it is exercising judicial power. Reticence is unlikely to suffice: the court's cupboard of traditional actions, primarily the written opinion, seems rather bare for this purpose. Only by acknowledging the difficulties encountered by the diverse groups with a stake in the outcome, clearly stating the motives and reasoning behind its actions, and presenting an explanation of why other options were rejected can a court hope to achieve a consensus and a genuine resolution in complex litigations. The court must actively lead, publicly as well as in the courtroom.

This posture, it may be argued, places the court in an undesirable, and unwinnable, competition for power or popularity. But the situation in institutional reform litigation may be better described as one of a vacuum of power. In enforcing the statutory norms relevant to the Boston Harbor case, the court became subject to the same tests of the public arena, the same contending swirl of interests and ideas, that affect the actions of other sectors of the government. The court, in such situations, must acknowledge that the media today provide the forum in which those who have economic or political power, not excluding the court itself, are rendered visible and accountable to the people.

With the benefit of hindsight, it is undeniable that the media played a crucial role in helping the court gather the necessary public support in *Quincy*. Nevertheless, as a prescriptive matter, the question of whether the court should resort to the media in order to influence public opinion—and by what means and how often it should be permitted to do so—is a difficult one. One danger is that the court will render itself irrelevant by conforming to the traditional mold of a silent and reactive judiciary; neither, however, can the court afford to ignore the potential of political backlash from being regarded as too proactive. If, at the end of the day, sufficient public support for a proposed reform remedy is not aroused, there is a risk that the public will perceive the court as unduly interfering.

This is a difficult balance to achieve. But as a general principle, in a clear case of a power vacuum and a deadlock in the democratic process, the court should not allow an excess of caution to immobilize it when compelling societal interests are at stake, and so hinder its ability to do what is right for the long-term public good.

All of this suggests that a successful outcome to complex public litigation requires a judge willing to wield the power of the court in the public interest. The prosecution of claims that turned out, under Judge Garrity's guidance, to be judicially enforceable rights finally led legislators to treat the environmental degradation of the harbor as an important and urgent matter. Americans take pride in the independence and rectitude of their judges. The judging of the Boston Harbor case, with the court's clarification of the common social purpose and willingness to act upon it, exemplifies those qualities. Judges who view themselves as purely procedural arbiters will miss significant opportunities to guide litigation toward its highest and best resolution. The Boston Harbor outcome vindicates an expansive view of the law and the bench, one that sees these institutions as instruments of communal and political betterment—a view, not incidentally, that has inspired generations of lawyers and that vitalizes the judiciary's moral claim to be heard.

CONCLUSION
The High Tide of Judicial Action

Sensitivity to one's intuitive and passionate responses, and awareness of the range of human experience, is . . . not only an inevitable but a desirable part of the judicial process, an aspect more to be nurtured than feared.

—William J. Brennan, Jr.

While this book concentrates on one particular environmental case of special significance, its reach is meant to be broader. It is concerned with the nature and consequences of judicial power when provoked by movements for reform. The dispute resolution process devised by Judge Garrity adapted the traditional rules of the judicial system to the needs and goals of those who live in a major metropolitan area. The successful outcome of this case reveals how, at crucial junctures, judicial lawmaking can become an indispensable part of the general process of solving social problems and institutionalizing otherwise evanescent reforms on a more permanent basis.

The Boston Harbor reform process exemplifies an emerging new model of governance that steps away from a rigid adherence to the orthodox doctrine of the separation of powers to stress the interdependence of the activities of government, in particular of legislating and adjudicating. Advocates of this approach view the separations between the branches as, at most, temporary categorizing lines. Like the movable lane-dividers used to channel traffic flow, they can be placed where required to stave off confusion or conflict, but removed or lowered when there is need for joint action. The spirit of collaboration that was invoked so successfully in the Boston Harbor litigation, with its call for an affirmative exercise of power by legislators, has always been part of the political theory upon which the Constitution of the United States was based. The Founders, seeking to prevent a concentration of power that would result in tyranny, nevertheless had no intention of sacrificing the ability to govern—or the provision of essential public services—on the altar of institutional separation.

In many ways, and so frequently that it is barely noticed but rather accepted as routine, judges intervene in legislative operations, establish limits on the behavior of legislatures, and reconfigure the policy-making environment of the states in which they serve. In the process the public role of the judge has been gradually transformed—without direct acknowledgment but with an immediate impact on litigation strategies, legal scholarship, and the training of new generations of lawyers. Ultimately, political philosophy, the intellectual basis for the reciprocal interaction of legislating and judging, is reformulated, reflecting the institutional adaptations that are made to meet changing collective needs and goals.

In a democracy public opinion will ultimately determine the success of a judicial intervention. State judges in situations of institutional breakdown may have to assume a powerful moral role, with an obligation not only to seek a remedy but also to convince the people—and the executive and legislative branches—of the rightness of their approach. Recognizing that, part of the court's ambitious agenda in the Boston Harbor case was to change attitudes and to encourage social learning. This effort is a supremely difficult task for judicial leadership, one that requires refinement through experience. This was certainly the case in the *Quincy* litigation. Here the court could build on the aspirations of John Adams, Theodore Roosevelt, and Lyndon Johnson—there is a striking continuity in American thought and feeling on preserving a vibrant living environment. But first the court had to overcome the pervasive invisibility and lack of glamour of the sewage issue. And as in any situation of institutional breakdown, the court faced the challenge of retaining the attention and mustering the continued support of local groups needed to organize and sustain support for its actions.

Political savvy—or, in the more genteel formulation of the U.S. Supreme Court, "a practical flexibility in shaping . . . remedies and . . . a facility for adjusting and reconciling public and private needs"[1]—is required to ensure that each interest group is heard, to some degree pacified, and left willing and able to follow through on the prescribed judicial remedies. Undoubtedly, the Massachusetts legislature and the Dukakis administration would rather have had clean waters than not, yet the political and financial price appeared too great for them to undertake the necessary reform without judicial prodding. This inertia was changed by the city of Quincy's action in going to court, seeking an injunction that would reallocate power between it and the state government by invoking the authority of the court and the law.

Why, in an area such as greater Boston that takes pride in its institutions and its traditions, have the courts so often been called in to remedy notorious cases of public mismanagement? In the case of Boston Harbor, the enormous cost of the remedy was one factor, and Judge Paul Garrity added, "It's political. Somebody has to take the heat for sewer rates which are going to double in the next ten years. The court can do that."[2] Not an entirely satisfactory answer to many. Others thought there were deeper roots, reflecting the social and ethnic history of the population. The answer is to be found, mused Judge Arthur Garrity of the U.S. District Court, in the state's wary relationship with its capital city. The city/state tension tends to generate stalemates that lead to failure by inaction. He talked about the Yankee-run state house retaining control over Boston as a way of keeping check on the Irish, who dominated city hall. "It may be," he concluded, "that the city became accustomed to having other people make difficult decisions for it."[3]

Perhaps the current contest over the proper limits of judicial power will one day be seen as part of a larger transition. At some future date the ideals of democracy may require that we resist the temptation of turning to the judiciary for remedial action in instances of political deadlock and instead reform the other two branches, making them more accountable, more directly responsive so that they are empowered—and motivated—to deal more rapidly with pressing issues like the pollution of a great harbor, the deterioration of public housing, the failure of the local educational system, or the mistreatment of the powerless.

By and large, neither local nor state government officials had seen, heard, or spoken evil of the adverse consequences of unguided development without infrastructure improvements in the Boston metropolitan area—the spillover effects in the social "commons" and the harms inflicted on the environment. Without the court's willingness to serve proactively as public educator and political goad, Boston Harbor would have died as an ecological system and as a center of civic life. The *Quincy* litigation underlined the court's potential role in breaking through the gridlock that frequently surrounds complex social issues in a democracy. When the city of Quincy brought its case before Judge Garrity in the Norfolk Superior Court, the complaint it filed did not allege an abuse of power or an improper use of authority—but rather a failure to act. Instead of the typical request that the court fulfill its role of providing a restraint on the actions of other branches of government, in this case the court was asked to spur them to action—to help push the lawbreaking Metropolitan District Commission to fulfill its statutory duties, and to move the state legislature to enact institutional reforms to resuscitate the dying harbor. As in other instances of institutional breakdown, the court, as a body of last resort, could help break the logjam; and as the tenured branch of government, it could bear the ensuing criticisms and pressures. The lesson to be drawn for environmental protection is that there exist many arrows in the quiver of reform, most especially the court as a powerful ally in institutional change.

To break the stalemate, Judge Garrity used both adjudication and mediation, means that have been traditionally available to the judiciary, but he modified and employed them in imaginative ways that can provide guidance to other courts in future cases. A continuing process of negotiation and mediation overseen by the special master was helped along by persistent reminders that the court could resort to the alternative of returning to adjudication should that prove necessary; the hovering presence of potential judicial sanctions made the special master's mediation efforts more persuasive than they might otherwise have been.

Application of the knowledge and talent of experts, trial by affidavit, negotiation techniques, ex parte communications, devising a procedural order rather than attempting to impose a consent decree—all combined to make the substantive injunctions issued by the trial court more than hortatory. The *Quincy* litigation refutes any charges that judges lack the capacity to formulate and implement complex remedies—in this case the court expanded a complaint over sewage washing ashore on a single beach to accomplish a major restructuring within state government without ever officially determining liability or ordering a permanent remedy.

Collective memory is spotty at best. Perhaps too much happens too fast in the modern world to be recorded in the collective psyche, much less recalled in tranquility. In the struggle over the fate of Boston Harbor, part of our society managed to find new meaning in its history; as it looked forward toward rehabilitation, it honored the memories of John Adams's harbor. With its power invoked, the court educated itself and the public at large that care for Boston Harbor was part of the life of the community, including the gifts of memory and of connection. It took a type of collective heroism to seek change, identify the causes of pollution, find ways around the technological obstacles pointed out by the engineers, overcome the shortsighted legislative maneuvers of politicians indifferent to the bigger picture, and finally begin to restore the harbor so that dolphins, sea lions—and humans—can swim in it. These are events out of which public lore is spun, and achievements that build a civic tradition.

Power is not simply a matter of constitutional allocation. A pronouncement from the bench has force not only because of the constitutional powers conferred upon it but by its moral weight. The issue raised by Stalin's famous retort, "How many divisions does the Pope have?" can also be invoked about the judiciary: How many voters does the court have? One argument is that to the extent judges become active on divisive social issues, their moral capital, and with it their political power, will decline.[4] But excessive caution in the exercise of judicial power can be just as damaging as an excess of zeal. Democratic governance calls upon the judiciary not only to protect rights but also to ensure adherence to and respect for legal principles. Power not deployed is power soon lost, perhaps irretrievably. If the court had refused to rise to the challenge presented by the lawsuit filed by the city of Quincy, or had been unwilling to remind the other branches of government of their obligation to bestir themselves, that would have left the social and legal problem untouched, the political stalemate unresolved, the building of a participatory process stymied. The surest way for the court to dilute its moral and legal capital and narrow its influence would have been to isolate itself from the harbor crisis.

I have argued that the need to stir into action the other branches of government constitutes a self-contained justification for Judge Garrity's actions in the *Quincy* case. The successful launch of the independent Massachusetts Water Resources Authority argues even more persuasively for the legitimacy of the court's conduct.

The *Quincy* outcome went beyond its local bounds, playing a part in bringing environmental issues to the forefront of national consciousness. It contributed importantly to the debate by making the economic case for a cleaner environment. By proposing a remedy that bore with it highly visible costs, Judge Garrity sparked discussions of the alternative costs of continued inaction, delayed infrastructure improvements, and deferred maintenance of the plants, and a realization that further delay would only increase the eventual costs. The publicity supported the creation of an independent authority that could spread increased costs by means of long-term financing. At the very least, the effort helped persuade citizens that the rescue effort was worth the cost.

But *Quincy* accomplished more than that. It ultimately renewed the deep historical—I would even say spiritual—connection between the region and its harbor. As contemporary Bostonians rediscover the waters at their doorstep, they forge a connection with the past: with the European settlers who made the harbor the hub of their fledgling colony, with the merchants and seamen who established Boston as a center of commerce, with the immigrants who streamed into the city in search of opportunity. Just as the harbor's expanse offers the eye relief from the relentless verticality of urban life, its natural rhythms offer city dwellers relief from their clock-bound routines, opening space and time for human contact and the building of civic bonds. In its beauty citizens find a focus for their sense of stewardship, of shared responsibility for a treasured resource. Bostonians were moved to appreciate that their lives and the life of the harbor were intertwined, and the court can take a measure of credit for this rediscovery.

The *Quincy* litigation taught a community about itself, about the value and vulnerability of its resources, about neglect and resilience. The state court made a vital contribution to the learning process, mobilizing the community's collective intelligence to address a threat to its well-being.

Regenerating Boston Harbor echoes the expansive vision of public service enunciated by John Adams in 1765: "Let us tenderly and kindly cherish, therefore, the means of knowledge. Let us dare to read, think, speak, and write. Let every order and degree among the people rouse their attention and animate their resolution."

And finally, as he emphasized, "let every sluice of knowledge be opened and set a-flowing."[5]

POSTSCRIPT
Boston Harbor Today

> We fray into the future, rarely wrought
> Save in the tapestries of afterthought.
>
> —Richard Wilbur

On September 6, 2000, marked by a champagne-toasted gala at 11:45 A.M., the Deer Island sluice gates leading to Boston Harbor were closed forever. Treated wastewater was directed into a new outfall tunnel to begin the 9.5-mile journey out to the middle of Massachusetts Bay, and so out to sea. By 3:00 P.M. that day, the cloudy harbor waters began to clear. Within a week, tests by Massachusetts Water Resources Authority scientists showed that bacteria levels were down, and soon large numbers of striped bass and bluefish schooled near Peddock's Island. After a long and tempestuous voyage, Boston Harbor had been reclaimed.

The September 2000 celebration highlighted only the surface layers of the pioneering innovations catalyzed by the lawsuit filed by the city of Quincy in 1982, and laid out in the ambitious agenda of Judge Garrity's procedural order in 1983:

- On Deer Island, a new state-of-the-art secondary treatment plant added the capacity needed to handle the millions of gallons of wastewater produced in the Boston area each day, replacing the failing Deer Island and Nut Island plants.
- An inter-island tunnel carried wastewater of the southern metropolitan area from Nut Island to Deer Island, allowing the demolition of the Nut Island treatment plant.
- Treated wastewater was dispersed in Massachusetts Bay be-

yond the harbor by means of a 9.5-mile outfall pipe, the longest one-way tunnel in the world.

• A new fertilizer plant at the former Quincy shipyard disposed of the perennial quagmire of sludge.

• An extensive discharge permit established legal and administrative requirements for continuous control of discharges into the harbor.

Every element of the task encountered obstacles—technical, political, scientific, and administrative. The court's resolve and the legislature's action in 1984 had only begun the effort.

The construction of the massive new Deer Island plant raised alarms in the city of Winthrop, which encompassed the only land connection to the island. To soften opposition there, the MWRA agreed that material and workers would not be transported over land. Some 3,000 construction workers, as a result, were barged daily to Deer Island. The new plant was built in stages, as the old plant was torn down.

A second major project, the inter-island tunnel, transported sewage flows of the twenty-three south system communities from Nut Island to Deer Island, where the necessary secondary treatment could be applied. This improvement enabled the MWRA to finally demolish the rickety Nut Island treatment plant.

The 9.5-mile outfall pipe was not as visible to the naked eye as the shiny purification plant it serviced. A triumph of modern technology, it is the longest tunnel of its kind on the planet: 400 feet below the Deer Island plant, the 24-foot-diameter, concrete-lined tunnel burrows east, out to Massachusetts Bay where it disperses treated wastewater through fifty-five discharge points. But it was a cause for concern to some environmentalists and many residents of Cape Cod who feared that the harbor's gain would be the bay's loss. The pipe ends just fifteen miles away from Stellwagon Bank, which was designated a National Marine

Sanctuary in 1992, and which is one of the nation's most fecund but delicate ecosystems, home to whales, sea birds, turtles, fish, dolphins, lobsters, and scallops.[1]

A catastrophic accident marred the project. On July 21, 1999, William Judge and Timothy Wordeen, two workers, died in the tunnel when their breathing equipment failed. Immediately closing off construction, the federal Occupational Safety and Health Administration fined four contractors $410,000 and forbade further work until a reliable air supply could be guaranteed. Already $202 million over budget and twenty-three months behind its deadline, the tunnel remained off-limits for a year until an air-circulation system was installed.

The sludge disposal problem was always at issue. It engendered a series of controversies that involved all the branches of government, at times requiring the judiciary to serve, literally, as a court of last resort. The first contention was presaged by the description in the special master's report of three alternative methods of sludge disposal, and the debate among experts about appropriate technology. Each method rallied its separate adherents; none could command a consensus.[2] In the end, the MWRA decided to recycle the sludge into compost for use as fertilizer or landfill.[3] Soil additive pellets shipped all over the country became the chosen mode for moving out of a seemingly impossible quandary.

The location of sludge treatment facilities, not surprisingly, caused some of the most intractable problems, as the mystique of a reinvigorated Boston Harbor proved small compensation to prospective neighbors for the possibility of objectionable odors, diminishing property values, and a blighted landscape. After a long search in which Malden, Lynn, Revere, Everett, Winthrop, Stoughton, and Avon fought location of the sludge treatment plant in their neighborhoods, the MWRA acquired the former General Dynamics shipyard in Quincy in 1991 and transformed it into one of the largest fertilizer plants in the world—but only after Quincy lost bids in two separate courts to halt the sale, and the MWRA agreed to pay compensation to the city.[4]

In addition, the Environmental Protection Agency insisted upon the designation of a landfill as a backup disposal option for unsold pellets and as a reserve dump for raw sludge. After a three-year, $10 million search that reviewed over 300 sites, the MWRA selected a 95-acre parcel in Walpole that was owned by the state. The choice provoked an explosive reaction.[5] Walpole brought suit, and its protests to the legislature led the Massachusetts House in June 1990 to vote to delay any decision on transferring the land to the MWRA. When the House, in its own singular fashion, missed its self-imposed December deadline and adjourned instead, the EPA requested that the court order the immediate transfer of the Walpole site to the MWRA. Building on the precedent set years earlier by Judge Garrity, Judge A. David Mazzone ordered a moratorium on new sewer hookups until the transfer was accomplished, warning that the stakes included "the credibility of the court's schedule for the clean-up and the public's faith in the integrity of the entire project." He rejected Governor William Weld's request for a 120-day suspension of the ban, decreeing that the moratorium would be lifted when the land was transferred for the sludge landfill, "and no sooner."

A three-judge U.S. Court of Appeals ruling affirmed the judge's moratorium, rejecting the state argument that the court was "acting too soon in this case." In a question from the bench, then Circuit Court of Appeals Judge Stephen Breyer, a member of the panel, pointed out, "It is very, very, very unlikely that the state will find another site and get it under construction within a year and a half" pursuant to the timetable set for the Boston Harbor cleanup.[6] And this was the leitmotif of judicial reaction: the progress of the regeneration of Boston Harbor would not be frustrated by parochial claims. The moratorium came to an end only in May 1991 when a reluctant Governor Weld signed the bill that authorized the transfer.

Still, that was not the end of the matter. Through the arguments and persistence of the Walpole residents, new factors came into play. The MWRA's board of directors reopened the search, this time including out-of-state sites even though the cleanup order mandated an in-state facility. At first the delay seemed to provoke yet another judicial confrontation with the other branches, including an order by the federal court to move forward immediately with the site. But suddenly the situation was defused; in a change of heart, the MWRA's board of directors approved a proposal to ship sludge to East Carbon City, Utah, rather than to the intransigent city of Walpole. Six years of relentless picketing, rallying, lobbying, letter-writing, and sound-bites by its citizens overcame the numerous studies by experts that had found the Walpole site to be safe and efficient.

"We're so happy," exclaimed the Walpole town administrator at this turn of events, "all these years, all that fighting—this is just fantastic." The bureaucracy, unwilling to concede defeat at the hands of ordinary citizens, retained its aplomb: "I believe," said the EPA attorney in the courtroom, apparently with a straight face, "I speak truthfully when I say political pressure had no impact in our decision."[7]

Finally, drafting an administrative permit to regulate discharges into the harbor required years of legal wrangling among public and private parties to ensure that the Deer Island discharges met strict environmental standards. Parties to the final settlement included the Environmental Protection Agency, the Massachusetts Water Resources Authority, the MWRA advisory board, the Executive Office of Environmental Affairs, the Charles River Watershed Association, the Fore River Watershed Association, and several Cape Cod groups. In announcing approval of the permit, the MWRA annual report concluded, "Everyone agrees with what the permit must prove: that the plant will run well, the outfall will be carefully monitored, and the ecosystem of Massachusetts Bay will be scrupulously protected."

Indeed, the permit was the most comprehensive and aggressive regulation yet adopted for municipal wastewater treatment. It set effluent limits, monitoring requirements, and pollution prevention standards. Results had to be reported monthly and made available to the public. In addition, the MWRA was required to create forty-three monitoring stations that would collect data on the impact on marine life and water quality. The permit, as another precaution, required that the MWRA develop and implement a pollution prevention plan that encompassed all users, including industrial, commercial, and residential. "I think we've developed one of the best environmental monitoring programs not only in the U.S. but in the world," proclaimed the president of the New England Aquarium and chair of the Outfall Monitoring Task Force.

Fifteen years of work yielded both steady improvements in marine indicators and a remarkable effect on the shoreline. Regeneration of Boston Harbor had an impressive effect on real estate development and values. The South Boston waterfront was converted into a stylish real estate market. A new federal courthouse adorned the Fan Pier; a $1.2 billion, 2.9-million-square-foot mixed-use complex and a museum of modern art are proposed for the remainder of the Pier. Spectacle Island, where the city once dumped its trash, was transformed into a recreational site, and the MDC led a $55 million effort to restore harbor beaches. South Boston's Carson Beach was refitted with an elegant bathhouse; the East Boston Pier Park was created. About 75 percent of the forty-three miles of a continuous public walkway along the edges of the harbor has been completed. A private group, the Island Alliance, raised millions for a new harbor islands national recreation area. Save the Harbor/Save the Bay, a community-based organization, rallied a Campaign for the Water's Edge to improve public access to the harbor. The 1998 Boston Harbor Project Annual Progress Report noted that none "of the major construction projects now being planned on the waterfront would be taking place without a revitalized Boston Harbor."

In reviewing the history of the *Quincy* litigation, one must be impressed by the enormous power of the judicial branch to act as a catalyst for change. All too often, existing governmental institutions fail to address the social conflicts that inevitably arise in a complex industrial society. Even noble efforts to reverse segregation in housing, or to achieve environmental justice, may bog down as they encounter the contending interests of elected officials, regulators, representatives of business, and private citizens. This is what happened in Boston. The legislative and executive branches of government blanched in the face of a problem that demanded large sums of money and the transformation (or demise and replacement) of an established, old-line government institution. "There is no more disgraceful monument to the inept timidity of a succession of Massachusetts governors and legislators than Boston Harbor," as a *Boston Globe* columnist summed up. "For some twenty years the commonwealth's top elected officials have watched this great harbor, from its inner waterfront to its outer islands, deteriorate in quality to that of an open sewer."[8]

The champagne toast of September 2000 marked a successful close, a solution that is both unique and yet can be generalized to other situations. The process and outcome of the *Quincy* case were a successful experiment that demonstrates the judiciary's ability to fashion workable mechanisms for coping with government gridlock. Environmental despoliation is not an inevitable trap from which society cannot escape.

I have watched with interest and admiration as the MWRA has taken shape, as Boston Harbor has been regenerated, and as the citizens of Massachusetts have rallied to the cause, paid the costs, and shaped the transformation of the complicated system of water use and disposal on which our society depends. The people of the Boston metropolitan area came together and worked together over a generation in order to protect their shared public realm. To assume responsibility for securing the quality of life under the crowded conditions of a modern metropolis is a demonstration of faith in the future. Indeed, the whole long process of salvaging Boston Harbor offers us a metaphor for a complexly interwoven society, the clear waters an image of ourselves and our deepest concerns, as we actually are, and of our abiding ideals.

Timeline of the *Quincy* Case _____

1982

17 December. The city of Quincy files suit in Norfolk Superior Court
against the Metropolitan District Commission (MDC) and the
Boston Water and Sewer Commission (BWSC), charging them
with polluting Quincy's beaches and waters.

1983

11 February. BWSC files first answer to Quincy's complaint.

20 April. MDC files its response, with a counterclaim alleging that
Quincy discharges pollution through its storm drains.

7 June. The Conservation Law Foundation files an antipollution suit
in federal court against the MDC and the EPA.

9 June. Judge Paul Garrity grants Quincy's motion to join additional
defendants to the case.

13 June. Quincy moves for a preliminary injunction.

15 June. Judge Garrity holds hearings on Quincy's motions: for a
preliminary injunction; to refer the case to a special master; to
order the MDC to give Quincy prompt notice of sewage discharges; and to restrain the MDC from adding new communities to its sewer system or allowing any major expansion of the
system.

17 June. Quincy requests a court order requiring a two-gallons-per-
day reduction in existing wastewater flow for every new gallon-
per-day added to the MDC system.

27 June. Judge Garrity issues initial "Findings, Rulings, and Orders"
determining that the violations alleged had more than likely occurred, that the MDC is discharging pollutants in violation of
permits, and that Quincy has asserted "enforceable legal claims."

6 July. Judge Garrity convenes a hearing on Quincy's request to appoint a special master to find facts, propose remedies, and draft a
comprehensive order.

8 July. The court issues "Further Findings, Rulings, and Orders" on
Quincy's request for a preliminary injunction, reaffirming its earlier findings. Judge Garrity appoints a special master to resolve
issues of fact, hear evidence, and report findings by August 9,
1983. Charles Haar and Steven Horowitz are named as special
master and deputy master.

14 July. Special master's three-day trial begins.

9 August. Special master's report is delivered to Judge Garrity. It describes faults in the MDC sewage treatment system and recom-
mends system-wide improvements in staffing, facilities, and
financing, and presents the alternative of a new water and sewage
treatment authority.

10 August. Special master requests that the MDC and Division of
Water Pollution Control submit legislative proposals for
infiltration/inflow removal, and that the MDC and Executive
Office of Environmental Affairs submit plans for conservation
measures and legislative proposals for financing treatment projects.

2 September. Judge Garrity accepts the special master's report.

9 September. Judge Garrity issues procedural order setting schedules
for regenerating Boston Harbor, and appoints Charles Haar to
monitor progress. The parties agree to develop a plan in cooperation with the EPA.

10 September. EPA lawyers pledge to support the parties' agreement.

1984

January. Senate President William Bulger's commission submits a bill
proposing a cleanup of the harbor and the establishment of a
new agency to handle sewage disposal.

8 February. The First National Bank of Boston releases a report on the
funding requirements of water and sewage treatment services in
the Boston area.

27 March. Judge A. David Mazzone of the U.S. District Court stays
the proceedings in the case against the MDC and EPA, in deference to the state *Quincy* litigation.

April. Governor Michael Dukakis proposes a bill to create a new metropolitan water and sewage treatment agency.

18 June. Charles Haar advises a legislative committee that in the absence of a political solution Judge Garrity would impose measures to end the pollution of the harbor.

10 August. The court holds a hearing to review the defendants' efforts to comply with the procedural order of September 1983.

4 October. The Bulger bill passes in the Senate.

9 October. The special master reports to the court that only slight improvements have occurred in the condition of the harbor.

16 November. Judge Garrity announces that without significant legislative progress by November 26, he will take steps to place the MDC sewer division into judicial receivership.

28 November. House-Senate conference committee postpones action on all legislation concerning the proposed Massachusetts Water Resources Authority (MWRA).

29 November. Judge Garrity imposes an immediate ban on all new tie-ins to the MDC sewer system, halts work on current MDC sewer projects, and announces a trial for December 4 to consider placing the MDC sewer division into receivership.

3 December. Representative John Cusack's alternative MWRA bill is reported out of committee. The House approves a compromise bill based on the Dukakis proposal. The Senate approves the Bulger bill.

4 December. Judge Garrity issues a moratorium order and convenes the trial on the issue of placing the MDC sewer division into receivership.

5 December. Justice Joseph Nolan of the Supreme Judicial Court overturns Judge Garrity's ban on tie-ins to the MDC sewer system.

10 December. Judge Garrity states that he has prepared a new moratorium order that would apply to future sewer connections, but that he will refrain from imposing it while the legislature considers the MWRA legislation.

11 December. The legislature renews debate on the MWRA bills.

12 December. The House passes a bill to create a sewer and water authority. The Senate authorizes a conference committee to work out differences between the House and Senate bills.

13–17 December. The conference committee works through the weekend and finally agrees on a compromise bill to create a combined water and sewer authority.

19 December. House and Senate pass the bill by large majorities, and
Governor Dukakis signs it that evening, creating the Massachusetts Water Resources Authority.

1985

9 January. Judge Garrity resigns from the bench, the case is assigned to
Chief Judge Thomas Morse, and Charles Haar is appointed monitor.

27 February. Governor Dukakis swears in eleven members of the
MWRA's board of directors.

1 July. The Massachusetts Water Resources Authority begins operations, taking over the MDC water and sewer divisions.

31 December. The *Quincy* case ends in state court.

Summary of Recommendations

I. Reduction of Flow to MDC Treatment Plants

  A. Planned Infiltration/Inflow Reduction Program
   1. Determination by the MDC and the DWPC by September 1, 1983, of acceptable infiltration/inflow rates for each community in the south and north system service areas.
   2. Utilization by MDC and DWPC of all enforcement powers to require performance of necessary infiltration/inflow studies.
   3. Design and implementation of those infiltration/inflow projects that are found to be cost-effective.
   4. Investigation and implementation by MDC of rewards to communities for removing infiltration/inflow and penalties for excessive infiltration/inflow. The court shall establish implementation date.
   5. Submission by DWPC to the court by September 30, 1983, of proposed legislation to allow awarding of state grants for infiltration/inflow removal beyond that called for under federal guidelines, and for communities not receiving federal grants.

  B. A 2:1 Reduction Program
   1. Implementation of a permit requirement for a 2-for-1 reduction of infiltration/inflow relative to new flow.
   2. Determination by September 30, 1983, of the feasibility of establishing a greater than 2:1 ratio for the removal of infiltration/inflow.
   3. Determination by September 30, 1983, of the feasibility of a MDC system-wide "banking/trading" program.
   4. Improvement of awareness and enforcement of sewer connection permit requirements (see Section V-B).

  C. MDC Municipal Assessments as a Conservation Device
   Submission to the court by January 1, 1984, of a proposal pre-

pared jointly by the MDC and the EOEA on the potential for using MDC and member-community sewer charges as a means of
encouraging the reduction of sewage influent to the MDC system.

II. Plan for Increased Capacity and Improved Treatment of Sewage
   A. Completion of Nut Island Upgrading
      1. Conducting of tests to determine if outfalls 101 and 102 can
         be cleaned and relined. Tests should be completed and sub-
         mitted to the court by January 1, 1984.
      2. If cleaning and relining are unfeasible, plans for replacement
         of these outfalls should be submitted to the court by March 1,
         1984.
      3. The potential for installing an effluent pumping station to
         eliminate the use of outfalls 103 and 104 should also be in-
         cluded in the report.
      4. Cost-benefit analyses of installing improved diffusers and of
         extending existing outfalls should also be conducted.
      5. A response by MDC, submitted to the court by November 1,
         1983, as to which of plaintiff's recommendations concerning
         physical improvements to Nut Island will be undertaken, in-
         cluding a proposed time schedule.

   B. Maintenance and Upgrading of Deer Island Treatment Plant
      1. Presentation to the court by January 1, 1984, of a plan outlin-
         ing the physical improvements to Deer Island that are neces-
         sary to greatly reduce the discharge of raw sewage from
         Moon Island. The report should include a consideration of (a)
         replacement of the defective Nordberg pump engines or con-
         tracting for the supply of sufficient replacement parts, (b) re-
         pair and/or cleaning of the engine smokestacks, and (c) im-
         provements to the facility's power system.
      2. Submission to the legislature of a supplementary budget re-
         quest for the repairs that are recommended in the plan.

III. Treatment and/or Reduction of Discharges from Moon Island
    Presentation to the court by January 1, 1984, of a plan and time-
    table to minimize the volume and environmental impact of
    Moon Island discharges. This plan should specifically examine

the options of chlorinating Moon Island discharges and renovating the holding tanks to enable the discharges to be released on outgoing tides.

IV. Quincy Storm Drains
  A. Implementation by the city of Quincy, in conjunction with the state defendants, of a testing program that will attempt to identify the volume of pollutants coming out of Quincy storm drains.
  B. Where necessary, development by the city of Quincy and the DWPC of a program to identify and eliminate the non-stormwater sources of pollution to Quincy's storm drains.

V. Improvement of Administration and Operations

  A. Operations and Staffing
    1. Submission to the court of MDC's operation, management, and maintenance plans.
    2. Presentation to the court and the legislature by January 1, 1984, of a plan and supplemental budget for the staffing needs of the Deer and Nut Island treatment plants.
    3. Presentation to the court and the legislature, on the above date, of the overall staffing requirements of MDC, including any additional personnel required to comply with the recommendations of the report.
    4. Assignment of MDC staff to promptly notify all local public health officials whose communities abut the Boston Harbor of events such as bypasses and discharges of untreated or partially treated wastewaters that may present a public health risk.

  B. Education, Monitoring, and Enforcement Activities
    1. Maintenance by DWPC of a record of all enforcement actions it takes with respect to NPDES permit requirements. Written determination of the validity of the explanation offered for all discharges and bypasses of untreated and partially treated sewage.
    2. Periodic reporting to the court by DWPC of all NPDES permit enforcement actions.
    3. Initiation by MDC of a system for immediate notification to

BWSC when the gates to the Columbus Park headworks are being closed and the wastewaters diverted to Calf Pasture for pumping to Moon Island.

4. Inclusion in the September 30, 1983 report on the 2:1 infiltration and inflow reduction program of a section on plans for enforcement of new connection permitting, covering (a) plans for assessing the level of compliance, (b) enforcement techniques, (c) staffing requirements, and (d) training needs.

5. Initiation within 60 days of an extensive educational program emphasizing the existence and scope of the requirements of the sewer extension and connection regulations, the penalties for disregarding them, and the incentives for compliance.

VI. The Discipline and Direction of a Financial Plan

A. Completion by the state defendants of a financial plan for obtaining the funds necessary to carry out MDC projects and programs. Expert, independent financial consultants should be employed to prepare and review this report.

B. Five measures relating to the financing of the MDC sewerage system should be evaluated:

1. An independent sewerage authority.

2. General obligation bonds or special revenue bonds.

3. Contract assistance, capital reserve.

4. Revising current system of charges.

5. The balance between sums collected by MDC and legislative appropriations.

Notes

Trial documents from the *Quincy* case—*Quincy v. Metropolitan District Commission*, Civ. No. 138,477 (Mass. Super. Ct., Norfolk County, filed Dec. 17, 1982)—are contained in the Quincy Litigation Papers (QLP) at the Harvard Law School Library (donated by the author). Trial documents are normally noted the first time they are used in a chapter but not repeatedly thereafter. Any trial document not specifically noted can be assumed to belong to the QLP collection.

Introduction

1. George Bush, 1 September 1988, quoted in Robin Toner, "Bush, in Enemy Waters, Says Rival Hindered Cleanup of Boston Harbor," *New York Times*, 2 September 1988, A16.
2. Garrett James Hardin, "The Tragedy of the Commons," *Ekistics* 27 (1969): 168–170 (originally published in *Science* 162 (1968): 1243–1248).

1. The Harbor in the National Political Campaign

1. Metropolitan District Commission, "Summary of Supplemental Draft Environmental Impact Statements on Siting of Wastewater Treatment Facilities in Boston Harbor" (28 and 31 December 1984).
2. Christine Chinlund, "In Boston, Bush Blames Rival for Delays in Harbor Cleanup," *Boston Globe*, 2 September 1988, 1 (hereinafter "Bush Blames Rival").
3. Robin Toner, "Bush, in Enemy Waters, Says Rival Hindered Cleanup of Boston Harbor," *New York Times*, 2 September 1988, A16 (hereinafter "Bush in Enemy Waters"); Andrew Miga and Jonathan Wells, "Mass. Poll Shocker," *Boston Herald*, 1 September 1988, 1.
4. George Bush, 1 September 1988, quoted in "Bush Blames Rival."
5. Ibid., quoted in "Bush in Enemy Waters." The Bush team also

made sure that the picture of their candidate on the filthy water was not compromised by images of Dukakis supporters in the background. As reported in the *Boston Globe*, "When [the flotilla] edged toward Bush's ferry, near the range of television cameras trained on the vice president, some of his supporters, New Hampshire Gov. John Sununu first among them, stood briefly to block the camera operators' view." "Bush Blames Rival."

6. Jim Maddy, 31 August 1988, quoted in Philip Shabecoff, "Environmentalists Say Either Bush or Dukakis Will Be an Improvement," *New York Times*, 1 September 1988, B9.

7. "Bush in Enemy Waters."

8. George Bush, 31 August 1988, quoted in Christine Chinlund, "Campaign 88: Bush Offers Proposals on Environment," *Boston Globe*, 1 September 1988, 19.

9. On the day of the harbor cruise, a Dukakis campaign spokesperson emphasized the point that "[t]his [Reagan-Bush] administration has twice vetoed the Clean Water Act. It slated the Waste Water Treatment Grants Program for termination." Any delays in the cleanup were attributed by the governor's associates to the EPA alone, which "dragged its heels for years" in deciding on the best approach for Boston Harbor. George Mitchell, the Democratic Senate Majority Leader, claimed that when Bush led the regulatory commission he had blocked efforts to cut lead levels in gasoline, set standards for hazardous waste disposal, and halt toxic discharges into waterways.

10. "Excerpts from the Interview with Dukakis," *New York Times*, 9 October 1988, 34.

11. Robert Healy, "Turning Negative into Positive for Bush," *Boston Globe*, 7 September 1988, 15. See, e.g., Walter V. Robinson, "Bush to Inspect Boston Harbor Pollution," *Boston Globe*, 31 August 1988, 11; T. R. Reid, "Dukakis Renews Attack, Is Soon Back on Defensive; On Eve of Bush Visit, Boston Harbor Pollution Overshadows Iran-Contra Affair as Issue," *Washington Post*, 1 September 1988, A16. See also Christine Chinlund, "Bush Offers Proposals on Environment," *Boston Globe*, 1 September 1988, 19.

12. After all, this was the administration that featured James Watt as its Secretary of the Interior, with scandals galore, and Anne Gorsuch Burford as administrator of the EPA, who was engrossed with the effort to "dismantle" that agency.

13. *Boston Herald,* 26 October 1988, 25.

14. Christopher Connell, "Bush Takes Breather after Ohio Tax-perience," *Baton Rouge State Times,* 22 October 1988, A1. Bush defended his Boston Harbor tactics as self-defense: "When you get beat around the head by a man who's got a record as dismal as this, I'm not going to stand there and take it. I've been proposing what I would do about it." "Bush Blames Rival." "Inasmuch as I hear a lot of sludge coming out, aimed at me by a person who's been a part of the problem here, I have to defend myself." Timothy McNulty, "Bush Fires Pollution Broadside in Dukakis Waters," *Chicago Tribune,* 2 September 1988, 20.

15. Chris Black, "Dukakis Sails on Dirty Water Off Jersey to Demonstrate against Ocean Dumping," *Boston Globe,* 30 May 1988, 10.

16. George Bush, quoted in David Nyhan, "Bush, Dukakis in a Water Fight," *Boston Globe,* 5 June 1988, A25.

17. Michael Oreskes, "Bush Lashes Back at Kennedy Taunt," *New York Times,* 3 September 1988, 7.

18. Michael Deland, quoted in Larry Tye, "EPA Official Says Dukakis to Blame for 6-Year Delay," *Boston Globe,* 11 August 1988, 1. (Deland would soon become the chairman of the Council on Environmental Quality in the new Bush administration.) In the shifting sands of official federalism, the strange claim emerged that Massachusetts was at fault for not obtaining its fair share of funding from Washington. In addition to the reduction of federal grant money under the Clean Water Act, the EPA's budget for water pollution was cut by as much as 43 percent, with the Reagan administration leading the fight that defeated congressional efforts to appropriate money for cleaning up Boston Harbor. In effect, the Reagan administration took the bat away and then blamed the player for not making a hit. See also Norman Boucher, "The Enforcer," *Boston Globe Magazine,* 30 October 1988, 24.

19. Larry Tye, "EPA Regional Head Draws Praise from Both Sides," *Boston Globe,* 28 September 1988, 25.

20. George Bush, quoted in *Boston Herald,* 25 October 1988, 5.

21. Charles M. Haar, "Mr. Bush Sinks the Truth in Boston Harbor," *New York Times,* 18 October 1988, A31.

22. While the Dukakis administration's inaction and second application for waiver may appear dilatory in light of the eventual denial of the waiver request, EPA officials apparently welcomed the addi-

tional information brought before them when Massachusetts submitted its second application. James Simon, Massachusetts's assistant secretary of environmental affairs, reported, "There was a lot of scientific uncertainty about secondary treatment of wastes in the mid-1970s." Simon went on to blame the EPA for delaying decision on the waiver requests for the six years in question: "Our task would have been a lot easier if the federal government hadn't sat on its hands." But the Bush campaign was not deterred. "If it takes the governor of Massachusetts eleven years to clean up his own harbor, Americans must question his commitment to the even-larger environmental questions which face our nation," Lee Atwater, Bush's campaign manager, fired back. Tye, "EPA Official says Dukakis to Blame."

23. See Dianne Dumanoski, "Bush Accused of Shunning Harbor; Groups Say President Has Reneged on Environmental Promises," *Boston Globe*, 4 September 1991, 17.

24. John Aloysius Farrell, "Congress Backs $100m for Boston Harbor," *Boston Globe*, 27 September 1991, 3.

2. Under the Judicial Lens

1. I served as chairperson of The President's Task Force on Natural Beauty, whose report to the president was made in 1964, and as an organizer of the subsequent White House Conference on Natural Beauty.

2. Neither did Dukakis's campaign issues managers, both professors at the Harvard Law School, appreciate how responsive voters would be to an active program to protect the environment for future generations.

3. In nineteenth-century Illinois, for example, every spring, after concluding the session of the Sangamon County Circuit Court in Springfield, the trial judge and an entourage of lawyers that once included Abraham Lincoln moved on for several months from one courthouse to another across the fourteen counties of the Eighth Judicial Circuit. We are told by biographer David Donald that Lincoln traveled in his own buggy, pulled (according to Carl Sandburg) by a horse named Old Buck. Accommodations were miserable. Enduring such circumstances together for anywhere from two days to two weeks in each county seat, the lawyers and the presiding judge developed a sense of camaraderie. See David Herbert

Donald, *Lincoln* (New York, 1995), 104–106, 146–149; Carl Sandburg, *Abraham Lincoln: The Prairie Years* (New York, 1926), 215. Something similar was to occur among many of the parties who found themselves thrown together in search of a resolution of the *Quincy* lawsuit.

4. Amended complaint, Sup. Ct. Cir. Action no. 138477.

5. Section 42 subjects violators to criminal penalties, a fine of not less than $2,500 or more than $25,000 per day of violation, and/or imprisonment for up to one year. The civil penalty is a fine of not more than $10,000 per day. If a publicly owned facility violates the conditions of a permit, section 44 gives the state's Division of Water Pollution Control the power to prohibit all additional connections to the system until the violations cease.

6. The state defendants, in their answer, claimed these statutes did not apply to the MDC, which was a state agency.

7. The defendants would further argue that these obligations could not be the subject of private enforcement actions.

8. *Mandamus,* from the Latin, means "we enjoin." A writ of mandamus is "issued by a superior court commanding the performance of a specified official act or duty." *Merriam Webster's Collegiate Dictionary,* 10th ed.

9. Judge Garrity, in applying the standard under Rule 65 (Massachusetts Rules of Civil Procedure), declined to grant a preliminary injunction regarding this finding.

10. Professor Albert O. Hirschman notes that the availability of better quality substitutes at higher prices may complicate this calculus by encouraging the rapid exit of quality-conscious consumers—a situation that paralyzes institutional dissent by depriving it of its principal agents. But Boston Harbor is a unique resource—they aren't making them anymore—and so quality-conscious consumers cannot forsake it for a readily available alternative. See Hirschman, *Exit, Voice, and Loyalty* (Cambridge, Mass., 1970), chap. 5.

11. A harbor constituency needed to be created. A comprehensive harbor cleanup plan, therefore, had to proceed on the assumption that a harbor constituency must be brought into being—not merely mobilized. To do otherwise would have been to presume (and take the chance) that the distinct interests of the individuals and of all concerned with the renewal effort were so similar that they could be readily organized into a cohesive front. It would have been overly

simplistic to assert that a general acknowledgment of the need to clean up the harbor would be sufficient to harmonize the diverse interests of those who make up a "harbor constituency."

12. *Perez v. Boston Housing Authority,* 400 N.E.2d 1231 (Mass. 1980).

3. Coping With Complexities

1. The judge's ruling provided that a party could forthwith appeal any adverse findings upon filing an affidavit asserting that the adverse finding "made by the Special Master is not supported by the evidence presented to him." A significant limitation, though, was added: "Sanctions will be imposed by this court," the opinion went on, "if what is asserted by affidavit turns out not to be the case." Further Findings, Rulings, and Orders on Plaintiff City of Quincy's Application for Preliminary Injunctive Relief, 8 July 1983, QLP.

2. Article XCVII, Massachusetts State Constitution. An earlier article, Article XLIX (superseded by Article XCVII in 1972), had been narrower in language and outlook.

3. *City of Camden v. Byrne,* 411 A.2d 462, 472–473 (N.J. 1980).

4. An analogy may be drawn to school desegregation cases. Following the election of President Nixon in 1968, the Department of Justice ceased to be the plaintiff in school desegregation cases, and responsibility devolved to civil rights organizations that did not have the resources to match the efforts made previously by the department. As a result, courts increasingly turned to special masters to fill the gap.

5. An estoppel is defined as "a legal bar to alleging or denying a fact because of one's own previous actions or words to the contrary." *Merriam Webster's Collegiate Dictionary,* 10th ed.

6. John Salmond, *The Law of Torts: A Treatise on the English Law of Liability for Civil Injuries,* 8th ed. (London, 1934), 233.

7. American Law Institute, *Restatement of the Law (Second): Torts* (St. Paul, 1989), §821B.

8. William Lloyd Prosser, *Handbook of the Law of Torts,* 8th ed. (St. Paul, 1964), 592; see the expanded version in W. Page Keeton et al., *Prosser and Keeton on the Law of Torts,* 5th ed. (St. Paul, 1984), 616. See also *Commonwealth v. South Covington & Cincinnati Street Railway Company,* 205 S.W. 581 (Ky. 1918) ("the doing of or the failure to do something that injuriously affects the

safety, health, or morals of the public, or works some substantial annoyance, inconvenience, or injury to the public").

9. An obvious analogy to pollution of the harbor is the traditional public nuisance of obstruction of a public highway. On the then-contemporary law of nuisance, see John D. Leshy, "Interlocutory Injunctive Relief in Environmental Cases," 6 *Ecology Law Quarterly* 639 (1977).

10. Scalia's suggestion goes further than Justice Kennedy's concurrence in *Lucas,* but is in its spirit of articulating the court's newly minted nuisance exception in a more expansive and flexible manner: "[t]he common law of nuisance is too narrow a confine [that is, domain] for the exercise of regulatory power in a complex and interdependent society." *Lucas v. South Carolina Coastal Council,* 505 U.S. 1003, 1035 (1992). Even though nuisance law is a matter of state law, and not for the federal courts to define, Justice Scalia took pains to cite instances where nuisance rules would be outcome determinative, and, in noting the significance of "changed circumstances or new knowledge," drew back from the absolutist view that can be found elsewhere in his opinion. Ibid., 1031.

11. As Justice Blackmun bluntly put it, "There is nothing magical in the reasoning of judges long dead." *Lucas,* 1055. See also the dissenting opinion of Justice Stevens in *Lucas,* using in his argument the phrase "arresting the development of the common law." Ibid., 1069. His fear was that the majority was freezing the police power to the concerns of some past period while the nature of nuisance law commanded an evolution to meet new conditions. See also *The Hecht Co. v. Bowles,* 321 U.S. 321, 329 (1944) ("The essence of equity jurisdiction has been the power of the Chancellor to do equity and mould each decree to the necessities of the particular case.").

12. In environmental law it is applicable most prominently to issues such as wetlands and endangered species.

4. The Setting

1. Metcalf & Eddy, "Wastewater Engineering and Management Plan for Boston Harbor—Eastern Massachusetts Metropolitan Area" (March 1976), 2–13 (hereinafter cited as EMMA Main Report).

2. The map of the harbor (page xiii) and some of the background information given below are drawn from Boston Harbor Inter-

agency Coordinating Committee, "Wastewater Management Planning for Boston Harbor" (August 1980), chap. 1.

3. John Adams, *The Adams Papers: Diary and Autobiography of John Adams* (Cambridge, Mass., 1961), 1:141 (diary, 25 June 1760).

4. Ibid., 2:375 (diary, 19 May 1779).

5. John Adams to Cotton Tufts, 29 March 1776, *Adams Family Correspondence* (Cambridge, Mass., 1963), 1:367.

6. *Merriam Webster's Collegiate Dictionary*, 10th ed. (sewage and sewer).

7. Eliot C. Clarke, *Main Drainage Works of the City of Boston*, 2d ed. (Boston, 1885), 7. This situation was not unique to Boston: the stench of sewage from the Thames River in 1858 was so bad that the drapes of the Houses of Parliament were soaked in chloride of lime in a futile attempt to make the air in the chambers breathable. *New York Times Book Review*, 1 January 2001, A11.

8. *Report of a Commission Appointed to Consider a General System of Drainage for the Valleys of Mystic, Blackstone, and Charles Rivers* (Boston, 1886).

9. According to the EMMA Main Report, the agency survived, through the duration of the *Quincy* litigation and beyond, as the oldest metropolitan service district in the United States.

10. "Preliminary Report of the Special Commission Directed to Investigate the Discharge of Sewage from the Metropolitan Sewerage Districts into Boston Harbor and Its Tributary Waters, November 1935" (January 1936).

11. "Wastewater Management Planning," 8.

12. EMMA Main Report, 2–19. The Alewife Brook, Charlestown, East Boston Electric, East Boston Steam, and Reading pumping stations served the northern system; the Braintree-Weymouth, Hingham, Quincy, Hough's Neck, and Squantum stations served the southern system.

13. Ibid., 2–29.

14. Studies commissioned by the Metropolitan District Commission concluded that dry-weather overflow was "the single most important pollution influence on water quality" in the Dorchester Bay, Neponset River Estuary, Charles River Basin, and Inner Harbor planning areas. MDC, "Combined Sewer Overflow Project: Sum-

mary Report" (April 1982), 4. Storm-related overflows were also considered a serious problem, but responsibility for dealing with them was pushed by the MDC back onto member municipalities; it was they, the report concluded, that should be charged with improving local collection systems that they owned and maintained. Another MDC study, this one for the Charles River Basin, completed in 1982 by Metcalf & Eddy, recommended spending $65.4 million for combined sewer overflow improvements in that planning area.

15. When the *Quincy* litigation began, the MDC's forty-three member communities owned and operated 5,300 miles of collection sewers joined to the metropolitan system's intercepting sewers. These municipal systems varied significantly in age and type of construction. Approximately one-third of the sewage treated by the MDC originated in the city of Boston's collection system. As of 1980, more than 70 percent of Boston's 1,400 miles of sewer pipelines in use had been built before 1900, including 28 miles of wooden pipe built before 1850. About 70 percent of its mileage as of 1980 consisted of combined sewers. Mary J. Miller, J. Chester Johnson, and George E. Peterson, *The Future of Boston's Capital Plant* (Washington, D.C., 1981), 40.

16. See "Wastewater Treatment Facilities Planning in the Boston Metropolitan Area: A Case Study" (1979); Urban Systems Research and Engineering, "Sludge Management Planning in the Boston Metropolitan Area: A Case Study" (1979); "Institutional Aspects of Wastewater Management: The Boston Case Study" (1979); and "Water Quality Goals, Objectives, and Alternatives in the Boston Metropolitan Area: A Case Study" (1979).

17. Federal Water Pollution Control Administration, "Report on Pollution of the Navigable Waters of Boston Harbor" (1968), 2, 4, 50. Two of the most comprehensive surveys ever done of Boston Harbor water quality were conducted in the early 1970s, following up on the work of the FWPCA. Thereafter the MDC maintained sampling programs that ran continuously during the spring and summer of each year to monitor the condition of the harbor and its public beaches. Another study was conducted during 1970–1972 under the auspices of the New England Aquarium for the state's Department of Natural Resources (published in two volumes in

1972 and 1973). To a great extent, more recent government-sponsored planning studies concerning the harbor relied on the environmental quality data drawn directly or indirectly from these sources.

18. The relevant information is contained mainly in technical data volumes 13A and 13G accompanying the EMMA Main Report (see note 1 in this chapter). See especially vol. 13A, pp. 4 and 96.

19. The EPA found serious nutrient overenrichment in the Inner Harbor and noted other evidence indicating pollution east of the President Roads area. Its review also classified winter flounder fin erosion as a "major Harbor problem" suggesting contaminated sediments. The federal agency also reviewed MDC studies done in 1982 that it had requested in order to supplement the MDC's 1978–1979 data. According to the EPA, these data indicated pollution-caused changes in sediment benthic communities and disturbing PCB concentrations in harbor sediments. EPA Office of Marine Discharge Evaluation, "Analysis of the Section 301(h) Secondary Treatment Waiver Application for Boston Metropolitan District Commission" (1983).

20. At the time of the *Quincy* case, however, only one project had been designed and was under construction, while the others had not yet even been designed.

21. Paul F. Levy, a former executive director of the Massachusetts Water Resources Authority, has expanded these observations to the operations of business affairs, both governmental and corporate. See Levy, "The Nut Island Effect: When Good Teams Go Wrong," *Harvard Business Review* 79, no. 3 (2001): 51–59.

22. Lewis Mumford, *The City in History* (London, 1961). See also Abby A. Rockefeller, "Civilization and Sludge: Notes on the History of the Management of Human Excreta," in "Toxic Alert" (1997, 1998), www.cqs.com/sewage.htm (originally published in *Current World Leaders,* 39, no. 6 (1996): 99–113).

23. The subterranean achievement, the second of Paris's engineering triumphs, became a tourist attraction—via a tour taking about an hour—for visitors ranging from Emperor Alexander II to nobles and commoners. So carefully maintained were the pedestrian paths in what had been the last refuge of the hunted lawbreaker (or resistance fighter) that "a lady might walk along them from the Louvre to the Place de la Concorde without fear of bespattering her dainty

skirts." David P. Jordan, *Transforming Paris: The Life and Labors of Baron Haussmann* (New York, 1995), 276.

5. The Cast of Characters

1. As the primary agency of Massachusetts for environmental planning, the EOEA is entitled to use the services and plans of regional planning agencies, conservation districts, conservation commissions, and historical commissions in order to fulfill its environmental planning responsibilities.

2. The MDC's powers and responsibilities are defined by Chapter 92 of the General Laws of the commonwealth. The commission is charged to "construct, maintain and operate main sewers and other works required for a system of sewage disposal" for communities in the Boston metropolitan area and is authorized to contract for the extension of services to additional cities and towns.

3. Charles Button affidavit, 20 July 1983, 3, ¶4, QLP.

4. See "A Statement of Mandate" in affidavit of James S. Hoyte, 15 June 1983, QLP.

5. Ian Menzies, "Sargent Takes the Harbor On," *Boston Globe,* 2 June 1983, 1.

6. In a letter to me dated 14 July 1983, William F. Weld, United States Attorney, District of Massachusetts, pointed out that Judge Garrity had ruled that the master was authorized "and in fact encouraged" to join as a party defendant (in the state case) the United States, that is, the EPA. He added that the EPA was willing to assist in a "friend of the court" capacity and ready to provide information and general responses to proposals, believing it could work cooperatively with the master without being made a party to the suit; otherwise, federal policy would necessitate its seeking removal to the federal court. As a final note, he added that the extent and timing of EPA's cooperation would be subject to a rule of reason, "in light of resource constraints and the extremely complex nature of the problem."

7. Earlier, the National Environmental Policy Act had been signed into law on January 1, 1970. It articulated high-minded goals for national environmental policy, including promoting harmony between "man and his environment" and increasing understanding of ecological systems. At first the law had minimal bite; it required

every federal agency working on a project to prepare an environmental impact statement (EIS) describing potential environmental effects in detail. Subsequently, the courts played a surprisingly powerful role in translating high-sounding principles into practice: cutting corners in an EIS could result in litigation that might block a given project.

8. The definition and significance of these characteristics of the effluent are described in the "Primer for Wastewater Treatment," cited by the court in *United States v. Metropolitan District Commission,* Civil Action 85-0489-MA, Civil Action 83-16214-MA:

> BOD is a measure of the oxygen requirement exerted by microorganisms to stabilize organic matter.
>
> TSS is an indicator of the physical quality of water. High levels of suspended solids can affect the ecology of a harbor by inhibiting light transmission needed for photosynthesis.
>
> SS, a measure of the volume of settleable solids in wastewater, is used as an indicator of the effectiveness of treatment plant clarifiers.
>
> Fecal coliform bacteria is used as an indicator of other bacteria, including pathogenic organisms that can cause diseases such as typhoid fever, dysentery, diarrhea, and cholera.
>
> Total coliform bacteria is a measure of both fecal and nonfecal coliform bacteria.

The governing 1976 permit used these measurements in setting effluent limitations for the Deer and Nut Island treatment operations.

9. A violation of NPDES permit conditions clearly is a violation of the Federal Water Pollution Control Act. *National Resource Defense Council v. Costle,* 568 F.2d 1369 (D.C. Cir. 1977).

10. 1977 Mass. Acts 292.

11. This process, called bioturbation, was discovered by Charles Darwin.

12. In 1983, when the EPA ruled on the MDC's sewage treatment variance request, 86 percent of the clam beds in Dorchester Bay were classified as "grossly polluted." Levels of fecal coliform bacteria were ten times higher than the level at which unrestricted clam digging was allowed.

13. When benthic ecologists such as Eugene Gallagher, of the Univer-

sity of Massachusetts at Boston, and Kenneth Keay, of the Massachusetts Water Resources Authority, study the effects of pollution on a given marine ecosystem, they typically focus on infauna rather than epifauna. Gallagher and Keay studied Massachusetts's benthic ecosystem extensively over many decades, and documented both its worst degradation and its partial recovery. They found that in the worst areas, only a few highly adaptive species of worm-like creatures (spionids and capitellids) could survive. Most of those that do are so notoriously resistant to pollution that benthic ecologists use their presence in large numbers as an indicator of benthic degradation.

14. "Richness" is a measure of the number of species found in a given sample, while "evenness" measures the distribution among species.

15. Amazingly, no data on the infauna of the harbor and bay were collected until the early 1970s. The first comprehensive study was conducted in 1982 by the MDC in connection with its application for a waiver from the EPA.

16. One may wonder how these opportunistic species can survive in oxygen-poor black mayonnaise. Some build breathing tubes that protrude upward into the water. Others live with their heads in the mud, where they feed on the organic deposits, while breathing through vascularized filaments that protrude above the sediment surface.

17. A 1982 study of samples taken from thirty-nine sites within the harbor and the bay found the worst benthic contamination not near pollution discharge points, but rather in sediment settling areas, some of which were far from any known source of pollution.

18. For example, the 1982 study revealed lower species diversity and lower levels of dissolved oxygen at a site several miles out into Massachusetts Bay than at a site immediately adjacent to the Nut Island sewage treatment plant.

19. As the noted political economist Albert Hirschman points out: "When a uniform quality decline hits simultaneously all firms [in a given market], each firm will garner in some of the disgruntled customers of the other firms while losing some of its previous customers to its competitors. In these circumstances, [institutional dissent] is ineffective in alerting management to its failings, and a merger of all firms would appear to be socially desirable—that is, monopoly would replace competition to advantage, for customer dissatisfac-

tion would then be vented directly and perhaps to some effect in attempting to improve the monopoly's management." Hirschman, *Exit, Voice, and Loyalty* (Cambridge, Mass., 1970), 26.

6. Turning the Tide

1. William Sloman, quoted in "The Litigation and Politics of Boston Harbor: From Superior Court to Beacon Hill" (student paper, Harvard Law School, 24 May 1985 draft), 10, QLP. See also the brief submitted by the Attorney General, "Reference of This Case to a Master Is Unwarranted and Inappropriate," 15 June 1983.
2. The opinion Sloman relied on in his brief is *Bartlett-Collins Co. v. Surinam Navigation Co.*, 381 F.2d 546, 551 (10th Cir. 1967).
3. 363 Mass. 256, 280 (1973).
4. See *Glynn v. City of Gloucester*, 9 Mass. App. Ct. 454, 463 (1980): "Only extraordinary circumstances should justify a reference." This is similar to Federal Rule of Civil Procedure 53.
5. *Southern Burlington County NAACP v. Township of Mount Laurel*, 67 N.J. 151, 336 A.2d 713, *appeal dismissed and cert. denied*, 423 U.S. 808 (1975). See Charles M. Haar, *Suburbs under Siege: Race, Space, and Audacious Judges* (Princeton, 1996).
6. In a conversation with law students researching the case, Steven Horowitz, the deputy special master, later suggested that "[t]he reason that Judge Garrity chose to appoint Charlie Haar as a special master, knowing obviously that he is not an environmental technician or even an environmental lawyer, was that he felt that a generalist with the kind of knowledge about the way that the court system and executive branch and the political system work would be more valuable than somebody who would have a quick grasp of the technical issues, because you can learn the technical issues." Steven G. Horowitz, quoted in "Litigation and Politics of Boston Harbor," 11.
7. Equity Rule 59 (1912) codified the authority for special masters before promulgation of the Federal Rules of Civil Procedure. Vincent M. Nathan, "The Use of Special Masters in Institutional Reform Litigation," 10 *University of Toledo Law Review* 419, 424 (1979). See *Morgan v. Kerrigan*, 401 F. Supp. 216, 227 (D. Mass. 1975). In the main, courts have been passive in the liability phase, but less so in the remedial phase, where there is diminished need for an artificial barrier between the judge and the parties.

8. Sloman, quoted in "Litigation and Politics of Boston Harbor," 20–21.
9. James Hoyte, conversation with the author.
10. See Abram Chayes, "The Role of the Judge in Public Law Litigation," 89 *Harvard Law Review* 1281 (1976).
11. James Hoyte, conversation with the author.
12. Timothy G. Little, "Court-Appointed Special Masters in Complex Environmental Litigation: *City of Quincy v. Metropolitan District Commission,*" 8 *Harvard Environmental Law Review* 435 (1984).
13. Curtis J. Berger, "Away from the Court House and into the Field: The Odyssey of a Special Master," 78 *Columbia Law Review* 707 (1978).
14. Sloman, quoted in "Litigation and Politics of Boston Harbor," 17.
15. On the issue of the EPA's role in the case and the question of state jurisdiction, Judge Garrity wrote to President Ronald Reagan on August 1, 1983:

Dear Mr. President:

The City of Quincy in Massachusetts recently commenced a civil action against various agencies of the Commonwealth of Massachusetts and other defendants seeking court intervention to require speedy rectification of the horrendous pollution of Boston Harbor.

The United States Environmental Protection Agency (EPA) will play a critical role, especially in terms of funding, in the cleanup of Boston Harbor which I estimate will require some years and substantial federal, State and local monies to accomplish. Enclosed is a letter that I just received from an Assistant United States Attorney in Boston representing the EPA, in which letter he states: "[F]ederal (I gather Department of Justice) policy would necessitate our seeking removal to federal district court if EPA were made a party to a state court action. Also, the extent and timing of EPA's cooperation must be subject to a rule of reason, in light of resource constraints and the extremely complex nature of the problem."

Although I could not agree more with the thoughts expressed in the second sentence, the policy expressed in the first sentence is inconsistent with the public interest.

I plan to request EPA's technical and funding assistance in marshalling State and local resources to solve a local problem. However, an Assistant United States Attorney indicates that if EPA is involved in any meaningful way then the federal government will dictate both the process and the results by federal judicial intervention. As you so well know, federal judges are never reluctant to interfere in State and local affairs especially in Boston.

I recall your inspiring inaugural address in which you said in part: "It is my intention to curb the size and influence of the Federal establishment and to demand recognition of the distinction between the powers granted to the Federal Government and those reserved to the States or to the people . . ."

I respectfully request that you give meaning to the admirable notion of federalism which you articulated in your inaugural address and which you have repeated on many occasions since that time. I request that you direct the EPA to intervene in the action currently pending before me and not to remove it to federal court.

The assistant U.S. attorney referred to in the letter was William Weld. Years later, as governor of Massachusetts and a candidate for the U.S. Senate, Weld leapt into the Charles River, fully clothed, to demonstrate, among other things, the newfound purity of its waters.

16. See Procedural Order, 9 September 1983.

17. "Because of a defendant's desire to obtain a court order requiring it to do something that it would like to do but does not have the political power to do absent a court order, . . . the parties may agree on a plan that is beyond the scope of the court's remedial power even broadly construed." William A. Fletcher, "The Discretionary Constitution: Institutional Remedies and Judicial Legitimacy," 91 *Yale Law Journal* 635, 653 (1982).

18. See Donald L. Horowitz, "Decreeing Organizational Change: Judicial Supervision of Public Institutions," in Bette Goulet, ed., *The Courts: Separation of Powers—Final Report of the Chief Justice Earl Warren Conference on Advocacy in the United States* (Washington, D.C., 1983).

7. A Dying Harbor?

1. Unless otherwise noted, the quotations from expert testimony in this chapter are from written affidavits submitted to the special master. These documents, as well as other papers cited in Chapters

8 and 9, including motions, briefs, and specialized reports, have been deposited in the Quincy Litigation Papers (QLP), Harvard Law School Library, where they are available for inspection and analysis.

2. Baratta further argued in his affidavit that, because of this dilution, the chlorination demand diminished by half, from 6 mg/liter normal sewage flow to 3 mg/liter, during storm flow conditions. He added that bypass discharges are made via the same outfall system as treated sewage "and so the diluted storm flows are mixed with and attenuated by treated plant effluent." Noel Baratta, affidavit, 5 July 1983, 3, ¶3.

3. David Standley, supplemental affidavit, 18 July 1983, 10, ¶20.

4. Ibid., 9, ¶17.

5. William Gaughan, affidavit, 5 July 1983.

6. Glenn Haas, affidavit, 5 July 1983, 7.

7. State Defendants' Proposed Findings of Fact and Conclusions of Law, 26 July 1983.

8. Robert Holthaus, affidavit, 15 July 1983.

9. Citing their finding that samples from Quincy's storm drains contained bacteria that may have come from human or animal waste, Vittands and MacKinnon further argued that Nut Island was not likely responsible for the high fecal coliform counts in Quincy for three additional reasons: First, discharges from the Nut Island plant during normal operating conditions had a markedly smaller coliform count than those found in samples from around Wollaston Beach. Second, the distance between the nearest outfalls and Wollaston Beach was between two-and-a-half and three miles, an unrealistically long journey for coliform. Third, regrowth from any bacterial matter from Nut Island would be inhibited by the salt content of Quincy Bay, weakening coliform organisms and preventing them from migrating upstream into Quincy storm drains.

10. Standley, supplemental affidavit, 18 July 1983.

11. Specifically, samples taken by the Carr team on July 7, 1983, indicated that the quality of the water coming out of the city's drains was far superior to that of the water in Quincy Bay.

12. David Standley also put forth another, perhaps less scientific and more risky, explanation for the city's claim that its storm drains did not significantly contribute to the pollution that afflicted the har-

bor as a whole: the "first flush" effect. Because the pipes within the North Quincy storm drain system had slopes close to, and in some cases less than, the recommended minimum slope, the flow velocities were often less than the three feet per second necessary to prevent the settling of solids in the drains. Hence, Standley claimed, during a heavy rainstorm the first surge of higher water flows might force settled solids out of its stormwater system, but these would be minimal and traceable mostly to animal sources (dogs and seagulls). Standley, supplemental affidavit, 18 July 1983, 9–10.

Jekabs Vittands of the MDC took issue with Standley's theory, claiming that the first flush effect was only relevant with regard to a limited number of combined sewer systems. Thus, Vittands hinted, it was unlikely that fluke rainfalls forcing out settled solids had contributed to an occasional increased level of coliform around the outlets of Quincy's storm drains; the city of Quincy itself was liable for the chronic pollution of its beaches.

13. This is what Justice Brennan must have had in mind in writing of "the important role that qualities other than reason must play in the judicial process. . . . I shall refer to these qualities under the rubric of 'passion,' a word I choose because it is general and conveys much of what seems at first blush to be the very enemy of reason. By 'passion' I mean the range of emotional and intuitive responses to a given set of facts or arguments, responses which often speed into our consciousness far ahead of the lumbering syllogisms of reason." William J. Brennan, Jr., "Reason, Passion, and 'The Progress of the Law,'" 10 *Cardozo Law Review* 3, 9, 17 (1988).

14. In the intervening years, the legal and the scientific communities have grappled extensively with this issue, as engineering and technological issues have played expanding roles not only in environmental litigation, but also in such areas as medical liability cases and disputes within the computing industry. The American Association for the Advancement of Science, working with the Federal Judicial Center, the research and education arm of the judiciary, has initiated a demonstration project on court-appointed scientific experts, aiming to assist federal trial judges in obtaining independent scientific and technical assistance. See Stephen Breyer, "The Interdependence of Science and Law," address at 1998 American Academy of Arts and Sciences annual meeting (16 February 1998). The *Quincy* litigation was among the earliest cases to supplement trial

testimony with court-appointed experts, and the issue will remain an important one for the courts for many years to come.

8. Report of the Special Master: Findings of Fact

1. Charles M. Haar, "Report of the Special Master Regarding Findings of Fact and Proposed Remedies *(City of Quincy v. Metropolitan District Commission),*" 9 August 1983, hereinafter cited as Haar, "Report." Trial documents cited in this chapter are in the Quincy Litigation Papers (QLP), Harvard Law School Library.

2. Population trends for the Boston metropolitan area were not uniform. Although the number of households in the metropolitan sewerage district continued to increase during the 1970s, the average number of persons per household decreased from 3.0 in 1970 to 2.5 in 1980. Outward migration from the older urban areas and resettlement in the suburbs led to a net population decrease of approximately 125,000 people during the decade prior to the *Quincy* litigation. Projections in 1979 indicated a continuation of the population decline, but at a lesser rate, in the older urban core areas, and stabilization in the inner suburbs bounded by Route 128. In the aggregate, the total MSD contributing population was expected to increase from 1,900,000 to 2,029,000 by the year 2010, with faster growth in the south metropolitan service area.

3. It was further estimated that by 2010, average sewage flows would be 152 mgd for Deer Island and 67 mgd for Nut Island; projected peak sewage flows came to 312 mgd and 131 mgd, respectively.

4. Sanitary sewer systems (except "force mains," which operate by pressure) are never completely tight and leak-free; pipes, tunnels, conduits, and manholes all leak to varying degrees, depending on their size, design, condition, and the extent to which they are submerged in ground or surface water. Because deterioration, and consequent leakage, is expected over time, sanitary sewer systems are commonly designed with an allowance for infiltration.

5. Metcalf & Eddy, "Site Options Study" (June 1982), 1:4–48.

6. Evidence indicated that in 1981, 77 mgd of infiltration and 171 mgd of inflow entered the south system alone. According to the plaintiff's expert, an additional 3.5 mgd of flow might have been added to the south system service area through illegal connections and through connections of less than 2,000 gpd (gallons per day) that did not require a permit and so were not recorded.

7. Estimates of the costs of transporting and treating the peak flow of I/I ranged from $0.12 to $40 per gpd, for the average and peak flows respectively. To these could be added the costs of community operations and maintenance, and should also include such considerations as the harmful impact on public health, recreation, the tourist industry, real estate values, or clam flats, not to mention the public's pleasure in the harbor. In practical terms, the fact that I/I was being transported and treated, rather than prevented, "cost" Massachusetts citizens far more than the official figures showed.

8. The DWPC ranked applications for sewer connection and extension projects from MDC member communities on the basis of a point system, which took into account health effects, environmental impacts, earlier court enforcement actions, and the amount of money budgeted for such projects. In sum, about $12 million per year was budgeted for sewer extension projects in MDC member communities. Thomas McMahon, affidavit, 15 June 1983, 3; David Standley, affidavit no. 1, 15 June 1983, 6, ¶11, 1–71. DWPC restrictions on MDC member-community sewer extension plans could include the allowance of new connections only where some amount of I/I had been removed from the system through rehabilitation or replacement of sewers and manholes. Although a 2:1 ratio of I/I removal was commonly used by DWPC, it was an arbitrary formula, chosen for the sake of consistency, and at times could be adjusted.

9. Jekabs P. Vittands, affidavit, 5 July 1983, 1–2. The EPA considered I/I "excessive" when its elimination through sewer system rehabilitation was less costly than the net cost of transporting and treating it at the receiving facility. Federal Water Pollution Control Act Amendments of 1972 (P.L. 92-500); Fay, Spofford & Thorndike, "Nut Island Infiltration/Inflow Study" (April 1979), S-2.

10. Rules and Regulations Covering Discharge of Sewage, Drainage, Substances, or Wastes to Sewerage Works within the Metropolitan Sewerage District, 12 December 1979. "Every municipality shall obtain a Permit from the Commission for all existing public or special discharges or connections from that municipality to the Metropolitan Sewerage System. . . . Permits may contain the following conditions: (1) Limits on the constituents and volumes of discharges into the system [and] . . . (2) Schedules for completing

inflow/infiltration studies and, when required, schedules for carrying out inflow/infiltration reduction programs."

11. The DWPC imposed the 2:1 restrictions on seven of the twenty-one communities in the south system service area.

12. State Defendants' Memorandum Concerning Remedial Measures, 20 July 1983, 4. As of the date of the trial proceedings in 1983, the federal government had granted $1,387,000 for I/I work directly related to Boston Harbor itself, and additional funds had been granted for I/I work in MSD upstream and member communities.

13. In particular, the report cited problems with electrical generators, screens, and sedimentation tanks. Haar, "Report," 69–70. Outfalls 101, 102, and 103 had become encrusted to the point that their functional capacity was reduced from 276 mgd to 165 mgd, leading to increased use of the emergency outfall 104. Outfall 104 discharged sewage less than 500 feet from Quincy's shores.

14. Discharges from outfall 104 during the fiscal year 1983 totaled 765 million gallons.

15. Fully 66 percent of the total number of bypasses from the Nut Island facility between July 1977 and March 1983 were attributable to increases in I/I related to wet weather; 34 percent were caused by operational and maintenance difficulties at the plant during dry weather.

16. Noel Baratta, affidavit, 5 June 1983, 6, ¶8.

17. Robert Daylor, affidavit, 15 June 1983, 7, §§14, 15.

18. EPA Office of Marine Discharge Evaluation, "Analysis of the Section 301(h) Secondary Treatment Waiver Application for Boston Metropolitan District Commission" (1983), 17; Daylor, affidavit, 16. Bacteria and other pathogens in Nut Island discharges affected shellfish flats as well. In Quincy Bay these flats lie even closer to the plant's outfalls than do the beaches.

19. U.S. Department of Commerce, National Oceanic and Atmospheric Administration, Boston Harbor Tidal Current Charts. If Moon Island discharged during the latter part of the outgoing tide, the effluent could first be swept out along the Quincy side of Long Island, and then return to Quincy Bay with the flood tides.

20. Daylor, affidavit, 11, 27.

21. Camp Dresser & McKee, "Report on Combined Sewer Overflows" (1982), 1:ix–21.

22. Further testimony traced the pattern. On the day following a major storm, strong northwesterly winds would bring sewage plumes from Moon Island under Long Island Bridge into the tidal currents of the western part of Quincy Bay. The ultimate result: vast quantities of raw, untreated sewage and contaminated stormwater reached areas used by swimmers, boaters, and fishermen.

23. By design, there were four points at Nut Island from which influent flows might be allowed to bypass the system; MDC studies described how these were being used at the time of the *Quincy* litigation. *Initial bypasses* took place when wastewater passed directly from the High Level Sewer to an emergency channel leading to outfalls 101, 102, and 103. Design specifications dictated that this condition would occur if influent flows exceeded 280 mgd, but in practice it took place at flow rates as low as 140 mgd—an amount only somewhat above the average daily flow—when intake screens became clogged. The wastewater received no treatment other than incidental chlorination when it was combined with treated sewage in the outfalls. *Comminutor overflows* occurred when influent overwhelmed the plant's grinders. Comminutor overflows through outfalls 101, 102, 103, or 104 resulted in the discharge of unshredded materials of the same general character as initial bypasses, except for the removal of larger objects and solids. Scum and suspended solids, debris, and fecal matter remained in the effluent. *Pre-aeration channel bypasses* occurred when influent exceeded the capacity of Nut Island's six sedimentation tanks. *Effluent channel bypasses* occurred whenever effluent volume exceeded the combined capacity of outfalls 101, 102, and 103; encrustation of the primary outfalls led to bypasses to outfall 104 at flows of only 165 mgd.

24. The commonwealth required that a wastewater treatment plant provide fifteen minutes of chlorine contact time (thirty minutes in shellfish areas) for effluent released through an outfall, whether or not that effluent bypassed primary treatment. Outfalls 101 and 102 did provide fifteen minutes; outfall 103, which carried half the plant's flow when all three were in use, did not. As the shortest, outfall 104 offered the least contact time of the four.

25. In 1982, several experts agreed, the minimum flow of sewage to Nut Island on any day was 56 mgd, the average daily flow was 124.62 mgd, and the maximum flow was 261.4 mgd. MDC, "63rd

Annual Report" (10 December 1982), 28. No separate data existed on the average level of dry-weather flow, but testimony suggested it was less than 100 mgd. Accordingly, in theory, when operating properly and in accordance with the intentions of its designers, Nut Island had adequate design capacity for dry-weather flow. But the plant's wet-weather design capacity could not handle the full amount of increased flow resulting from I/I during periods of heavy rainfall, even if it was operating at full efficiency. On balance, wet weather resulted in more harm due to bypasses than benefit from dilution. According to the MDC, an average of 48,000 lbs/day of suspended solids, 38,000 lbs/day of grease and petroleum, and 6,200 lbs/day of settleable solids were released into the waters off Nut Island between June 1981 and June 1982. MDC, "63rd Annual Report," 28.

26. EPA, "Analysis of the Section 301(h) Waiver Application," 11, 27.

27. To the astonishment of many who learned of it only at the *Quincy* trial, no treatment whatsoever was ever provided to the sewage discharged from Moon Island. BWSC, Statement of Disputed Facts Pertinent to the Interlocutory Relief Sought Against It, 20 July 1983.

28. According to a BWSC witness at the *Quincy* trial, "The tanks are in a state of disrepair: the granite walls need repointing and some replacement, and the gate-mechanisms are totally rusted out and would have to be entirely replaced." The conclusion: aside from some seepage, the holding tanks were entirely blocked up. Charles Button, affidavit, 20 July 1983, 10, 13.

29. The main pumping station contained nine wastewater pumps. Of these pumps, eight were powered by twelve-cylinder radial, dual-fuel engines, one by an electric motor. The balance of the influent was delivered to the plant by the Winthrop Terminal Facility. Like Nut Island, the Deer Island plant was designed to provide primary sewage treatment only. The treatment processes included screening and grit removal, aeration of the influent for a ten-minute period, primary sedimentation, and post-chlorination of the plant effluent prior to ocean discharge through two long submerged outfalls. Treatment of sludge was accomplished through sludge thickening, primary digestion, and chlorination. MDC, "63rd Annual Report," 31-32.

30. In response to Deer Island's low pumping capacity, the EPA issued

an administrative order in August 1981 requiring the MDC to maintain five pumps on-line continuously, thus mandating a peak capacity at approximately one-half the peak design capacity of the plant. Nevertheless, the MDC failed to meet even this lowered requirement. MDC, "63rd Annual Report," 35.

31. Aside from inadequacies at the main pumping station, the Deer Island treatment plant was found to be deficient in many other respects as well. For example, the sedimentation tanks were undersized, the control system in the primary effluent channel had been abandoned, only two of the four sludge thickeners were in operation, so-called "detention" periods within the scum concentration tanks and the sludge digestion system were insufficient, and the electric generators were in poor condition. Metcalf & Eddy, "Site Options Study," 1:4–15, 25.

32. During the period from January 1, 1982, to June of 1983, for example, there were ninety-five discharges from Moon Island. Of these, sixty-three took place as a result of increased effluent volume during wet weather, and thirty occurred as a result of "operational difficulties at Deer Island" during comparatively dry weather. And as the operating capacity of Deer Island decreased, wet-weather discharges from Moon Island became more frequent and contained more concentrated levels of pollutants. The effluent was described by eyewitnesses and experts as a brown, murky fluid, carrying vast quantities of ammonia (toxic to fish), phosphorous (responsible for algae blooms), highly toxic trace metals such as mercury, pesticides, carcinogenic organic chemicals, grease, and suspended solids, which included tampon applicators, condoms, and pieces of human excrement. Its fecal coliform count was ten times higher than that found in the most contaminated of Quincy's storm drains.

33. Cited by Paul Levy, "The Nut Island Effect: When Good Teams Go Wrong," *Harvard Business Review,* 79, no. 3 (2001): 51–59.

9. Report of the Special Master: Remedies and Recommendations

1. Charles M. Haar, "Report of the Special Master Regarding Findings of Fact and Proposed Remedies *(City of Quincy v. Metropolitan District Commission),*" 9 August 1983; hereinafter cited as Haar, "Report." Trial documents cited in this chapter are all in the Quincy Litigation Papers (QLP), Harvard Law School Library.

2. Plaintiff's Memorandum to Special Master Regarding Remedies, 18 July 1983, 3.

3. A five-year projection of new construction suggested an addition of at most 30 mgd, or approximately 15 percent, to the existing average sewage flow system-wide.

4. State Defendants' Memorandum Concerning Remedial Measures, 20 July 1983; Glenn Haas, affidavit, 5 July 1983, 3–5; Noel Baratta, affidavit, 15 July 1983, 7–8, ¶9.

5. Plaintiff's Memorandum to Special Master Regarding Remedies, 6, §c.

6. In particular the state defendants maintained that it was not possible to limit the peak flows in the High Level Sewer to 250 mgd. Jekabs P. Vittands, affidavit, 15 July 1983, 2.

7. T. C. F. MacKinnon, affidavit, 5 July 1983, 2. Running the numbers, it seemed that removing 28 percent of the calculated peak flow of 179 mgd of inflow and 30 percent of the calculated peak flow of 77 mgd of infiltration would reduce the total peak flow of 310 mgd to 237 mgd, thus casting doubt on the claim that peak flows to Nut Island could not be reduced to 250 mgd.

8. Ibid.

9. Ibid., 6.

10. Baratta, affidavit, 8–9.

11. David Standley, affidavit, 2 July 1983, 1, ¶5. The similarity to transferable development rights (TDRs) in the land-use planning area is obvious.

12. The report noted that the DWPC had the authority to implement such a program through its power to approve, deny, or conditionally approve all new connections to community systems.

13. Beginning in 1982, the MDC charged the municipalities according to volume, peak flow, and effluent strength. But this process was a cost allocation program only, not designed as a conservation device.

14. "The legal posture of BWSC is complex and intriguing," the report stated. "To the extent the court finds no liability on the part of the BWSC, for purposes of efficiency the BWSC should confer with the MDC on actions to ameliorate the harmful effects of Moon Island discharges. This is consistent with BWSC's current status as an indispensable party."

15. Haar, "Report," 153.

16. Baratta, affidavit, 7, ¶9; Haas, affidavit, 4–5; Haar, "Report," 152.
17. Charles Button, affidavit, 20 July 1983, 2–314; Haar, "Report," 153.
18. I was reluctant to accede to the defendants' claims that other projects might prove more cost-effective than chlorination or tank restoration at Moon Island. Recognizing, however, "the traditional restraint of the court in these matters," the report recommended that "if the defendants are able to devise a realistic solution for Moon Island discharges, other than renovation of Moon Island itself, which is not only cost-effective but pollution-effective, the court should stay its hand. It should accept such a response and assure that it is accomplished expeditiously, rather than dictate any specific remedial measures."
19. On August 2, 1983, the court ordered the master to "look into the possibility of remedial orders directed to the improvement of conditions at Moon Island," and ordered BWSC to remain in the action as an "indispensable party." None of the remedial proposals spoke to the question of which agency would bear the cost of improving conditions at Moon Island. Whether or not the BWSC, as distinct from the MDC, had this obligation was a matter of legal responsibility to be resolved by the court.
20. Baratta, affidavit, 7–9, 59; Haar, "Report," 148–149.
21. Vittands, affidavit, 1–241; Haar, "Report," 149.
22. The report also noted that the state's Department of Environmental Quality Engineering and Division of Water Pollution Control could enforce the requirements of the NPDES permits; it was therefore suggested that the DEQE's enforcement actions in this regard be periodically reported to the court.

10. The Judge Lays Down the Law

1. Charles M. Haar, "Report of the Special Master Regarding Findings of Fact and Proposed Remedies *(City of Quincy v. Metropolitan District Commission),*" 9 August 1983, 165–166.
2. Judy Foreman, "Court Gets Plan to Clean Boston Harbor," *Boston Globe,* 11 August 1983, 1.
3. "A Starting Point," *Boston Herald,* 12 August 1983.
4. "Hope for the Harbor," *Boston Globe,* 13 August 1983, 14.
5. "A Cleaner Boston Harbor: Something the State Cannot Afford to Postpone," *Christian Science Monitor,* 1 November 1984, B2.

6. "Hope for the Harbor," 14.
7. Editorial, *Quincy Patriot Ledger,* 12 August 1984.
8. James Hoyte, conversation with the author.
9. Michael Sloman, quoted in "The Litigation and Politics of Boston Harbor" (draft paper, 24 May 1985), 30, QLP.
10. Judge Garrity, *Boston Globe,* 25 August 1983, 21.
11. Judge Garrity, Findings, Rulings, Opinion, and Orders, 9 September 1983.
12. A significant drawback of consent decrees is that they are difficult to modify as circumstances change, whereas the procedural order was subject to simple change by the parties or the court. Overall, compensating for the lack of legally binding effect on the parties, the procedural order was a far more flexible instrument.
13. Procedural order, 9 September 1983.
14. Ibid.
15. In a letter presented to Judge Garrity on September 10, 1983, EPA lawyers pledged to "fully support the parties' agreement within the limits of its authority and resources."
16. Francis W. Sargent, "All Must Help Clean Up the Harbor," *Boston Globe,* 16 September 1983, 15.
17. Chris Black, "Panel on Sewer Services Sought," *Boston Globe,* 17 September 1983, 32.
18. Editorial, "Harbor's Ebbing Tide," *Boston Globe,* 3 December 1983, 18.
19. Charles Radin, "Cleanup of Boston Harbor Defies Effort at Tidy Solution," *Boston Globe,* 22 April 1984, 1, 22.
20. Public Finance Group, First National Bank of Boston, "Protecting Water Resources: A Financial Analysis—A Report Analyzing the Funding Requirements of Water and Sewerage Services in the Boston Metropolitan Area" (8 February 1984).
21. James Hoyte, conversation with the author.
22. Charles Radin, "Harbor Help Insufficient, Monitor Says," *Boston Globe,* 13 April 1984, 21.
23. Ibid., 26.
24. "The Court and the Harbor," *Boston Globe,* 16 April 1984, 18.

11. Awash With Ideas

1. This sentence is a paraphrase of section 1(b) of the Massachusetts Water Resources Authority Act (hereinafter MWRAA), the state

statute that set up the MWRA. (Enacted as chapter 372 of Acts of 1984, *Acts and Resolves Passed by the General Court of Massachusetts in the Year 1984,* 1:753–833; §§1–30 (only) were also published in *Massachusetts General Laws Annotated* (hereinafter *MGLA*) (2001), 11B:360–414 (c.92 App. §1–1 to 1–30).)

2. See §1(c), MWRAA.

3. Public Finance Group, First National Bank of Boston, "Protecting Water Resources: A Financial Analysis—A Report Analyzing the Funding Requirements of Water and Sewerage Services in the Boston Metropolitan Area" (8 February 1984).

4. See Jameson W. Doig, *Empire on the Hudson: Entrepreneurial Vision and Political Power at the Port of New York Authority* (New York, 2001).

5. *Boston Globe,* 11 October 1984, 27.

6. As regards the potential administrative savings from integration of the water delivery and sewer systems, an example that came readily to hand was that of the Boston Water and Sewer Commission, which had recently combined the two systems at the local level. The savings achieved through consolidation were estimated to range between 2.5 and 3 percent of the BWSC's budget. Assuming that the proposed MWRA would have an operating budget of $50 million annually, this suggested a potential yearly savings of $1.5 million. Moreover, the financial viability of the combined system could be enhanced if it had a single, integrated revenue generation and collection mechanism.

7. To obtain favorable terms, the MFAB sometimes needed to hold back agencies from issuing bonds, while at other times it made sense to accelerate the process. The MFAB job and my work as chairperson of the state commission appointed by Governor Dukakis to rescue the Massachusetts Housing Finance Authority from a debt crisis that threatened to put it into bankruptcy, and, later, as a consultant on the cash flow problems of New York's Urban Development Corporation, were undoubtedly factors in Judge Garrity's decision to select me as special master.

8. The initial tentative draft of the MWRA bill, done by the law firm of Mintz, Levin at my behest so that we could better understand the issues that would be raised by such an enabling act, assumed a combined system. Over time there were some eight versions of the bill as Francis Meaney and I worked out details.

9. Philip Shapiro, a one-time interim executive director of the MWRA and currently a managing director of Standard & Poor's, explains it as a difference in the level of essentiality: drinking water must be available to people within thirty-six hours, whereas the results of an inadequate sewer system can be tolerated for decades. Furthermore, there is a clear local responsibility for drinking water, whereas the federal grants program and the EPA made the sewer picture more uncertain.

10. First National Bank of Boston, "Protecting Water Resources," 61–62.

11. The first draft of 10 November 1983 termed it "The Metropolitan Boston Water Resources Authority."

12. Section 10, MWRAA.

13. Sections 3(b) and 13(d), House bill 5915 (Dukakis bill).

14. Section 3(b), Senate bill 2272 (Bulger bill).

15. In various other provisions the Bulger bill carried over important elements of the Dukakis bill aimed at augmenting the governor's powers of appointment.

16. In fact, if one examined the Bulger bill closely, it emerged that merely by blocking appointment of the Quincy and Winthrop recommendations, the governor would be able to control a majority of the remaining members. Section 3(d). And those powers were further augmented in the Bulger bill by giving the chairperson, the secretary of EOEA, a special veto over official board actions.

17. Reported out of the House Committee on Ways and Means on December 3, 1984.

18. The tilt toward localities in the Cusack bill was highlighted by other factors: the quorum was increased to five, and the bill did not grant any special veto to the chairman.

19. Section 3(c), House bill 6319 (Cusack bill).

20. The statute makes explicit that these two represent "water resources protection interests." Communities in the Connecticut River Valley retained an historic memory of diversion of flows to the Boston water supply, and they sought insulation from MWRA actions that might carry a similar impact. This explains the inclusion of a Connecticut River Basin representative, who could be expected to protect that watershed. Section 69 prohibits interbasin transfers without legislative approval; sections 9 and 42 create the Division of Watershed Management to retain state control over all watersheds and water rights.

21. Section 3(c), MWRAA.
22. Section 3(b), MWRAA.
23. The definition of "minority" appears at *MGLA*, c.7, §40N(2): "a person with permanent residence in the United States who is American Indian, Black, Cape Verdean, Western Hemisphere Hispanic, Aleut, Eskimo, or Asian." The language is replete with difficulties. There could be claims that being a white male constitutes "misfeasance, malfeasance, or willful neglect of duty" as cause for removal as defined in section 3(d). And some of the language can be read so as to imply that only one director may be a minority person—a constitutional nightmare if that were the case.
24. John H. Mollenkopf, *The Contested City* (Princeton, 1983), 149.
25. The breadth of power conferred on the MWRA's board of directors may be explained as a lesson the legislature drew from its reading of the consequences of more restrictive earlier enactments, such as the Massachusetts Bay Transportation Authority (*MGLA*, c.161A), which adhered too tightly to the literal text of its enabling statute.
26. The full assortment of provisions in section 6 of the legislation makes the MWRA's board of directors responsible for adopting and amending by-laws, choosing an official seal, maintaining an office, determining a fiscal year, adopting and enforcing procedures and regulations in connection with performance of duties, entering into contracts and agreements, obtaining insurance and entering into agreements of indemnification, and applying for and administering grants or gifts. In addition, the board is granted the power to sue and be sued, employ personnel, engage architectural, engineering, accounting, management, legal, financial, environmental, and other professional services, appear in its own behalf before other public bodies, and acquire, take, and hold title to property. Also in the act as a final blessing is the all-embracing clause, "to do all things necessary, convenient or desirable for carrying out the purposes of this act or the powers expressly granted or necessarily implied by this act." Section 6(r), MWRAA.
27. Section 3(d), MWRAA.
28. Section 3(a), MWRAA. Section 8(i) is also pertinent: "The Authority and division shall be subject to the provisions of, and to regulation by the department of environmental quality engineering and any division thereof as may be duly exercised over an independent public authority of the commonwealth."

29. The collapse of New York's Urban Development Corporation, often attributed to its large number of ex officio directors, posed many caveats to the framers of the MWRA.

30. See Lawrence Susskind, Sarah McKearnan, and Jennifer Thomas-Larmer, eds., *Consensus Building Handbook* (Thousand Oaks, Cal., 1999).

31. See §23, MWRAA.

32. The original Dukakis draft provided for two nonvoting gubernatorial appointments representing environmental expertise and the Connecticut River basin. The Cusack bill, perhaps to an unwieldy extent, gave all sixty cities and towns a voting representative and included seven additional voting representatives from the Metropolitan Area Planning Council, the Connecticut River basin, and the Quabbin, Wachusett, and Ware watersheds.

33. The Dukakis and Bulger bills provided for total community votes to equal one hundred; in the Cusack bill that number was ninety-five (§23(b) of the Dukakis bill, §22(b) of the Bulger bill). In the MWRAA, as finally passed, the cities and towns together were allocated ninety-five votes, with five more divided evenly among the other seven members of the advisory board, bringing the total to one hundred.

34. Section 4(e), MWRAA.

35. All three drafts set up the same funding framework for the advisory board. Regular meetings were to be held, and special meetings could also be called by the MWRA or by fifteen members of the advisory board. A quorum was to consist of representatives holding a total voting strength of fifty or more votes; action may be taken by a majority of the votes represented in the quorum. A different set of procedures, aimed at balancing the power of metropolitan Boston and the rest of the state, governed the selection of the advisory board's three nominations for the MWRA's board of directors. The MWRAA provided for a total of sixty-seven votes—one to each community and one for each of the seven additional members—for the election of the three advisory board appointees to the board of directors.

36. Sections 8(c) and 8(d), MWRAA. The approval of the governor and the legislature was also required for these extensions.

37. Section 8(a), MWRAA.

38. Sections 8(a) and 8(b), MWRAA.

39. Section 23(d)(v), MWRAA.

40. A final and unique addition to the legislation, present in all drafts and in the final act, was the appointment by the advisory board of an ombudsman to represent the board "in all matters" relating to the MWRA's "programs, operations, finances and charges" (§23(h)) and to analyze for the board the authority's current expense budgets, capital expenditure budgets, and capital programs and their effect on charges (§23(i)). The ombudsman was to report regularly on the affairs of the authority and on the effect of its program and operations on the costs to consumers of water and sewer services (§23(iii)). Strangely, this office has turned into more of a paper job than a reality.

41. Section 7(a), MWRAA. The final act offered a slightly shorter list of possible fields of expertise from which to choose than did earlier drafts, although the original Dukakis bill did not require expertise in any particular area.

42. The Cusack and Bulger bills were more restrictive in that they provided for a shorter, three-year term and allowed for removal without cause.

43. Upon recommendation of the executive director, the board of directors establishes reasonable compensation, benefits, and other terms of employment for other employees of the MWRA.

44. Section 7(a), MWRAA.

45. Section 7(h), MWRAA.

46. Section 8(i) of the Cusack bill and of the act. Similar provisions were proposed in section 8(f) of the Bulger bill.

47. Not only was the attorney general ambitious for higher office; he was also of the view, justifiable from his perspective, that a recent run of consent decrees costly to the commonwealth constituted a fiscal hemorrhage that had to be stopped.

48. Sections 27 and 24, MWRAA.

49. This element of section 24 may raise constitutional issues. However, the Supreme Judicial Court is the only constitutionally provided tribunal in the commonwealth. The legislature has the power to establish, alter, or abolish any other court in its jurisdiction. See *Opinion of the Justices to the Senate*, 372 Mass. 833, 363 N.E. 2d 652, 664 (1977). Moreover, since the legislature has left one forum for such cases, it would not appear to have infringed the right to legal recourse. In the interim after passage of the MWRAA and be-

fore transfer to the federal district court, there was considerable analysis by the parties of the legislative language. Agreement emerged among all the parties that the Supreme Judicial Court, which was totally unused to acting as a trial court, after receiving the *Quincy* case, should remand it to the Superior Court.

50. A vast array of interests continue to wield unchecked powers in the spheres in which they operate, sustained by support from the legislature and within virtually every agency. The need to centralize yields to a still more intense desire to have as many interests as possible represented in decision-making.

51. This model is a refinement of approaches previously tried in the commonwealth, most notably in the Massachusetts Bay Transportation Authority, but the initiative represented by the final MWRAA is unique.

52. Sections 8(c) and 8(d), MWRAA.

53. Section 22(a), MWRAA.

54. Section 22, MWRAA. The reports, which can go quite far, even to the extent of including recommendations for statutory changes and alterations in the authority's activities and administrative procedures, are to be made to the heads of the executive and legislative branches.

55. Section 9, MWRAA. Extensive powers of eminent domain are conferred: the authority may acquire real property, or any interest or rights therein, that it deems essential for operation, improvement, or enlargement of its sewer and water works systems, subject only to prior approval of the governor and the legislature in some situations.

56. Section 42, MWRAA.

57. Sections 8(c) and 8(d), MWRAA.

58. Section 7(c), MWRAA. The final act follows the Cusack bill in detailing certain inherent management rights that the MWRA may not limit or forgo as part of any collective bargaining agreement.

59. Section 69 of the act also prohibits any capital expenditures likely to create a new interbasin water transfer without the express approval of the legislature.

60. Massachusetts Fair Share, "Position Paper on the Proposed MWRA" (5 October 1984), 2.

61. This thesis runs counter to Professor James Q. Wilson's pessimistic argument contrasting business management's focus on the bottom

line of profits to government organizations' stress on the top line of constraints. Since the government agencies are shackled by bond covenants, judicial review, and legislative conditions, their energies, runs the argument, are expended in overcoming obstacles rather than in concentrating on their mandates. See Wilson, *Bureaucracy: What Government Agencies Do and Why They Do It* (New York, 1989), 115. This is hardly true of the MWRA's approach or actions or achievement.

62. The classic discussion can be found in Annmarie H. Walsh, *The Public's Business: The Politics and Practices of Government Corporations* (Cambridge, Mass., 1978). See also Alan Rabinowitz, *Municipal Bond Finance and Administration: A Practical Guide to the Analysis of Tax-Exempt Securities* (New York, 1969), and William B. Sims, *The Security of Municipal Bonds: Utility Revenues versus Full Faith and Credit* (New York, 1976).

63. 348 U.S. 26, 32 (1954): "[W]hen the legislature has spoken, the public interest has been declared in terms well-nigh conclusive. . . . [T]he legislature, not the judiciary, is the main guardian of the public needs to be served by social legislation."

64. *Hawaii Housing Authority v. Midkiff,* 467 U.S. 229 (1984).

65. See *Wein v. State of New York,* 347 N.E.2d 586 (N.Y. 1976). Authorities are also held free from accordance with legislative appropriation requirements, the nondelegation doctrines, and local government home-rule concepts.

12. Safe Harbor

1. The impossibility of insulating a public authority from the world of politics has been noted by several analysts. Robert Caro found that, contrary to the myth that Robert Moses operated at a "higher level," in truth he ran "a political machine oiled by the lubricant of political machines." Caro, *The Power Broker: Robert Moses and the Fall of New York* (New York, 1974), 17. See also John E. Osborn, "New York's Urban Development Corporation: A Study on the Unchecked Power of a Public Authority," 43 *Brooklyn Law Review* 237 (1977).

2. Section 2 of the MWRA Act (hereinafter MWRAA), *Acts and Resolves Passed by the General Court of Massachusetts in the Year 1984,* 1:753–833.

3. "The charges of the Authority, whether of general or special appli-

cation, shall not be subject to supervision or regulation by any office, department, division, commission, board, bureau or agency of the commonwealth or any of its political subdivisions." As a separate unit apart from the state, the MWRA was free of other, everyday governmental restrictions on the creation of debt, such as requirements of extraordinary majorities or those of local debt ceilings. One provision that raised the eyebrows of observers was section 12(b) of the act. Under it, the board of directors can delegate §12 (bond issuance) determinations to any single director or officer. Given the breadth of the discretionary powers and given the capital market pressures, this power seems potentially open to abuse of the public interest.

4. Section 10(a) provides that the charges shall be fixed and adjusted so as to provide funds sufficient to (1) pay all current expenses; (2) pay all debt service; (3) maintain all reserves reasonably required by any bond resolutions; (4) pay all costs of maintenance and replacement of the system, and costs of improving, extending, and enlarging the system; (5) cover payments to the commonwealth for debt service; and (6) pay all amounts that the authority is obligated for by any law or contract, including any bond resolution.

5. Section 19 of the MWRAA provides that MWRA bonds are exempt from taxation by and within the commonwealth.

6. See "Comment: An Analysis of Authorities—Traditional and Multicounty," 71 *Michigan Law Review* 1376 (1973).

7. See Section 12(a) of the MWRAA on bond issuance. Crucial terms such as interest rates and maturities are determined by the authority acting on its own; it need only "advise" the Executive Office for Administration and Finance and the state's Finance Advisory Board of the timing and terms. A further and sweeping conferral of power was the standard authorization to "sell its bonds in the manner, either at public or private sale, for the price, at the rate or rates of interest, or at discount in lieu of interest, as it may determine will best effect the purposes of this Act." Section 12(b), MWRAA.

8. The enabling statutes of public authorities generally contain express disclaimers of direct state liability to fund deficiencies.

9. From the very outset, in the draft bill of 10 November 1983, the legislation emphasized that the credit of the commonwealth was not pledged for the payment of MWRA debts.

10. An ameliorating step was taken to expand the market for the MWRA's bonds: standard language qualified them as legal investments for public officers and agencies, and for banks, insurance companies, trust companies, trustees, executors, and other fiduciaries. Section 14, MWRAA.

11. Section 12(c), MWRAA.

12. Section 12(g) of the MWRAA states that bondholders "may enforce and compel performance of all duties required by this act or by such bond resolution."

13. Section 21, MWRAA.

14. Section 13, MWRAA.

15. Sections 12(d), (f), and (g), MWRAA.

16. The team consisted of a financial adviser, bond counsel, a consulting engineer, and an underwriting group. In order to select the underwriting team, MWRA staff and the financial adviser visited twenty investment banking firms in New York and Boston and collected background information to use in their request for qualifications. Firms were asked to describe their response to specific issues facing the authority, including introduction of a new credit to the market and the designing of a new bond resolution. The process broadened the authority's understanding of municipal finance and, more to the point, helped it understand how others in the financial world viewed the MWRA. The agency's financial planning tasks included developing a general approach to the rating agencies, advice on engineering and financial feasibility studies, a marketing plan to sell the agency's debt, and assistance in preparing the necessary legal and financial documents.

17. To aid in the authority's early financing, the enabling act provided a state loan as well as state credit support. During the start-up period, the authority was permitted to borrow up to $65 million from the state, to be repaid by June 30, 1986; the second part of this transition aid came in the form of a full faith and credit guarantee of MWRA notes by the state, extended through June 30, 1990. Section 5, MWRAA. The assumed outstanding debt of the MDC was made subordinate to any outstanding MWRA debt.

18. A bizarre aspect of the invisible infrastructure phenomenon emerges in a front-page *New York Times* story. It describes a secret sewage project in Baghdad. To the disappointment of its workers, an engineering triumph in treating the sewage pouring into the

Tigris river is cloaked in obscurity. The fear is that publicity could make the project a target for sabotage. "It's a Dirty Job, But They Do It Secretly in Iraq," *New York Times*, 10 June 2004, 1.

19. A potential conflict exists here. Collecting sewer charges can be seen as a form of taxation; in that case, the effect is to shift the tax burden from the general public to those obliged to use the sewer facility. The state might adopt a strong conservation policy and would then desire to schedule charges accordingly, whereas the authority and its bondholders might desire only a total of revenues that covers use of the facility and thus may have an interest antagonistic to the state's policy. Various requirements of federal law act as a constraint on user charges for sewer systems. Recipients of federal wastewater construction grants must comply with the cost recovery requirements of the Federal Water Pollution Control Act Amendments of 1972; each recipient of wastewater treatment services must pay its proportionate share of the costs of operation and maintenance, including replacement; and each applicant must obtain the EPA regional administrator's approval of its user charge system.

20. See §10(a), MWRAA.

21. Sections 10(a) and (b), MWRAA.

22. Section 10(a), MWRAA. MWRA's wholesale charges for water are based on metered water use for the immediately preceding calendar year. Costs are divided by the total number of gallons sold to communities, to derive an average unit cost; this unit cost is multiplied by each municipality's metered water use to derive the total water bill for that municipality. The costs of operations are allocated to each municipality in accordance with (1) its proportion of the population served by the local sewer system (the "contributing population") to the total contributing population in the MWRA sewer system; and (2) the proportion of the "population equivalents" of a municipality's retail users that contribute 25,000 gallons or more of flow per day ("industrial users") to the "population equivalents" of all industrial users in the system.

23. The retail option was considered attractive by some because it facilitates an annual review of local charges to ensure consistency in rate setting and compliance with requirements, if any, of the EPA. But taking this course would weaken the collection power for user charges, given the authority's dependence on municipal intermedi-

aries to carry out its most powerful enforcement mechanism, the shut-off of services. Also, the retail billing alternative is the most costly and administratively complex option to implement; furthermore, it would extend the authority's start-up phase by a period of two additional years, thereby extending the need for the commonwealth's credit enhancements for a longer period of time.

24. Section 26(e), MWRAA.

25. Public Finance Group, First National Bank of Boston, "Protecting Water Resources: A Financial Analysis" (February 1984), 49–56.

26. A wrinkle in the system as adopted should be mentioned. The new authority would not collect its first revenues until November of 1985, although it would begin operating in July of that year, resulting in a temporary cash flow problem. The end result was a $65 million loan by the commonwealth to cover the gap.

27. See, e.g., William J. Quirk and Leon E. Wein, "A Short Constitutional History of Entities Commonly Known as Authorities," 56 *Columbia Law Review* 521 (1971).

13. Parting of the Waters

1. Jerry Ackerman, "New Agency for Harbor Is Called Superfluous," *Boston Globe,* 12 October 1984, 67.

2. Judy Foreman and Andrew Blake, "MDC Harbor Receivership Eyed," *Boston Globe,* 10 October 1984, 23.

3. Jerry Ackerman, "Legislature Faces Deadline for Harbor Cleanup Vote," *Boston Globe,* 15 November 1984, 27.

4. It later came out that the Ways and Means Committee's members had bickered over provisions of the various bills, then voted to postpone action until December 5 so that an amended version of the Dukakis bill could be printed by December 3; that would allow lawmakers the customary forty-eight hours to consider the revisions.

5. *Perez v. Boston Housing Authority,* 400 N.E.2d 1231 (Mass. 1980).

6. See the earlier cases of *Turner v. Goolsby,* 255 F. Supp. 724 (S.D. Ga. 1965), and *Newman v. Alabama,* 466 F. Supp. 628 (M.D. Ala. 1979). See also *Morgan v. Kerrigan,* 409 F. Supp. 1141 (D. Mass. 1975), *aff'd sub nom. Morgan v. McDonough,* 540 F.2d 527, 533 (1st Cir. 1976) ("The more usual remedies—contempt proceedings

and further injunctions—were plainly not very promising, as they invited further confrontation and delay.").

7. *Morgan v. McDonough*, 533.

8. The *Perez* case decided that the state could not be forced under statute to fund the rehabilitation of BHA property, while *Bromfield v. Treasurer and Receiver General*, 459 N.E.2d 445 (Mass. 1983), indicated that Massachusetts might be ready to move in an affirmative direction: "We may contemplate a departure from tradition by permitting levy of execution upon the Commonwealth's property," the court stated. In that case, however, the court ultimately chose to wait for the time being, confident that the legislature would pay its own debt. The Massachusetts constitution provides that "[n]o moneys, shall be issued out of the treasury of this commonwealth, and disposed of . . . but by warrant under the hand of the governor for the time being, with the advice and consent of the council." Article XI, Massachusetts Constitution.

9. Further Order on Plaintiff City of Quincy's Application for Preliminary Injunction, Sup. Ct. Civ. Action No. 138477 (29 November 1984).

10. Dudley Clendinen, "Judge Restricts Boston's Sewers to Clean Harbor," *New York Times*, 30 November 1984, A1.

11. Judy Foreman, "Court Bans Tie-ins to MDC Sewers," *Boston Globe*, 30 November 1984, 1.

12. "Boston Horror; Clean It Up, a Judge Demands," *Time*, 10 December 1984, 37.

13. "Sewage Ruling Bans Building in Boston," *New York Times*, 2 December 1984, E2.

14. Judy Foreman, "Receivership Threat for Harbor Cleanup," *Boston Globe*, 16 November 1984, 7.

15. Laurence Collins, "Aftermath of the Harbor Ruling," *Boston Globe*, 1 December 1984, 1.

16. Clendinen, "Judge Restricts Boston's Sewers," B9.

17. Foreman, "Court Bans Tie-ins to MDC Sewers."

18. Ibid.

19. Ibid.

20. Collins, "Aftermath of the Harbor Ruling."

21. Clendinen, "Judge Restricts Boston's Sewers."

22. This was due to the efforts of Senate President Bulger himself, who

explained in personal terms his sudden and unexpected desire to take action. The fresh northeast wind blowing across Castle Island and along the length of Carson Beach reminded him that autumn had arrived. In too many past years he had seen public interest in the harbor die with the coming of fall. This year, he had resolved, would be different.

23. Laurence Collins, "Panel Sends Harbor Bill to House," *Boston Globe,* 4 December 1984, 1.

24. *Boston Herald,* 5 December 1984.

25. "Ban on Boston Sewer Hookups Is Overturned," *New York Times,* 6 December 1984, A23.

26. Ibid.

27. Margot Hornblower, "Boston Harbor Sewers Back Up into Litigation," *Washington Post,* 9 December 1984, A6.

28. Deland also blamed former EPA officials for not filing suit earlier. "Nobody's hands are clean," he said.

29. Judy Foreman, "Sewer Tie-ins Ban Is Lifted," *Boston Globe,* 6 December 1984, 1.

30. See "Judge Prepares Ban on Boston Sewer Links," *New York Times,* 11 December 1984, A18.

31. Andrew Blake, "House Begins Debate on Sewer Authority Bill," *Boston Globe,* 11 December 1984, 19.

32. Andrew Blake, "House-Senate Panel Agrees on State Water Authority," *Boston Globe,* 14 December 1984, 29.

33. Andrew Blake, "Ultimatum Given on Harbor Bill," *Boston Globe,* 15 December 1984, 1.

34. *Boston Herald,* 16 December 1984.

35. Andrew Blake, "Conferee: Harbor Bill Is 'Close,'" *Boston Globe,* 17 December 1984, 1.

36. Andrew Blake, "Panel OK's Harbor Bill," *Boston Globe,* 18 December 1984, 1.

37. Ibid., 10.

38. "Panel Passes Bill on Boston Harbor Cleanup," *New York Times,* 18 December 1984, A23.

39. Ibid.

40. Andrew Blake, "Harbor Bill OK'd, Signed into Law," *Boston Globe,* 20 December 1984, 1.

41. Ibid.

42. Blake, "Panel OK's Harbor Bill," 1.
43. Blake, "Harbor Bill OK'd, Signed into Law," 7.
44. Ibid.
45. Ibid.
46. *Washington Post*, 21 December 1984, A17.
47. Ibid.
48. Andrew Blake, "MDC Now Facing Federal Harbor Suit," *Boston Globe*, 21 December 1984, 7.
49. This appointment as monitor represented a far stronger measure of court control than that proposed by state officials, who had wanted me assigned only as a consultant to the EOEA.
50. *United States v. Metropolitan District Commission*, 1985 WL 9071, *16 (D. Mass. 1985) (unpublished opinion).

14. The Commons Restored

1. See Walter F. Murphy and Joseph Tanenhaus, *The Study of Public Law* (New York, 1972), 65–70.
2. See also James L. Oakes, "The Judicial Role in Environmental Law," 52 *New York University Law Review* 498 (1977). This insightful review by Judge Oakes presents a working hypothesis: "There is little to be feared and much to be gained from a more active judicial role in this area." Ibid., 499.
3. *Baker v. Carr*, 369 U.S. 186, at 270 (1962).
4. Professor Carl Friedrich argues that the three basic functions are natural and inherent in governance. See Friedrich, *Constitutional Government and Democracy* (Boston, 1941); Herman Finer, *The Theory and Practice of Modern Government*, rev. ed. (New York, 1949).
5. See Gerald N. Rosenberg, *The Hollow Hope: Can Courts Bring About Social Change?* (Chicago, 1991), and Nathan Glazer, "Should Judges Administer Social Services?" *Public Interest* 50 (1978): 64. Much of the debate centers on whether courts have the self-confidence, the patience, the competence, or the structure to act in complicated, drawn-out situations. See Helen Hershkoff, "State Courts and the 'Passive Virtues': Rethinking the Judicial Function," 114 *Harvard Law Review* 1833 (2001).
6. See Laurence Tribe, *American Constitutional Law*, 3rd ed. (New York, 2000), 118.

7. In his dissenting opinion in *Morrison v. Olson,* 487 U.S. 654 (1988), Justice Scalia quoted Article 30. A separation of powers amendment modeled on it was proposed as part of the U.S. Bill of Rights but was rejected by the Senate. See Bernard Schwartz, *The Bill of Rights: A Documentary History* (New York, 1971), 1151.

8. See Paul M. Bator, "The Constitution as Architecture: Legislative and Administrative Courts under Article III," 65 *Indiana Law Journal* 233 (1990).

9. James Madison, "Federalist No. 47," in *The Federalist* (New York: Modern Library, 2000), 307–315. The framers of the U.S. Constitution did not wish for the doctrine to impose on the branches a rigid specialization of function; what they intended was to prevent the accumulation of unchecked power in one branch to the exclusion of the others. "Where the *whole* power of one department is exercised by the same hands which possess the *whole* power of another department," Madison wrote, "the fundamental principles of a free constitution are subverted." Ibid. (italics in original).

10. Ibid.

11. *Mistretta v. United States,* 488 U.S. 361, 381 (1989).

12. *Bowsher v. Synar,* 478 U.S. 714, 749 (1986).

13. *Risser v. Thompson,* 930 F.2d 549, 552 (7th Cir. 1991).

14. *Rice v. Draper,* 93 N.E. 821 (Mass. 1911).

15. The court pointed out "the strange spectacle" of a court direction "to the executive forces of the government to . . . punish the chief executive officer of the state, who commands and controls the military forces that are ultimately relied upon for maintenance of law and order." The better course, the court recommended, was that for official acts the governor answer "only to his own conscience, to the people who elected him, and in case of the possible commission of a high crime or misdemeanor, to a court of impeachment." *Rice,* 823.

16. See William B. Gwyn, "The Indeterminacy of the Separation of Powers in the Age of the Framers," 30 *William and Mary Law Review* 263 (1989).

17. *Hannigan v. New Gamma-Delta Chapter of Kappa Sigma Fraternity,* 327 N.E.2d 882, 885 (Mass. 1975).

18. *Blaney v. Commissioner of Correction,* 372 N.E.2d 770, 774 and n. 4 (Mass. 1978).

19. *Perez v. Boston Housing Authority,* 400 N.E.2d 1231, 1252 (Mass. 1980).
20. Ibid., 1248, quoting *Ex parte Peterson,* 253 U.S. 300, 312 (1920).
21. Ibid., 1252.
22. In affirming this broad assertion of judicial authority, the Supreme Judicial Court left a loophole by making special mention of the "hybrid character" of the Boston Redevelopment Authority, based on its unique relation with the federal government. *Perez,* 1252 n. 36.
23. See Roscoe Pound, "Justice according to Law," 14 *Columbia Law Review* 1 (1914).
24. *Myers v. United States,* 272 U.S. 52, 84 (1926).
25. Woodrow Wilson, *Constitutional Government in the United States* (New York, 1921), 56–57; the book was first written before Wilson became president.
26. Ibid.
27. *Rice,* 823.
28. "Quotation of the Day," *Boston Globe,* 12 December 1984, 2.
29. Judy Foreman, "Sewer Tie-in Ban Lifted," *Boston Globe,* 6 December 1984, 1.
30. As stated by Justice Benjamin Kaplan in *Perez.* For a comparative analysis of how the judiciary functions in Europe in such situations, see Alec Stone Sweet, *Governing with Judges: Constitutional Politics in Europe* (New York, 2000).
31. As noted earlier, an analogous set of criteria has been devised by the Massachusetts court for justifying the receivership remedy: "repeated or continuous failure of the officials to comply with a previously issued decree; a reasonable forecast that the mere continued insistence by the court that those officials perform the decree would lead only to confrontation and delay; [and] a lack of leadership that could be expected to turn the situation around within a reasonable time." *Perez* at 1250–1251. See also *United States v. Detroit,* 476 F. Supp. 512 (E.D. Mich. 1979).

15. The Call of the Bugler

1. Alexander Hamilton, "Federalist No. 78," in *The Federalist* (New York: Modern Library, 2000), 496.
2. For example: "[W]e should be glad that judges themselves remain

firmly attached to a limited conception of their own powers."
Marc L. Miller, "Wise Masters" (book review), 51 *Stanford Law
Review* 1751, 1816 (1999).

3. Robert A. Dahl and Charles E. Lindblom, *Politics, Economics, and
Welfare* (New Brunswick, 1992).

4. *Southern Burlington County NAACP v. Township of Mount Laurel*, 336 A.2d 713 (N.J. 1975) *(Mt. Laurel I); Southern Burlington
County NAACP v. Township of Mount Laurel*, 456 A.2d 390 (N.J.
1983) *(Mount Laurel II); Hills Development Co. v. Township of
Barnards*, 510 A.2d 621 (N.J. 1986) *(Mount Laurel III)*. See
Charles M. Haar, *Suburbs under Siege: Race, Space, and Audacious Judges* (Princeton, 1998).

5. See Vincent M. Nathan, "The Use of Special Masters in Institutional Reform Litigation," 10 *University of Toledo Law Review*
419 (1979).

6. The Boston school finance case is a consummate example of the
usefulness of the special master as a finder of fact. Steven Horowitz
and I were appointed by Chief Judge Thomas Morse as masters in
Board of Education v. City of Boston, Suffolk Superior Ct. No.
47326 (1981). See Charles M. Haar, "The Role of the Special Master: A Helpful Judicial Tool," *National Law Journal*, vol. 4, no. 18
(11 January 1982), 11.

7. In cases of mass torts litigation, Margaret G. Farrell concludes,
special masters can "help courts deal with the time-consuming process of evaluating thousands of claims." The appointment of a
master "permits the participation of a facilitator who can spend
many hours becoming familiar with the facts and the parties."
Farrell, "The Function and Legitimacy of Special Masters," 2 *Wid-
ener Law Symposium Journal* 235, 265 (1997).

8. Canon 3(A)(4) of the Massachusetts Judicial Code provides that a
judge should not permit private interviews, arguments, or communications designed to "influence his judicial action . . . except in
cases where provision is made by law for ex parte application."

9. Compare Stephen P. Ware, *Alternative Dispute Resolution* (St.
Paul, 2001), §3.26.

10. This is a view advanced by Ellen E. Deason in "Managing the
Managerial Expert," 1998 *University of Illinois Law Review* 341,
395. Dealing primarily with managerial tasks, but by implication
extending to other areas of the special master's responsibilities,

Deason disagrees with the limiting approach of the Federal Rules of Civil Procedure, arguing that there is no consistent approach for deciding the appropriateness of appointing an expert. Ibid., 391.

11. There are thought-provoking observations (and differences) over the value of expert assistance to the courts. See James S. DeGraw, "Rule 53, Inherent Powers, and Institutional Reform: The Lack of Limits on Special Masters," 66 *New York University Law Review* 800 (1991); Farrell, "Function and Legitimacy of Special Masters." "In *City of Quincy*," DeGraw writes, "the court first extended discretionary powers to the special master and then allowed him to appoint additional experts—functional masters. In doing so, the court further eroded its own control over the judicial process and potentially imposed additional, unanticipated costs upon the parties responsible for paying the master's fees. This was, in effect, a delegation of the court's own inherent powers." DeGraw, "Rule 53," 827. Putting aside the question of fees—irrelevant in *Quincy*, since the experts donated their time—strenuously seeking to avoid employment of experts, especially objective professionals, in these complicated litigations is a strange frolic and detour. See *Morgan v. Kerrigan*, 530 F.2d 401, 426–427 (1st Cir. 1976). Judges should be relatively free to assign such duties to the special master as match the needs of a particular case and to modify that assignment as events develop. By design, inflexible rules do not honor the context of a particular situation, and in these situations context is all.

12. See Haar, *Suburbs under Siege*, 72–86, 188.

13. DeGraw, "Rule 53," 826.

14. An example of regulation is the attempt to install a reporting mechanism to ensure that a record of communications is established. See DeGraw, "Rule 53," 844. What if such a rule were to be applied to a national security adviser? Would a proposal that the professional relationship between President Bush and Condoleezza Rice be set down in formal prescriptions at the outset, as a check upon her actions, be regarded as either feasible or useful?

15. Canon 3(A)(6), Massachusetts Code of Judicial Conduct.

16. In such cases a judge cannot rest on the romantic belief that in the marketplace of ideas, right will somehow naturally prevail over wrong—a legal parallel to Adam Smith's faith in the "invisible hand" of self-interest.

17. See Haar, *Suburbs under Siege,* 172.
18. From their experience in the ordinary litigation experience, many lawyers avoid the press in the belief that the client is better off that way, but it is necessary to realize the difference in a political case and to change gears accordingly.

Conclusion

1. *Brown v. Board of Education,* 349 U.S. 294, 300 (1955).
2. Dudley Clendinen, "About Boston: The Buck Stops Here, Says Judge Garrity," *New York Times,* 2 October 1984, A18.
3. Ibid.
4. The brilliant Alex Bickel coined the term "passive virtues" as describing the essence of a proper judicial function. Alexander M. Bickel, "The Supreme Court, 1960 Term—Foreword: The Passive Virtues," 75 *Harvard Law Review* 40 (1961). See also Christopher J. Peters, "Adjudication as Representation," 97 *Columbia Law Review* 312 (1997). This restrictive view has often dominated the intellectual discussion on the nature of adjudication and the role of the courts in a majoritarian democracy.
5. John Adams, "Dissertation on the Canon and the Feudal Law," in *The Works of John Adams* (Boston, 1851), 3:462–463.

Postscript

1. At the center of the outfall debate was the northern right whale, the world's most endangered whale species, which visits Massachusetts Bay each spring. Members of STOP (Stop the Outfall Pipe) vowed to make the whale "the spotted owl of the east coast."
2. At first the EPA demanded incineration. The MWRA backed a plan to recycle the sludge into fertilizer pellets. Moreover, different recycling methods were advanced by other environmental groups.
3. See Larry Tye, "MWRA Chief: Sludge Should Not Be Burned," *Boston Globe,* 19 January 1989, 27, for the agreement on recycling by various state officials.
4. Even the word "sludge" sounds loathsome, connoting a stomach-turning primordial ooze. Many communities said "no," including Quincy, which rejected two separate plans to build plants to recycle sludge. Spectacle Island became the popular first choice—since it was in no one's backyard.
5. Demonstrations were mounted by as many as 1,000 bused-in resi-

dents—including hundreds of high school students let go from classes for "a political science seminar day." *Boston Herald*, 5 January 1989, 1. A bartender helped people drown their sorrow in a new drink, the Sludge Deluxe Frappe. In Washington, Representative Barney Frank noted that "I can't think of any governmental issue that has reached farther into people's lives." Claims and counterclaims in the court papers, such as one that odors from the landfill would incite riots at a neighboring state maximum security prison, multiplied forebodings.

6. Ross Gelbspan, "State Asks Court to Lift Sewer Ban but Judges' Queries Signal Reluctance," *Boston Globe*, 17 April 1991, 1.

7. Michael Grunwald, "Judge OK's Plan to Ship MWRA Sludge to Utah," *Boston Globe*, 2 October 1993, 13.

8. Ian Menzies, "Boston Cleanup Suit Justified by State's Inaction," *Boston Globe*, 16 May 1983.

Acknowledgments

This book was launched in Martha's Vineyard in the late 1990s, following conversations with my dear friend and polymath, Daniel Bell. One afternoon he inquired about the Boston Harbor litigation of a decade past that had once been so prominent. This stirred up memories and took me back to the tumultuous events that had put Boston Harbor at the center of the public stage. I perused documents and newspapers of that time, conferred with colleagues from that earlier voyage, and found myself caught up once again in the details of the litigation that had been featured in the media day after day. This could be the subject of a study, many suggested, that would contribute to understanding the role of the judge in modern society, as well as the place of law in contemporary environmental struggles. And so this book was born.

It is with genuine appreciation that I express my gratitude to the scientists, experts, and fellow companions in the struggle to regenerate Boston Harbor. The following were most generous with their time and talents as they, too, revisited and reappraised the past: E. Eric Adams of the Massachusetts Institute of Technology; Noel Baratta of the Metropolitan District Commission; Charles Button of Rizzo Associates; Paul Levy, president and chief executive officer of Beth Israel Deaconess Medical Center; Steven Horowitz of Cleary, Gottlieb; Francis X. Meaney and Gregory Sandomirsky of Mintz, Levin, Cohn, Ferris, Glovsky, and Popeo; and Philip Shapiro of Standard & Poor's.

Judge Norman Stahl of the First Circuit Court of Appeals shared his wisdom. Theodore Cross; Hilbert Fefferman, legal counsel; Peter Lewis of Lazard Freres; and Michael Wolf of the University of Florida provided critical insights.

Professor Jerold Kayden of the Harvard Graduate School of Design, longtime friend, adviser, and collaborator, gave the manuscript his customary meticulous attention. Thanks are also due to an anonymous reviewer for his careful appraisal.

Matthew Seccombe is in a class by himself; it is my good fortune to benefit from his extraordinary editorial expertise. The opportunity to work with him was an exceptional learning experience.

I am grateful to Thompson Potter, a marvel of good will and skills, who typed and retyped the manuscript, always with perceptive comments.

Richard Audet, Harris Collingwood, Chris Kochansky, and Benno Weisberg improved the writing. Maggie Goud Collins added considerably to the overall effort from her extensive familiarity with water administration. I thank Michael Aronson, editor at Harvard University Press, for his counsel. Students at the Harvard Law School provided invaluable research: Justin Cooper, David Gold, Cori Parobek, and Rick Su.

David Cobb, of Harvard's Pusey Library Map Collection, was most helpful in suggesting maps and charts from the unique collections entrusted to him. The work of the Massachusetts Water Resources Authority, notably that of Barbara Allen, Rita Berkeley, and Tim Watkins, who supplied maps, slides, and diagrams, is gratefully acknowledged. The Harvard Law School Langdell Library, especially in the person of Janet Katz, assiduously pursued newspaper accounts, memoranda, and legal records. I am indebted to Stephanie Lovell, Massachusetts Deputy First Assistant Attorney General, for locating original documents relating to the litigation.

Special acknowledgment is due to the University of Miami Law School, where I teach as Distinguished Visiting Professor, for its hospitality and intellectual stimulation over the past seven years, and to the American Academy of Arts and Sciences, especially its executive officer, Leslie Berlowitz. The Academy also sponsored a meeting to discuss the implications of the Boston Harbor case. I want to record my thanks to the Harvard Law School for its continuing encouragement and for providing financial assistance for crucial editorial work.

Finally, there is my gratitude for the loving presence of my wife, Suzanne Keller, brilliant scholar and magnificent natural writer. Her perceptive wisdom, generosity of spirit, and patience restore my hope for individual and societal betterment.

My dear friend Paul Garrity died suddenly on August 21, 2004. He is of course central to the book and had read the several drafts over time. We both had looked forward to celebrating its publication and sharing yet another aspect of this ongoing adventure. He was truly a force of nature. I feel his absence deeply.

Index

Adams, E. Eric, 92, 146
Adams, John, 49, 50, 153, 255, 256, 257, 260, 262, 291, 294, 297
affirmative action, 179, 188, 344n23
American Academy of Arts and Sciences, 92
American Association for the Advancement of Science, 332n14
Army Corps of Engineers, 59
attorney general's office. *See* Massachusetts: attorney general's office
Atwater, Lee, 318n22
authorities, public: autonomy and role of, 197–199, 203, 215–217, 348nn65,1; financing of, 174–175, 198–199, 203, 204–205, 207–208, 214, 215–217, 349n8; governance of, 180, 182, 183, 187, 215–217, 348n1; metropolitan and regional authorities, 200–201
Avon, 300

Bacon, Francis, 189
banking and trading of flow reduction credits, 120, 140, 141, 339n11
Bank of Boston, 163–164, 172, 174, 180, 214
Baratta, Noel, 89–90, 101–102, 331n2
Basius, Frank, 225

Bellotti, Francis, 190, 226–227, 346n47. *See also* Massachusetts: attorney general's office
benthos (benthic ecosystem), 73–75, 110, 125, 326n13
Berger, Curtis, 94–95
Bickel, Alexander, 360n4(top)
black mayonnaise (pollutant), 74, 105, 327n16
Blackmun, Harry, 321n11
bond market. *See* private capital markets
Boston: benefits of harbor cleanup in, 303–304; city agencies with harbor jurisdiction, 67–68; effect of moratorium on, 240–241; harbor park plan, 68, 226; housing authority case in, 32–33, 98, 223, 259–260, 353n8; institutional breakdowns in, 292–293; and MWRA boards, 177, 178, 179, 180, 184, 345n35; port of, 49; resistance to treatment facilities in, 72, 143; school finance case in, 39, 275, 276–277, 358n6; sewer system of, 50–54, 67, 323n15; in state politics, 179, 292–293. *See also* Boston Harbor
Boston Globe, 15, 18, 20, 155, 156, 162, 165, 222, 224, 263, 286, 304
Boston Harbor: agencies with harbor jurisdiction, 66–68, 150, 325nn1–2; benthic ecosystem of,